Walking the old ways of east Breconshire and the Black Mountains

Walking the old ways of east Breconshire and the Black Mountains

The history in the landscape explored through 26 circular walks

Andy & Karen Johnson

LOGASTON PRESS

LOGASTON PRESS
The Holme, Church Road, Eardisley, Herefordshire HR3 6NJ
An imprint of Fircone Books Ltd.
www.logastonpress.co.uk

First published by Logaston Press May 2022

ISBN 978-1-910839-55-3

Printed and bound in Poland

Logaston Press is committed to a sustainable future for our business, our readers and our planet.
This book is made from paper from sustainable sources.

British Library Catalogue in Publishing Data
A CIP catalogue record for this book is available from the British Library

Contents

Key for the maps accompanying the walk routes

- A road
- B road
- Other tarmacked road
- Stream or river
- Building or group of buildings
- Woodland
- Boundary of open access land
- Indication of hill slopes
- Route of walk
- Other paths
- (1) Point on map relating to same point in walk description
- Pub
- Tea room
- Castle with stonework
- Castle, earthwork remains only
- Cathedral or priory
- Church or chapel of interest
- Mansion
- Prehistoric tomb or standing stone
- Hillfort or other earthworks

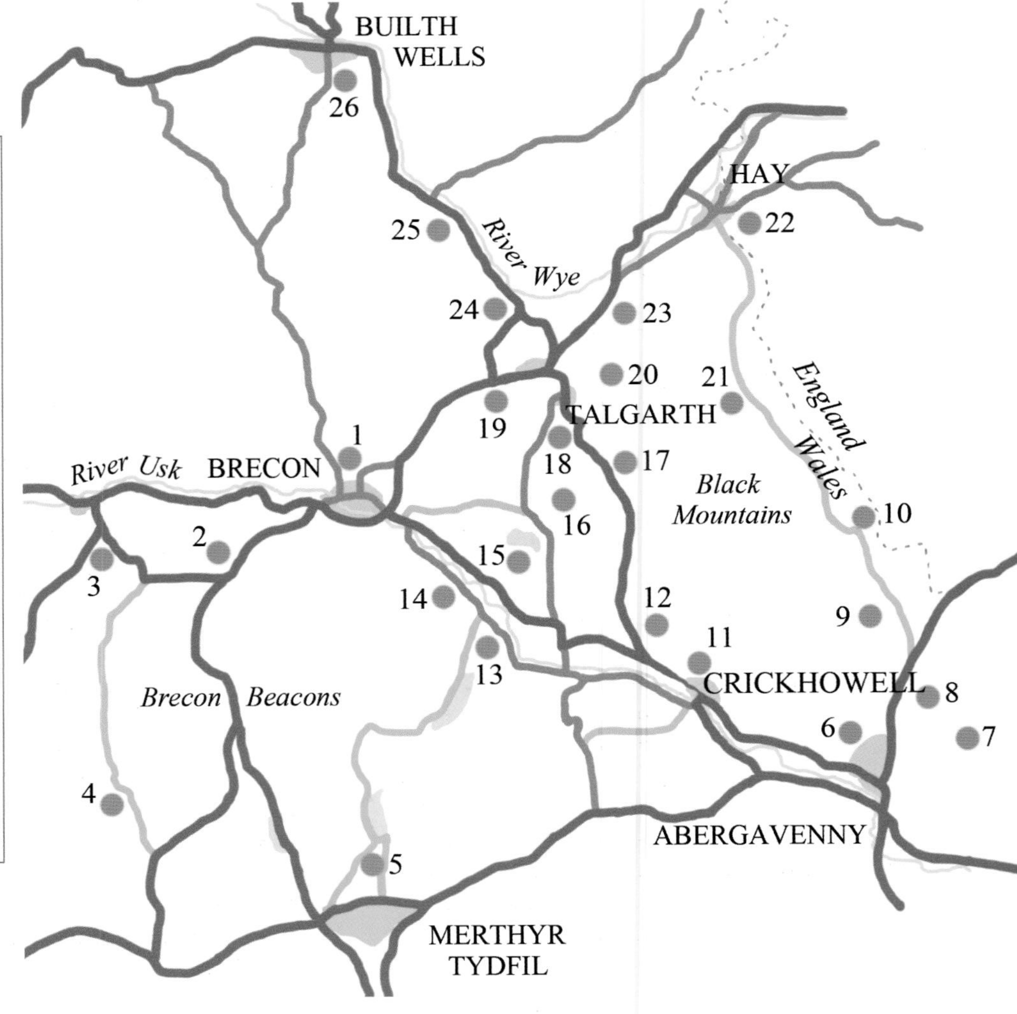

Map showing the locations of the walks

Introduction

In devising these 26 walks we have tried to cover a broad range of features so as to explore various aspects of the area's history. As fewer historical features are to be seen on the high stretches of open land, the walks are concentrated around the valleys and lower slopes, though the number of hillforts clustered around the valleys of the Wye and Usk means that there are plenty of hill climbs and good views to be had. The walks will also take you into some of the less well known areas of this rural landscape.

We ruled out some walks or routes because of the state of the paths, and we had to relinquish some historic sites because we couldn't find a way of including them on a pleasing circular walk. The walks as described should be suitable for all seasons, but be alive to weather forecasts and conditions if tackling any of the hilltop or ridge walks, and of course many paths will become boggy and slippery in places in or after wet weather. We have walked each of the walks in the book at least twice, in part to test the directions in different seasons; 'head for the church spire' may be an easy direction to follow in winter but impossible in the leafy summer. Paths change, too: they can be (legally) diverted, new tracks may be created for ever larger farm machinery, stiles are replaced by gates, and so on. Likewise, pubs, cafés and museums open, close, re-open. Nearly every time we've gone back to do a walk again, we've found that something is different. Bear this in mind when following a walk, but also remember that you are legally allowed to find an alternative route round an obstruction if you find one on a public path. Of course, make sure that you close any gates you open, that if you're walking with a dog, you keep him or her under control when you're walking among horses or sheep, though for safety reasons you may choose to allow the dog to run free when in a field of cattle. Do follow all the other aspects of the Countryside Code too.

We've imagined that you'll probably be driving to the start of the walk, and have given the location and a grid reference to most of these, together with other directions where we have felt they will be helpful. Within the major towns, rather than a grid reference we have given details of the road junction or feature near to which the walk begins. Point 1 on each map marks the point where the walk starts and often also the place where we've suggested you could park. The sketch map for each walk includes an approximate scale.

It is advisable to take the relevant Ordnance Survey map with you as a back-up, even just to help you to identify hills or features that you can see in the distance. We have marked the position of pubs and tearooms on

the maps but haven't included such symbols in the main towns, as they would tend to cover much of the map. In the case of some walks the only hope of sustenance en route will be to take it with you.

Each walk starts with a brief paragraph that gives its distance, an idea of the type of terrain underfoot, an indication as to how many stiles you are likely to face, and the historic features that the walk includes. It also indicates places en route which are open to the public at certain times of the year or day, to give you a chance to plan in advance when to do the walk if you want to include such places. A further idea of the historical features of the walk can be gained by leafing through it and seeing what is included in the boxes of information. The walk descriptions also often include a line or two about buildings or other features encountered. We have tried to give a reasonable depth of information about the places seen en route, but you may want to supplement it from other sources; excellent church guides are available in many churches, for example. All the photographs included with each walk have been taken on that walk, sometimes, but as rarely as possible, using an element of zooming in to counter the effect of the object appearing much smaller in print than when encountered outdoors.

Researching and writing the book has been fun. We hope that the places it will help you to visit (many of them only accessible on foot) will provide you with a great deal of interest and pleasure. And if the walking is too much, we hope the information and photographs will allow you to enjoy the landscape and history of this beautiful area in the bramble-free comfort of your own home.

We are very grateful to Sarah and John Zaluckyj, Paul Remfry, George Children, George Nash, Colin Lewis, Malcolm Thurlby, Roy Palmer and Paul R. Davis for their historical research which Logaston Press has published down the years and which has been of help in sorting out details included in this book. We thank our friends who have accompanied us on some of the walks and joined in considerations of whether a route is worth including in the book. In particular, many thanks to John Rogers and Rafa Cruz, Richard Johnson, David Styan, Richard Wheeler, Gavin McInerney, Trevor Wilson, Peter Cowin and Terry Pipe. And of course many thanks to Richard and Su Wheeler of Logaston Press for their encouragement and finesse.

Andy & Karen Johnson
February 2022

BRECON

During the Iron Age there were hillforts to the east of the town at Slwch Tump, north of the town at Pen-y-Crug (see p.3) and also about 2 miles to the west. Around 80AD the Romans established a cavalry fort at Y Gaer slightly further west still and then in 1096, after the Norman campaign in the area under Bernard de Neufmarché, a castle was established above the confluence of the rivers Usk and Honddu and today's town was founded. Neufmarché also established a priory (now cathedral, see pages 11–13), in part as an encouragement for the economic success of the town as it would then be granted endowments. In the 13th century walls were built to enhance the defence of the town, with the Watton gate in the east, the Strowed (Struet) gate in the north, the Bridge gate towards Llanfaes and the Water gate at the crossing of the Honddu. A further gate gave access to the River Usk, over which the first bridge is mentioned in 1461. During the 1500s and 1600s the town underwent a period of rebuilding, the more wealthier residents erecting large houses in Glamorgan Street whilst artisans and traders constructed premises and homes in Ship Street and across the river in Llanfaes. The town walls were partially dismantled during the Civil War in the 1640s, and in 1776 an Act of Parliament permitted the destruction of the gates at Watton, Usk Bridge and Struet. This in part reflected the town's growing importance as an administrative centre for a wide geographical area, as a county town, holding Assizes and Quarter Sessions, with flourishing markets and the need for easy ingress and egress. The Industrial Revolution saw the construction of a canal that linked the town to the developing industries to the south, but it was the development of these industries elsewhere that turned Brecon into something of a backwater compared with the earlier centuries. The town nevertheless now acts as the regional centre for a large rural hinterland and gains additional business due to the presence of army barracks and nearby training grounds, and from visitors to the Brecon Beacons national park.

Walk 1 Brecon & Llanddew

7 miles. Largely on paths, generally in good order, and some roads and lanes. Some stiles. Set in rolling country with a gentle climb to Pen-y-Crug hillfort, the return path following the river Honddu. Includes Brecon cathedral (but not the town), Pen-y-Crug hillfort, Llanddew church and bishop's palace.

Park near the cathedral on the road called Pendre (the B4520).

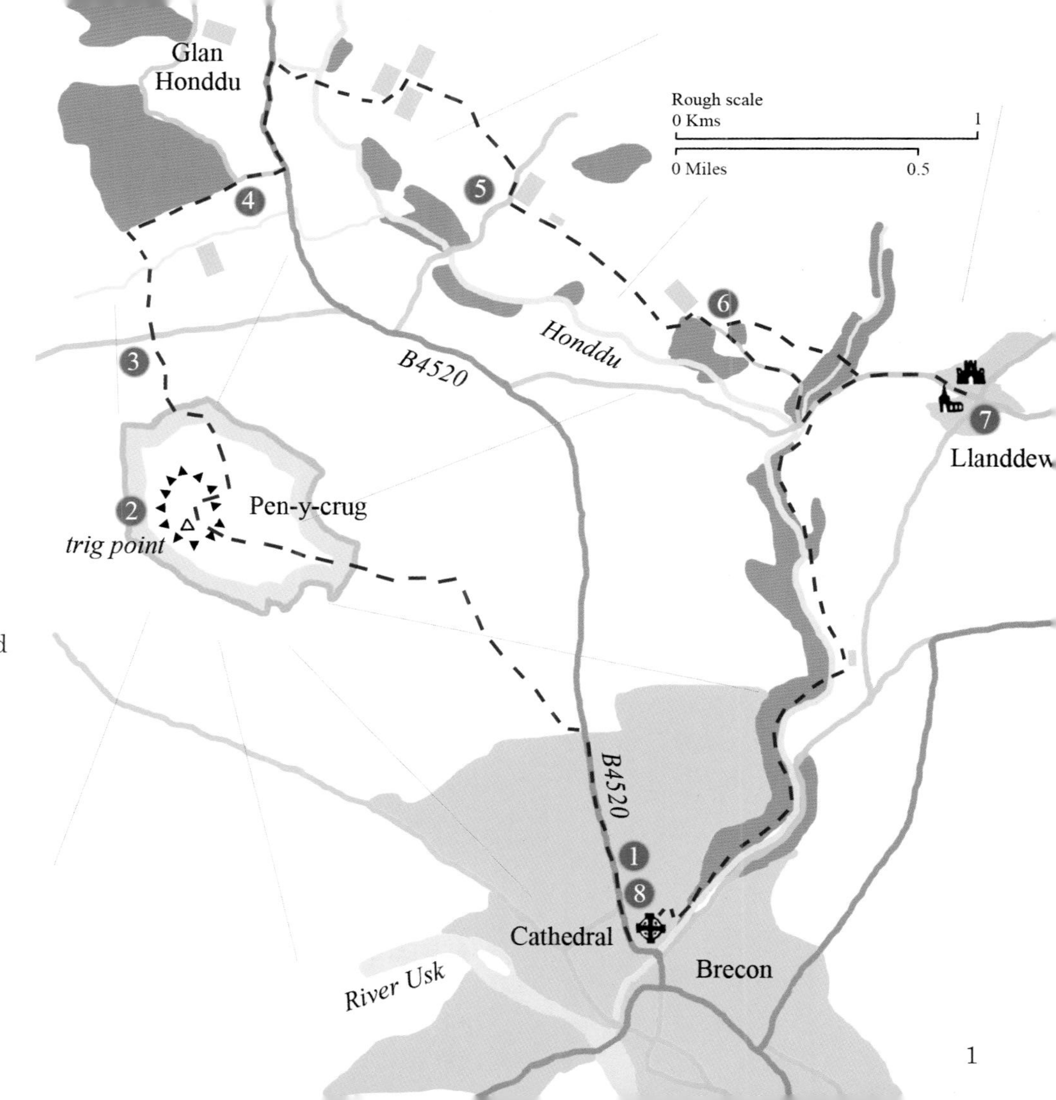

1 Walk north up Pendre, aka the B4520, the road heading north out of Brecon. Just past the last houses on the left, and just before a road called Pontgwilym off to the right, turn left on a track. This soon bends to the right and leads gently uphill. Just before a gate to Rowanoak Crug Farm crosses the

2

PEN-Y-CRUG HILLFORT

This oval-shaped multivallate Iron Age hillfort, whose name means 'top of the mound' (certainly the site is both commanding and conspicuous), internally measures some 182m north-south and 134m east-west. There are five ramparts on the eastern and northern sides, reducing to four on the western side, where the ground slopes away more steeply. There is a point on the north-western edge where the outer two ramparts merge into one. The steepness of the inner two ramparts suggests that their core is built of stone, which has apparently been confirmed at times when erosion has exposed the original rampart face. This we have never seen – just isolated pieces of stone here and there. Lengths of the outer ramparts often consist of what appears to be little more than a palisade footing with an intervening terrace. There is a simple entrance, probably originally inturned, on the south-eastern side where the present path enters the hillfort, and where there is a small annexe. The ramparts have been damaged in places by quarrying. At their highest, they rise some 5.2m. The size of the hill-fort has led to suggestions that it might have served as the administrative centre of the surrounding territory.

Photos on opposite page:
Bottom left: Looking over the annexe outside the entrance
Bottom right: Evidence of possible stonework walling now buried in the embankments

track, take another track off to the left. This continues uphill. Past a house on the left, keep straight on up a footpath and through a gate to enter the public access land on which stands Pen-y-Crug fort. Follow the path up into the fort (at one point crossing another footpath) and stand near the trig point to take in the full 360 degree view.

2 Having had a look around, face the trig point from the direction from which you approached it and turn right along a track which crosses the ramparts and picks up a prominent track that curves round the north-eastern corner of the fort and then drops downhill. The track passes through a gate to become hedged on both sides and soon leads out onto a road.

3 Cross the road and the stile on the far side and then walk across the field to a stile on its far side some 30 yards to the left of the far right-hand corner. Cross the stile and then the brook beyond and another stile into the next field. Here you head to the far right-hand corner, where you go through one of the gates into the field on your right. Then walk up to the fence alongside the wood, and turn right to follow this around the hillside. Cross one stile into another field, and then a further stile and descend some steps onto a minor road.

4 Turn right on the road, and then left at the junction ahead. You will be walking along this road for about a quarter of a mile and you need to take care as car drivers will only see you shortly before they pass you.

Having passed the entrance lodge to Glan Honddu on your left, go through the next field gate you reach on your right. (Glan Honddu was built *c*.1820-30 in late Georgian style for a John Jones, who died in 1857. The house remained with his heirs into the late 1900s.) The gate will lead you into a field near a spring which feeds a stream; follow this stream and gully on your left to reach a footbridge across the Honddu in the valley bottom. Once over this the path heads away from the river to cross a field and join a track which slants up the hillside. This will swing left to enter a farmyard, which you go through, to turn right immediately past the last barn on your right and just before a silage pit with a bungalow beyond to take a concreted way that leads to a gate into a field. Carry on slightly right across this field and pass to the left of a corner of hedgerow that juts into the field to reach a gate into the next field. Go through this and follow the hedge on your right, crossing two field boundaries to reach a road on the last field's far side.

5 Turn right on the road and then left just before the last of the group of houses on the left. Walk through the car parking area and then take a track just to the right of another house. Keep to the track, passing a small modern barn on your left, go through a gate, then another gate into a field. Follow the field boundary on your right and at the far end of the field you will reach two stiles in quick succession that will lead you into a field above which lies a collection of barns. Cross this field, passing just below

the barns, to a stile on the far side. Once over this, keep to the top of the bank and follow the fence along on your left and this will lead to another stile. Over this, follow the fence on your right and then the side of a barn on your left and you will soon reach an old stone stile out onto a lane. Turn right on this and follow it along past a house on the right to reach, where the lane bends to the right, a footpath gate and sign on the left.

6 Here you have a choice. The footpath leads along field edges before dropping steeply downhill in woodland to ford a stream by stepping stones and then clamber up the far side of the gully. In or after periods of wet weather the paths will be slippery and the stream quite deep. If you choose this route, go through the footpath gate then head to the gateway on the far side of this paddock to a gate in its corner into the next field. Through this, continue following the hedge on your left and cross the stile into the woodland at the far end. Over this, the path continues ahead to drop steeply downhill (there are some small steps cut into the hillside at places) just to the right of a gully. This path will lead to some stepping stones across the stream and thence a path up the far side. This passes to the left of a wire fence that surrounds a small sewage works and then meets a road, on which you turn left to walk into Llanddew.

If you feel that the route described is too full of obstructions, stay on the lane and follow it till it meets a road near a bridge across the Honddu. But don't cross this bridge: instead turn left and walk up the road into Llanddew to see the church and the remains of the bishop's palace.

LLANDDEW

It is recorded that Aled or Eluned, daughter of Brychan, took refuge in Llanddew church in AD500, suggesting that Llanddew's early church was a 'clas' foundation – a church organised independently and run by its own community of clergy, often within just a single building, such churches being able to offer sanctuary. The curved nature of the churchyard boundary also suggests an early foundation, Ty Gwyn (White House) and the more recent Church House having, it is thought, once stood inside the churchyard. The settlement first appears in the records as 'Llando', meaning 'Church of God', becoming Llanddew ('the church of St David') by 1249. The settlement was granted the right to hold a weekly market by Edward I in 1290-1, the market probably being held in the space between the church and the bishop's palace. Standel farm, about 1km to the south-east of Llanddew, is believed to be one of the places where Henry VII's army camped on a journey that ended with the Battle of Bosworth in 1485, the farm's name thought to derive from 'Henry's Royal Standard'.

LLANDDEW CHURCH

Parts of the tower and chancel date from the 1200s, but most of the building belongs to rebuildings in the 1400s and 1500s and a refurbishment in the 1800s. Fragments of post-medieval wall paintings were uncovered in the chancel during work in 1883, but these have since been lost. There are two elaborately carved stones in the porch which might have formed lintels or door posts in the earlier church. These are similar to two stones in the church at Llanfilo (see p.176) and might represent the work of the same stone-mason. Some have dated the carving of these stones to the 800s, but the geometrical patterns bear relationship with early work carried out under the Normans, such as lintels at Bredwardine church over the border in Herefordshire.

A stone carved with an incised cross and a faint inscription that was once built into the south transept is now kept inside the church. It might be a Christian reworking of an earlier monument.

LLANDDEW BISHOP'S PALACE

The fortified bishop's palace was built during the 1100s by the bishop of St David's as a home for the archdeacon of Brecon and is largely known to history as the home of Giraldus Cambrensis or Gerald of Wales, who occupied it, when archdeacon, between 1175 and 1204. Born into the nobility at Manorbier in Pembrokeshire, Gerald was educated in Paris and entered the service of Henry II *c.*1184. He is primarily known as a result of a number of books he wrote, two of them about Ireland as a result of accompanying the military campaigns of Henry's son, Prince John, in 1185-6. These were followed by two on Wales, *Itinerarium Cambriae* (An Itinerary of Wales) and *Cambriae descripto* (A escription of Wales), written after he accompanied Archbishop Baldwin of Canterbury on a recruitment campaign in 1188 for what became the Third Crusade.

The palace was partially updated during the 1340s by Archbishop Gower, who also extensively remodelled the bishop's palaces at St David's and Llamphey. It fell into disuse after the Dissolution of the monasteries and was described as 'an onsemelie ruine' by Leland in 1550. Llanddew vicarage was built on the site in the mid 1800s, parts of a rectangular building measuring some 22m x 5m (perhaps the 'small residence' of Gerald of Wales) surviving on the vicarage's lawns, together with parts of the surrounding curtain walls that include a semi-circular bastion. The building work around a well on the outside of the south-west curtain wall is believed to have been carried out on the orders of Archbishop Gower. Originally designed so as to allow access to its water from both inside and outside the palace, the internal access is now blocked. The cast-iron hand pump dates to 1908.

The photograph was taken on a visit to the palace with the owner's permission.

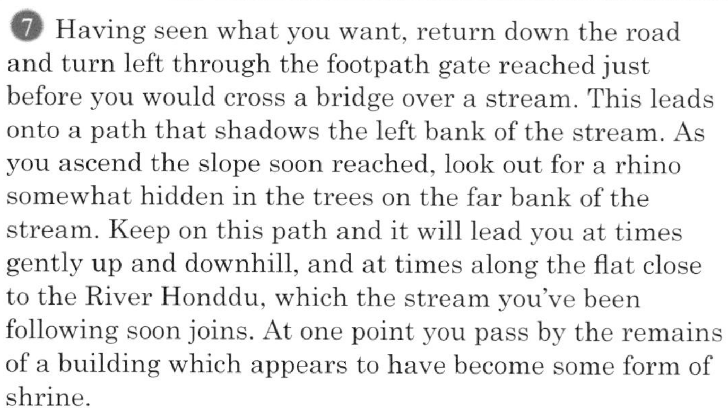

⑦ Having seen what you want, return down the road and turn left through the footpath gate reached just before you would cross a bridge over a stream. This leads onto a path that shadows the left bank of the stream. As you ascend the slope soon reached, look out for a rhino somewhat hidden in the trees on the far bank of the stream. Keep on this path and it will lead you at times gently up and downhill, and at times along the flat close to the River Honddu, which the stream you've been following soon joins. At one point you pass by the remains of a building which appears to have become some form of shrine.

PRIORY MILL

Also known at one time as Burges Mill, this was a fulling mill, then woollen mill, that was working between at least the mid 1600s and the early 1900s. It certainly became a very successful mill, and was perhaps profitable for most of its life, for when John Handley, the then owner, died in 1890 he left £6,825 in his will, one of the highest recorded amounts left by any craftsman, mercer or gentleman at that period. The current owners have sought to preserve and restore the buildings and their setting, running a small campsite and converting space above the old stables for holiday lets. The mill is the only surviving water-powered mill on the Honddu.

In due course the path will pass below a white painted house. At the end of this field, cross a stile to join another path. Turn right on this to cross the Honddu by a footbridge, and then left to follow the river to your left: at all the junctions then reached take the left-hand option, so keeping the river close to your left. You will pass Priory Mill and its campsite and in time you will reach a T-junction of paths, at which you turn right towards the cathedral, then left at the next junction.

BRECON CATHEDRAL

A priory of St John the Evangelist was founded as a cell of the Benedictine abbey of Battle in Sussex by Bernard de Neufmarché in the late 1090s. It was designed so that the nave served as the parish church, the abbot appointing the parish priest. Despite being granted land around the town and further afield in the Marches and in Wales, the priory only ever numbered its monks in single figures. In c.1225 there was a major refurbishment during which the chancel (used by the monks) was lengthened and the transepts and chapels were rebuilt. It became a place of pilgrimage, holding a number of relics, though it was best known for its rood screen topped by a golden cross, which was made c.1408. At the same time the chancel and the aisles became home to a number of guild chapels, of which only that of the corvisors (leather-workers) survives on the northern side, now dedicated to St Keyne; near the chapel is a display of tools and modern examples of the work of medieval corvisors involved in the shoe trade. At the Dissolution, many of the priory buildings (including the prior's lodgings, a guest house, an almonry and a tithe barn) were adapted to secular use, but the church survived as it also served the town's inhabitants. The cloisters were demolished in the 18th century (though part of the battlemented precinct walls and entrance gateway were retained) and by early in the following century the church was in need of urgent repair, with many of the windows boarded over. Some repairs were carried out in 1836 to prevent further deterioration and then, in the 1860s and '70s major restoration was carried out under Sir George Gilbert Scott, the current chancel vaulting and other roofwork being of his design. In 1923 the church became the cathedral of the new diocese of Swansea and Brecon and over the following 20 years many nearby buildings that had belonged to the former priory were reacquired, either by purchase or through gift, for use by the diocese. Further renovation has since been carried out, including the strengthening of the central tower, the rebuilding of St Lawrence's chapel, and the provision of a reredos to the high altar, the architect being W.D. Caröe.

In the nave is a font with carvings in the style of the Herefordshire School of Romanesque Sculpture, the craftsmen of which were active in the 1130s and early 1140s. The sources of inspiration are many and varied. *The Bestiary*, the Book of Beasts derived from the Greek *Physiologus* which was translated into Latin in the 5th century, is considered the primary source. This gives shape to many mythical beasts, to which have been added elements of Celtic, Anglo-Saxon and Romano-British styles, enriched by encounters with sculptures seen on the pilgrimage trail to Santiago de Compostela. The master craftsmen seem to have received their training at Hereford Cathedral, where forerunners of the work of the Herefordshire School can be seen. Here at Brecon, the bowl of the font originally had six beaded medallions that issued from the mouths and ears of gaping faces, themselves derived from classical masks. Only four of the medallions now survive, one depicting a dragon curled on itself, a second a long-necked bird, often a feature of the School (shown in the photograph here), a third a strange biped, again with a long neck, and a fourth showing symmetrical foliage growing from a central stem.

8 Having visited the cathedral, with your back to its door, walk straight ahead along an avenue of yew trees, then leave the graveyard and cross the road. Turn left, then at the T-junction turn right along Pendre and head back to your car.

Close to the font, by one of the nave pillars, is the largest cresset stone so far known in the UK; it has 30 shallow cups for holding tallow and wick so as to provide light in the church (see photo below). Also nearby, in the south aisle, is the tomb of Sir David Williams (d.1613) and his wife, their effigies carved from alabaster. The pulpit incorporates parts from the 15th-century rood screen, and two fragments of wall painting remain in the west crossing arch. In the south transept is a 17th-century cupboard with panels carved in relief that are reputed to have come from Neath Abbey. In the Havard Chapel (to the east of the north transept) there is a memorial to Walter and Christina Awbrey of Abercynrig dated 1312, comprising a single slab carved with two recumbent effigies. Near the entrance to St Keyne's chapel is a rare wooden recumbent figure (dated *c.*1555) of the wife of one of three men of the Games family, once commemorated by an all-wood three-tier tomb.

Walk 2 Mynydd Illtud

7.5 miles (if walking from Libanus, less if walking from the National Park Visitor Centre) mainly on lanes and grassy tracks, with paths across fields when returning to Libanus, the only section where there are also stiles. If you start from the National Park Visitor Centre the walk is very gentle, though if you start in Libanus the climb onto Mynydd Illtud is not overly strenuous. Includes a couple of standing stones, the site of an early church and saint's possible grave, an Iron Age hillfort and a castle motte.

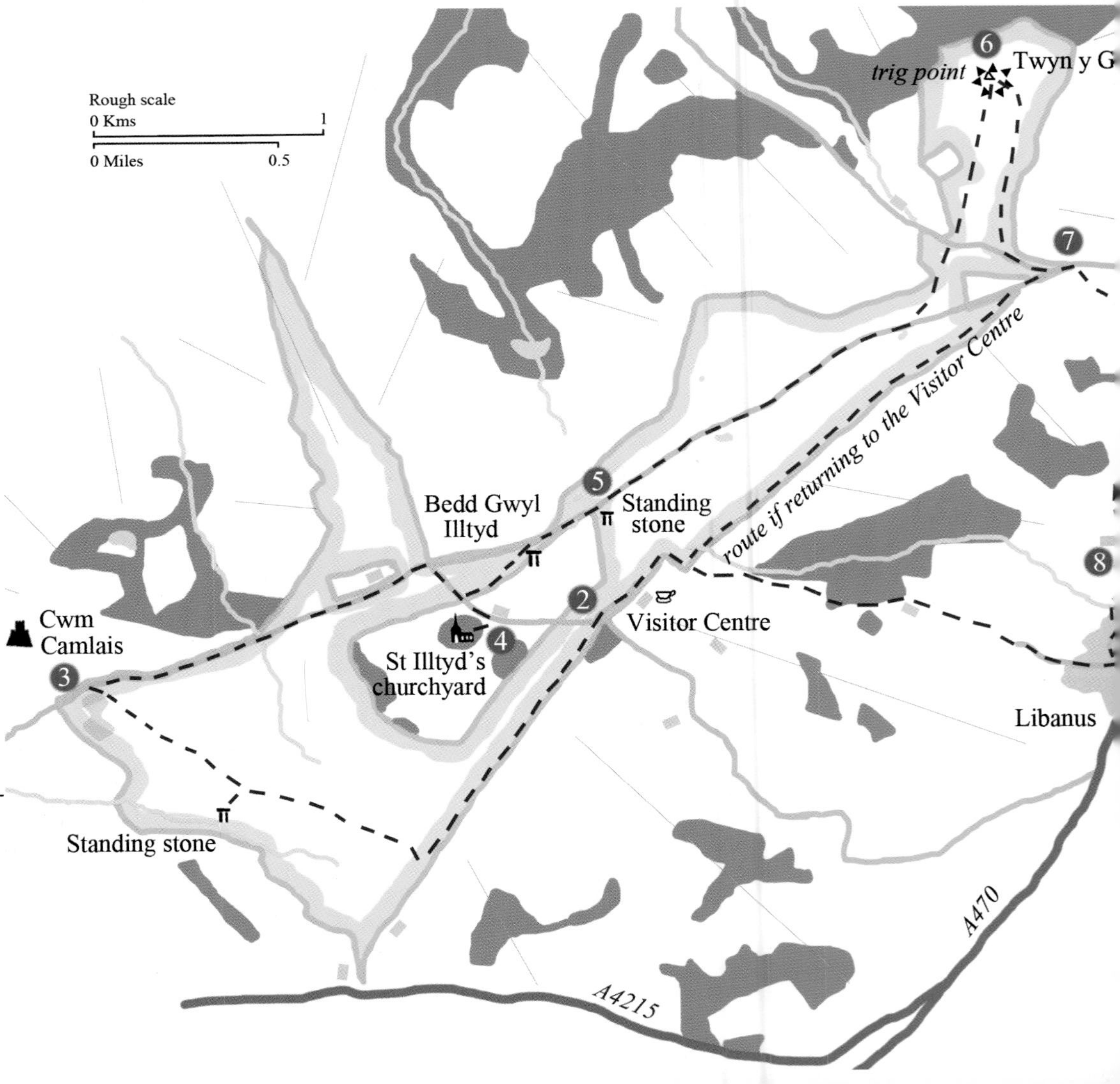

You can do this walk either from Libanus (grid ref: 995 260) or from the National Park Visitor Centre (follow the signs off the A470 in Libanus) up on Mynydd Illtud.

If you start from Libanus you can choose to time your walk to start or finish at the Tai'r Bull Country Inn and use its car park, or you can park in the village slightly to the north of the pub (in the direction of Merthyr Tydfil) in a crescent of road, near the red telephone box. If you start the walk from the National Park Visitor Centre, (see overleaf), there is a charge for parking here, but it gives you the option to avoid the (not overly strenuous) climb up onto Mynydd Illtud, the only slight climb then being to the Twyn y Gaer hillfort. There is also a tea room at the National Park Visitor Centre.

1 If starting the walk from Libanus, first head to the red telephone kiosk! With your back to its door turn left and in a few yards take the road called Glan Tarrell, to the right just past the converted chapel. The road soon meets a road turning off to the right with a footpath sign pointing along each option: keep straight ahead here (you will return by the other path). Follow the road, which becomes a gravelled and then stony track as it heads uphill, passing Argoed Lwyd, a mountain centre run by Hampshire County Council, on the left. Follow the track up onto the area of open access land on Mynydd Illtud, and almost immediately you'll come to the parking area on the left for the National Park Visitor Centre, around

which you turn left and then follow the road serving the visitor centre to a T-junction.

MYNYDD ILLTUD

Mynydd Illtud is formed from a mixture of mudstones and sandstones, the latter having been quarried in places. During the last ice age the area was covered in ice, resulting in a spread of glacial till over the hill and the occasional erratic block of sandstone. Traeth Mawr and Traeth Bach, two rock hollows towards the south-western end of the common, are now filled with peat.

If you parked at the visitor centre, head out of its car park on to the common and turn left to follow the road serving the visitor centre to where it meets a T-junction.

❷ For both options, at the T-junction keep ahead on the wide track which passes alongside a conifer plantation on your left, and beyond that the field boundaries that mark the edge of the common. As you approach a set of farm buildings directly ahead of you (standing just beyond the boundary of the common) and a few hundred yards before you would reach them, look out for a footpath gate in the fenceline on your left. When you are adjacent to this gate, your route turns right on an initially narrow path which gradually widens into a track.

Keep following this track until it reaches a road on the far side of the common, across which you can see the remains of Camlais Castle, though before you reach this point you might wish to make a diversion to visit a standing stone, and also see if you can spot the line of Sarn Helen, the Roman road which crosses the track.

To reach the standing stone, keep an eye out for where the track starts to pass bracken to its immediate left. At the end of this patch of bracken, reached in a few yards, a narrow path leads off to the left, following the edge of the bracken. Keep on this path till you reach the end of the bracken. The standing stone is some 25 yards off to your left and 20 yards away from the edge of the patch of bracken. Having visited the stone, return to the track.

STANDING STONES

There are two standing stones on the common, of which this is the southernmost. The other lies about halfway between this stone and the hillfort of Twyn y Gaer and will be seen later in the walk. Both stones are thought likely to be waymarkers, relating to some long-ago use of the common, the northern stone standing at the meeting place of four tracks. Nevertheless, in 1996 Cadw added the northern stone to the Schedule of Ancient Monuments giving its placement a supposed Bronze Age date (*c*.2300 – 800BC). For ley hunters, a line drawn between the two stones passes through the Celtic churchyard that stands on the common (and will be visited later in the walk). Folklore says that the stones were once robbers who stole a herd of pigs from Saint Illtyd, turned into stone as their punishment. The petrification of thieves is a common theme in the lives of Celtic saints, though sometimes it is just that their limbs are made to go stiff.

CWM CAMLAIS CASTLE

The castle mound hides the base of a circular tower *c*.12.5m in diameter externally with walls *c*.3.3m thick, set on a rocky outcrop, and surrounded by a ditch and outer bank. The whole site spans some 60m across, and there is no trace of any buildings other than the tower. A doorway was discovered in the eastern side of the remains of the tower during excavations in the 1980s. It is uncertain who built the castle, also known as Camlais, Blaencamlais, Maescar and Defynoch. However, it is thought to be the castle destroyed by Prince Edward in 1265, when Llywelyn of Wales was in alliance with Simon de Montfort and Edward was conducting military operations with Roger Mortimer and other Marcher lords. If so, the castle might have been built by Llywelyn, though the de Bohun earls of Hereford are other contenders, for the younger Humphrey de Bohun was a close companion in arms of Simon de Montfort, and Mortimer would have enjoyed discomfiting the family. At some point the de Bohuns granted the land hereabouts to Einion Sais to give him the wherewithal to strengthen the castle, and the Humphrey de Bohun who was earl in the 1270s ordered him to repair it. But it seems never to have been touched after its destruction in 1265. It's possible that the de Bohuns built the tower as a fortified hunting lodge when visiting the expanse of Fforest Fawr.

We have been unable to discern the line of Sarn Helen here (it is very clear later in the walk), but it crosses the track almost at a right angle somewhere near the track's highest point, and shortly before the track makes a slight bend to the left.

3 When you reach the road, turn right and walk along it, or follow a grass track just to its right. The road drops downhill and crosses a stream, just beyond which you join the line of Sarn Helen, which bends to the right at this point, having crossed the ground on your right, the modern road now following Sarn Helen's course across the common. The Roman road would have gone to the Roman fort at Y Gaer, some 2.5 miles to the west of Brecon.

Keep following the road, passing a small farm on your left, till you reach a turning off to the right. Take this, and as you walk along it, look slightly to your right to see the roughly circular and now wooded enclosure that indicates an old Celtic Christian churchyard. Cross a cattle grid and walk past the farm on the left-hand side of the road, and go through the first of two adjacent gates on your right and then through the gate into the old churchyard.

ST ILLTYD'S CHURCHYARD

The earlier recorded names of the site – Eglwysceyll in the 14th century, Capel ylldyt on Christopher Saxton's map of 1579 and Illtid Chapel on an estate map of *c.*1781 – show that its name means the chapel of St Illtyd, and tradition has it that this was where the 5th-century saint was martyred and then buried. A mound a quarter of a mile to the east on the common (which the walk will pass) is known as Bedd Gwyl Illtyd, 'bedd' being the Welsh for 'grave'. Whether this is the saint's grave is unknown, but what is certain is that the chapel stood in a remote location high on a stretch of hill, albeit only 500m from a Roman road that was still in use. A settlement never seems to have grown up in its vicinity, just a scattering of farms (the one over the road from the church probably dating to the late 1700s). The church was rebuilt in 1858 and repaired in 1888, yet described in 1911 as 'an ancient building of stone in the Early English style'. By the 1990s this was beyond sensible repair and was taken down almost to ground level, the process destroying anything of the earliest church that still remained above ground. The rise and fall in the ground level in the churchyard suggests other early use of the site, perhaps for burials; if the site had once been deemed especially holy due to its being believed to be the site of the martyrdom and burial of Illtyd, it may well be that for centuries people chose to be buried here. Knowledge of Illtyd comes from the *Life of St Samson*, which says that 'Illtud was of all the Britons the most accomplished in all the Scriptures, namely of the Old and New Testaments, and in those of philosophy of every kind, of geometry namely, and of rhetoric, grammar and arithmetic, and of all the theories of philosophy. And by birth he was a most wise magician, having knowledge of the future.'

4 Once you've seen the churchyard, return to the road and turn left (so initially retracing your steps). Once you have crossed the cattle grid back onto the common, turn right on a grassy track. Just after passing a gate into a field on your right, look out for a mound in the bracken between the grassy track you're following and the field's fence some 25 yards from the gateway; this is supposed to be the burial place of St Illtud. Continue along the track to rejoin the road, or follow the grassy track that shadows it to its right. When you pass the end of the fields on your right, turn right to walk a few yards to see the second standing stone.

5 The walk keeps following the road (or its neighbouring grassy track). When the road starts to gently slant downhill and before it makes a slight bend to the

right, you should be able to see slightly to the left of straight ahead the rise on which sits the hillfort of Twyn y Gaer, marked by its low earthen rampart, which is your next destination. Follow the road as it bends right, then take the first track off to the left, almost immediately turning right onto another, smaller, track. Follow this and it will join a larger track on the far side of the common. Turn right here to follow the track down into the valley bottom, cross the road here and then we suggest you take the main left-hand track up to the hillfort (you will be leaving it by one of the tracks seen to the right).

TWYN Y GAER

This oval hillfort measures roughly 100m by 85m and consists of a single bank with an entrance on the east, slightly inturned on its northern side. The bank appears to be a slight enhancing of the natural slope, with the only evidence of a ditch outside the bank being near the entrance. Is this simply evidence of the marking out of the site, construction never having progressed very far? Part of the northern side has since been quarried, whilst on the north-eastern side of the rampart there is evidence for the site of a hut, possibly of medieval date. On the southern and eastern approaches to the hillfort are several pillow mounds that date to around the 18th century, when rabbits were reared here for their meat. (For more on pillow mounds and rabbit farming, see PANT MAWR, p.34.)

Top left: One of the pillow mounds remaining from the days of rabbit farming, seen under a covering of bracken to the right of the path
Bottom left: This shows the exit you should take from the hillfort, along with the line of the long pillow mound in the bracken in the centre foreground

6 Having explored what you want of the hillfort, with your back to the trig point and facing Pen y Fan, take the track off to the left, which soon swings to the right. Look out for the mound off to the left part way down the hillside, and the long mound ahead of you where you pass through the fort's rampart – these are both pillow mounds, artificial mounds created for the rearing of rabbits in warrens; you may have noticed others, less visible, as you approached the hillfort.

Keep following this track as it bends to the right, passes the remains of a dead tree and then meets a road on which you turn left. At the T-junction with another road, turn left if returning to Libanus, or right if returning to the National Park Visitor Centre. If the latter, follow the road, but bear left off it when you reach a grassy track which will then shadow the left-hand side of the common and bring you back to the visitor centre.

7 If returning to Libanus, having turned left at the T-junction, cross the cattle grid, and immediately past the house on the right turn right where there is a footpath sign to take a lane that is initially tarmacked but soon turns to a gravel surface. This will lead you to a house where you keep right and head down a grassy bank between trees and a hedge to take a narrow path that soon leads to a stile alongside a ruined stone building. Cross the stile, then keep ahead across the field, following the sunken lane alongside the right-hand field boundary. At the far end of the field cross a stream and go through a field gate to then head across this next field, aiming slightly to the right of the peak of Pen y Fan. You will come to a stile into the next field, where Libanus is now visible below you. Over this stile, cross the top corner of the next field, aiming generally for Libanus but specifically for an oak tree which stands at the left-hand edge of a patch of old woodland on the far side of the field. Cross into the next field near the tree and head towards the farmhouse you can now see between you and Libanus. This will lead you to a stile to the right of a gate into the next field. Over the stile, head just to the left of the farmhouse where you will find a gate that will lead you to the farmyard in front of the house.

8 Cross the yard to join the lane that serves as the farm's access road, but when this almost immediately bends left, take the stile ahead into the next field. Then aim for a point just to the left of the white gable end of one of the houses that form Libanus (as a check, the point you want is some 50 yards up from the far left-hand corner of the field). Having crossed the field, you will find a wooden footbridge across a stream. Cross the bridge and follow the path on the other side to join a road. Turn left on the road and follow it along till it meets another road, turning left on this to return to where you parked.

Walk 3
Defynnog

4.25 miles, mainly on lanes and good quality tracks and grassy paths. Includes the village of Defynnog and an Iron Age hillfort. Few stiles. The walk is relatively easy with the ascent to the hillfort being long rather than steep and has sections with panoramic views (in clear weather). You could time the walk so as to also visit the Tanners Arms inn.

Park near the church in Defynnog (grid ref: 925 279).

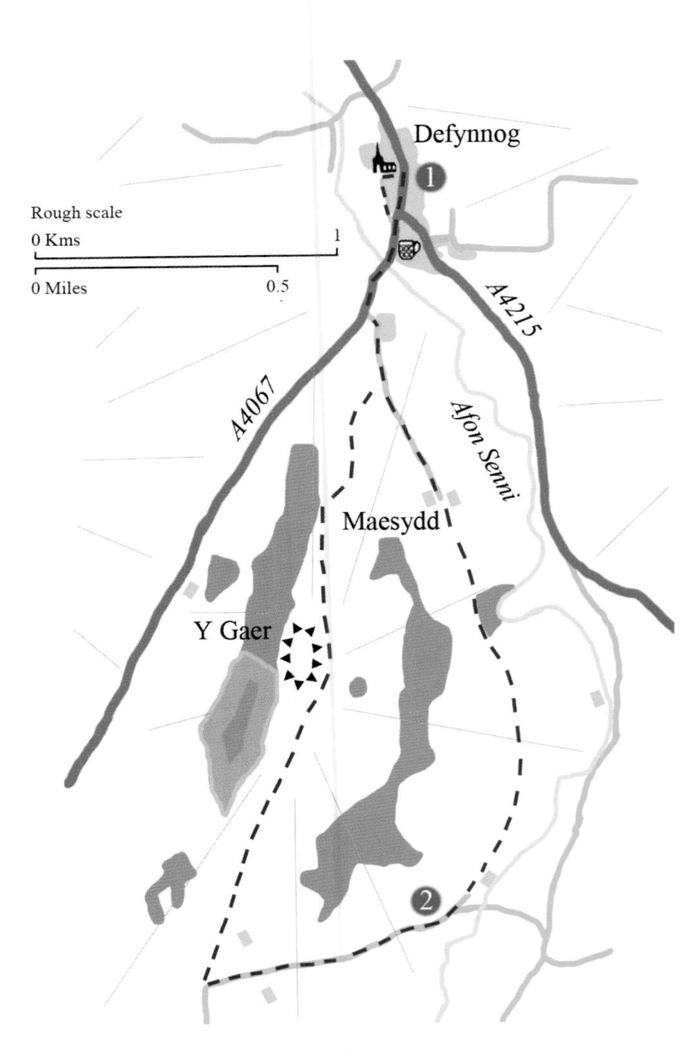

DEFYNNOG CHURCH

A pre-Norman foundation of the church is surmised from the dedication, its siting near the ancient yews that are in the churchyard, and various pre-Conquest features. These include an incised stone (now kept in the porch) which carries the 5th- or 6th-century Latin inscription Rugniatio [Fi}li Vendoni ('Rugniatis, son of Vendonius') and which some believe to carry possible Ogham marks down one edge, this indicating an early Irish language. This stone was later turned upside down and a ring cross added sometime between the 7th and 10th centuries. There is also a stone carved with a 9th- or 10th-century cross that has been reused as a lintel in the ringing chamber of the tower. Other probable pre-Norman features include the font, which has two inscriptions on the bowl, one in Lombardic lettering reading 'Siwurd + Gwlmer', and one in Runic lettering. The latter is strange, as it infers Viking authorship in an area not known for a Viking presence. Also early is the stoup. In addition the church seems to have acted as the minster church for the area, another sign of early foundation.

The north wall of the nave is considered to be part of the earliest structure and may retain a window that could have been constructed in pre-Norman days. The first time a church was recorded here was in 1254, and it is also mentioned in 1291. Most of the existing fabric dates to the late 1400s, however, in the Perpendicular style (though many windows are later). The building was restored in 1888-91 and further minor work was carried out in 1905. For a time, the west end of the nave was partitioned off and used as a schoolroom. Furnishings include an 18th-century pulpit on a later stone base, and an ornate reredos and east end panelling dating to the early 1900s. The yews (or technically just one yew) standing in the churchyard to the north of the church are thought to be possibly 5,600 years old, but in any event would already have been ancient trees and a significant feature of the landscape when the first church was built, and they may indicate that what was once a pagan site lies nearby. The lower branches include some rare golden boughs which must be left undamaged.

❶ Standing on the A4067 with your back to the path that leads to the church, turn right and walk along the pavement, staying on the A4067 at its junction with the A4215 (signposted to Merthyr Tydfil) and then passing the Tanners Arms on the left. Stay on the A road across the Afon Senni, then take the minor road (Glannau Senni) soon reached off to the left.

Follow this and in due course it will head through a gate between a set of farm buildings at Maesydd. After a while the road will lose its tarmac surface and become a grassy track, but just keep following the clear line of the track ahead. For a while it will narrow to become a stony path, but then it broadens into a grassy track once more and eventually leads past Wern Ddu, becomes a lane and reaches a minor road.

2 Turn right on the road and follow it uphill. Where the road makes a right-angled turn to the left near the crest of the hill, turn right onto a bridleway (through the right-hand gate of the two metal gates). Follow this along the ridge of the hill and you will gradually approach the ramparts of Y Gaer hillfort, which stands just to the left of the bridleway on the crest of the hill. As you walk along the ridge, remember to turn around from time to time to take in the wide views behind you.

Just past Y Gaer the bridleway enters a field, which you go straight across, aiming initially for a small rowan/ mountain ash that stands in the field. On the field's far

Y GAER (shown in the photograph below)
This consists of an oval-shaped main enclosure measuring roughly 110m by 80m defended essentially by enhancing the natural slope of the hill, with a bank and ditch on the north. To the south is a smaller annexe which is now more visible in the landscape than the main part of the hillfort. This was entered from the south-east, as was the main enclosure once one had passed through the annexe. Some of the entrance ways have been damaged by subsequent quarrying (the hill is composed of mudstones and siltstones with bands of sandstone, it being the latter that has been quarried in various places on the hill). There are no signs of any other recognisable features.

side the bridleway becomes a track and heads down the hillside, passing through several gates. Near the bottom, you will enter a field; walk along its left-hand edge. Eventually you will meet the road to Maesydd that you were on earlier. Turn left on this and then right on the A4067 to return to Defynnog. Turn left off the A road before returning to where you parked to visit the church, if you haven't done that yet. You may also wish to walk down the A road beyond where you parked to see Church Row.

CHURCH ROW
The row of houses was built *c.*1840 in Tudor style, presumably for one of the local estates, on the site of earlier buildings shown on a map of 1829.

Walk 4
Ystradfellte & Sarn Helen

6.75 miles with a 1 mile possible extension. On a mixture of roads, wide tracks and paths across fields. Few stiles. The route is rolling, the main ascent being the stretch along the road heading north from Ystradfellte. Includes walking on the line of a Roman road, a standing stone, evidence of a rabbit-farming enterprise, a Bronze or Iron Age hillfort, a Norman castle site and other historical features.

You can either park Ystradfellte (there's a car park near the centre of the village, grid ref: 930 135) and start the walk from there (point 8), or use the car park at the top of the road heading north from Ystradfellte at Blaen Llia (grid ref: 927 165) and start the walk from there (point 1). If you wish to visit the New Inn in Ystradfellte at some stage in the walk, check current details on the website www.waterfallways.co.uk.

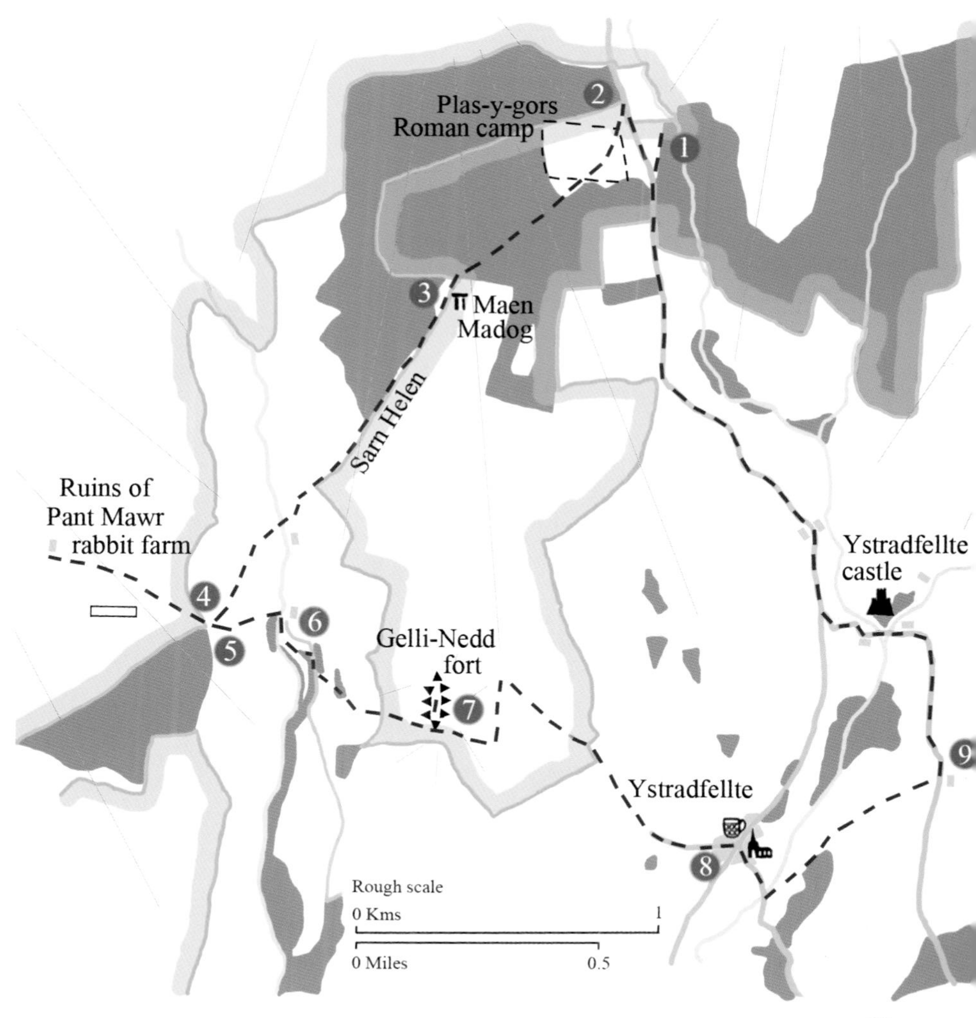

❶ Walk back up the track you drove down to reach the car park, and turn right on the road. After 450 yards you will reach, on the left, a wide gravelled area leading to a signposted track.

❷ Take this track, which follows the line of the Roman road known as Sarn Helen. Just before you reach a track off to the right and a wide turning area you will pass through a bank. It is difficult to be certain because of all the subsequent disruption to the ground here, but this is at least close to where the boundaries of a Roman marching camp should lie, and it does seem that the bank on the left soon makes a near right-angled turn to the right and then runs along the hillside above the current road. Any other putative remains of the outline of this camp have been obscured by the subsequent forestry.

Ignore the aforementioned track off to the right and keep following the well-stoned track that follows the course of Sarn Helen. Just over the crest of the hill you will reach the standing stone called Maen Madog on your left.

❸ Keep on along Sarn Helen, and when it loses its recent crushed stone surface, you may be able to spot stones that may have formed part of the original Roman paved surface. In due course Sarn Helen will adopt a zig-zag course down the hillside, passing through a gateway on the edge of the open access land and then descending to meet the waters of the Nedd Fechan. Cross

MAEN MADOG

This stone stands 11 feet tall and is inscribed on one edge with the Latin text Dervacus filius justi [h]ic jacit (Dervacus, son of Justus, lies here). This suggests that it may have been erected as a grave marker to someone who died when travelling this road, probably during the Roman period and before the adoption of Christian practices, or it may be a prehistoric megalith that was adopted for this use. The stone is not in its original position, however. In *c.*1800 it was reported as lying on its side, but it was stood up *c.*1850 next to a pit thought to indicate the place of Dervacus's burial. It was moved a short distance in 1940, presumably when work was carried out on the track. The stone was known as Maen Madog by at least 1500, when it appears as such in the earliest surviving farm leases for the area. Curiously, in 1798 a chance discovery was made about 100 yards away of another burial stone incised with a cross and an inscription in Ogham that translates as 'Of Gluvoca', suggesting an Irish Christian burial. This stone is now kept in the museum at Cyfartha Castle in Merthyr Tydfil.

ROMAN CAMP AND SARN HELEN

Sarn Helen is the name given to a number of Roman roads in Wales which take their name from Elen, a Romano-British princess and the wife of the emperor of Britain, Maximus, *sarn* being the Welsh for a causeway. Maximus, known in Welsh as Macsen Wledig, was proclaimed emperor by his soldiers in 383AD, when governor of Britain. He took many of the troops stationed in Britain over to Gaul where he defeated the Emperor Gratian, and in a settlement the following year he was recognized as Emperor of Britain, Gaul, Spain and Africa. Liked by his troops, but ambitious and prickly, he invaded Italy in 387 but was defeated and killed in 388. Unfortunately for folklore, the Roman roads in Britain would have been constructed before the era of Maximus and Elen. This stretch of Sarn Helen was part of the route from a fort in what is now Neath in south Wales all the way to a fort near Conwy in the north.

The Plas-y-gors Roman marching camp covers an area of 8.47ha and probably predates the road. Such camps were built by the army to protect the soldiers when camping overnight and were sometimes occupied only for that single night. The line of the ditch and earth ramparts of the camp was discovered by an aerial survey, with some exploratory trenches subsequently being dug. Analysis of a pollen sample taken from beneath a rampart indicated some tree-clearance prior to construction. The track you walk on through the camp does not necessarily strictly follow the original course of Sarn Helen. It is likely that the present track enters the camp at what would have been its north-eastern corner, roughly at the point where the existing two tracks meet, and then bends to the south-west and crosses the camp to pass through the centre of what would have been the southern rampart. The outline of the camp, already difficult to discern, is now further hidden by forestry activity. Few Roman artefacts have been found in the area.

the bridge and follow the track on the far side, which turns half left and heads uphill. Keep right at a fork reached just before a small copse and later on follow it uphill past a young forestry plantation on your right. Near the end of this, and just before you reach a gate across the track, you will come to a tall footpath sign on the left-hand side of the track.

4 Here you have a choice. The circular walk continues by taking the path to the left, but you may wish to take a pleasant excursion to the right to view the remains of Pant Mawr farm and possibly see the remains of a rabbit farming enterprise carried out in the mid 1800s (details on p.34). 'Possibly' because the remains are hidden in the vegetation, and one more obvious feature, a rectangular walled enclosure that is marked on Ordnance Survey maps, is almost as difficult to discern, in part because the footpath that passes through it is difficult to find.

To take this side excursion of about a mile there and back, turn right through the gate and follow the clear, stony track. In over a quarter of mile, take the footpath that leaves the track off to the left (the junction should have a standing footpath post) on a grassy sward and soon reaches the remains of Pant Mawr Farm. Alongside is a plan of the rabbit farm remains that have been identified in this area, the most visible being the rectangular enclosure, the photo above the map indicating the remains of this feature, which is believed to have been

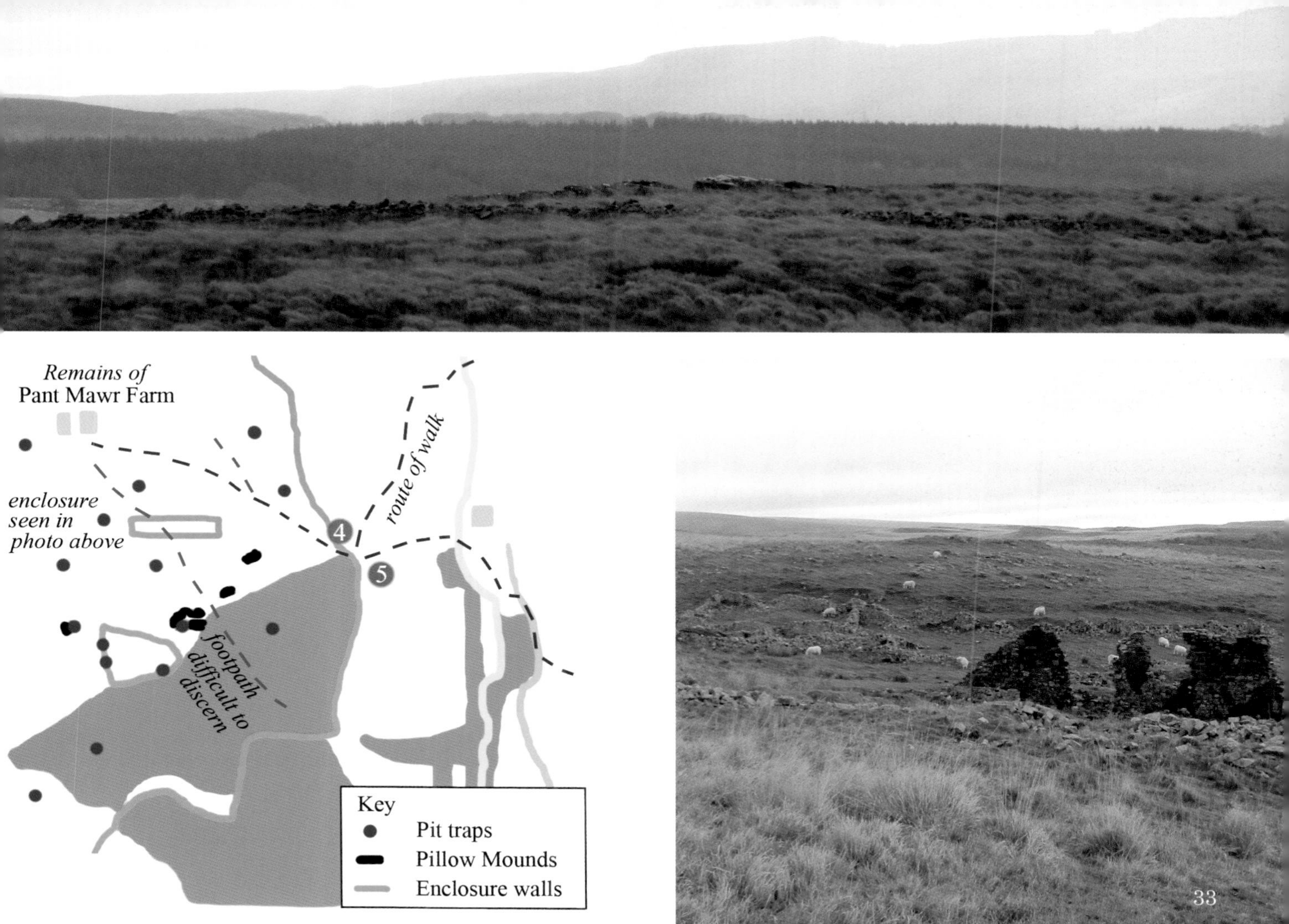
Remains of
Pant Mawr Farm
enclosure
seen in
photo above
route of walk
4
5
footpath
difficult to
discern
Key
Pit traps
Pillow Mounds
Enclosure walls

PANT MAWR RABBIT FARMING

In the 1800s there were a number of short-lived rabbit farms in the Brecon Beacons which raised rabbits for their fur rather than their meat. The Bells, a Scottish family, moved from Lincolnshire to Pant Mawr in the 1830s and between then and the late 1850s, when the land was acquired by the McTurk family, they developed an extensive rabbit warren. The area enclosed for the total warren was enormous, some 690 hectares being enclosed by stone walls. Within these, 93 pillow mounds of varying sizes, artificial mounds created for rabbits to make their burrows, have been identified, with further artificial mounds probably having been created in the areas to the south that have since been afforested. Scattered around are walled enclosures which created rabbit-proof places for cultivating fodder. Since creating rabbit-proof gateways was difficult, in most cases it seems that parts of the walls were taken down when the area was turned over for the rabbits to graze. Some of the enclosures suggest that near the tops of the walls there was a course that projected into the enclosure, which suggests that these were designed to keep rabbits from escaping; they appear to have been used to house breeding does. Smaller enclosures housed pits constructed to catch the rabbits. Some of these were simple affairs, others relatively sophisticated, with trap doors set into wooden floors which tipped the rabbits into the pits. The pit enclosures hereabouts are often quadrilateral in shape, typically 20m in length, 13m wide at one end and tapering to 6m at the other. Many of the pits were simply covered with brash (small twigs and other plant debris) on which small pieces of turnip and swede were scattered to lure the rabbits. The brash could not support the weight of the rabbits, which would fall into the stone-lined pits below. The larger rabbits would be killed and skinned, the smaller rabbits released. The rabbit meat appears to have been sold locally as a side income. The rabbits were normally killed in the winter months, when their fur was thickest, and it may be that the Beacons were favoured for such farms as it was felt that the harsh climate would make the rabbits develop thicker fur.

an area reserved for growing crops to feed the rabbits. Having completed whatever explorations you want, return to where the gate crossed the track at the start of this side trip, then keep ahead down the hillside.

5 The circular walk continues by following the field boundary on your right downhill, passing through a pair of small metal footpath gates as you go, to then follow the edge of a small piece of woodland to a footbridge back across the Nedd Fechan. Across the bridge, the path bends to the right and enters the field ahead through a small gate. Head across this field, keeping to the left of a group of trees that grow on the flanks of a tall bank that runs through the field shadowing the course of the river. When adjacent to this group of trees, look at the fenced field boundary on your left, in which you should see a stile almost immediately above you. Head for this stile, cross it, walk up the steps on the far side and emerge onto a lane on which you turn right.

6 Walk along the lane, and you'll soon be walking alongside a field on your left. You want to take the bridleway that starts by going through the gate that enters this field and then heads to the far right-hand corner of the field. Here a path leads through a patch of ground to a small gate. Go through this and follow the path that slants uphill through woodland, which it leaves through another small gate to enter an area of rough grazing. Cross this, bearing right when the path forks, to a small gate on the far side to re-enter the area of open access land.

Cross the first part of this by following a track to a gate on the far side of a fenced area, avoiding the assorted shake holes as you go. Through this next gate, climb up the rise ahead of you and at the top bear left to discover, perhaps somewhat surprisingly, an area of limestone pavement, created by acidic rainwater eating away at the limestone and creating underground streams and cave systems. The limestone would have been quarried for building material and for the extraction of lime for agricultural purposes in lime kilns. This is also an area deemed once to have been a 'fort' (named Gelli-Nedd) and if you walk through the area of limestone pavement you'll come to what could be the line of an embankment on the far side delineating part of the fort's curtilage.

GELLI-NEDD FORT

The site, measuring, roughly 60m from the north-west to the south-east by 45m, has a steep natural rock escarpment defence on its west and a less steep one to its east, leaving the south and north as especially requiring man-made defences. The rampart is formed of partly grass-covered roughly coursed limestone rubble, which may originally have been constructed as a wall, strongest on the north (the photograph below looks out across this rampart); loose blocks of limestone likewise might have provided some of the original building material. The entrance was on the north-east. In 1976 the Ordnance Survey identified two small scoops in the ground that it was thought were the bases for the construction of two huts, but these are now generally considered impossible to make out.

7 The photograph above shows the route you follow from the 'fort'. Essentially you head down the far side of the fort from the valley from which you approached it to another gate. Then follow the path that heads directly downhill from this gate to meet, just beyond the low point in this 'valley', a track running at right angles to the direction you've been following.

Turn left on this and follow it up the 'valley'. Shortly before you would reach an area of limestone rocks, you will meet another track. Turn right on this and follow it across and round the hillside. In due course, as you start to gently descend the hillside, you will pass through an

area which is marked on the OS map as having pillow mounds and cairns. The path will lead you alongside a short section of wall on your left to a gate which leads out onto a track between fields. Walk down this track and it will lead you out to join a road on which you continue downhill into the village of Ystradfellte.

YSTRADFELLTE CHURCH

The current church is thought to date from the 1500s, there being an absence of any earlier architectural features. It could be that some of the walling was constructed earlier, but no records suggest an earlier building. In 1809 it was reported that the church was in a poor state, with an uneven floor, broken windows and 'decayed' seats. It appears to have been in better condition when the antiquary Sir Stephen Glynne visited in 1855, though he noted that the interior was gloomy. Restorations were carried out in 1870 and 1882 when pews were installed, whilst the reredos and existing altar were added around 1900. In 1971 the chancel (which has a fine panelled barrel roof) was redecorated and the lychgate restored.

8 Cross the road junction to the church, turning right to walk past the post office and village hall down to a bridge across the Afon Mellte. Immediately across the bridge, take the path off to the left, which goes through a gate or over a stile (the choice is yours!) and follows a stony track uphill. Keep following this track across the hillside. It passes an area off to the right that provides a feeding station for livestock and then enters an area strewn with the remnants of black plastic silage bags, on the far side of which you need to look for a stile that marks the continuation of the track which you continue to follow. You may need to walk along the edge of the field above the line of the track where the track itself has become overgrown. Yet further on, the track is used as a sheep handling area. Here you need to spot the stile that will get you through the various sheep pens. In many places, however, this is a rather lovely path, and it will lead you out, via two metal field gates, onto a road just in front of a stone house.

9 Turn left on the road and follow it down to a bridge across the Afon Dringarth. Between this river and the next, the Afon Llia, is the site of a motte and bailey castle, now rather obscured by trees. The wide gravel track between the castle site and the Afon Dringarth is a public bridleway, and you may want to walk a short way along this to get other views of the castle site, best seen in winter when the trees are bereft of leaves.

YSTRADFELLTE CASTLE

The castle site lies in the trees behind and to the right of the buildings

The castle, also known as Castell Coch after the red (*coch*) sandstone of which it was built, has a form that suggests that it was built by the Welsh rather than the Normans. It sits on a triangular-shaped piece of raised ground, the apex of which points at the road along which you walk past it and at the junction of the Afon Llia and Afon Dringarth. Facing the road would have been a round tower, probably three storeys high, with walls some 2.5m thick and an internal diameter of 6m. The tower would have jutted out from the flanking walls which ran along the tops of the two banks above the stream valleys for some 35m in the case of the western wall, and 45m in that of the eastern wall, for it includes a dog-leg turn at one point. These were joined at their far end by a wall running from bank to bank in which there was a gateway. This curtain wall appears to have had no other towers, but a large freestanding hall block abutted the western wall. Beyond the northern wall that ran across the isthmus of the hillside was a large bailey, protected at its northern end by a massive earthen rampart and ditch. Use of poor quality earthen mortar has not aided preservation of the castle's walls.

The freestanding hall and all but freestanding southern tower are certainly more akin to Welsh castle design than Norman, yet the castle is in Norman hands when it is mentioned in the records. In 1230 it is mentioned as being in the hands of the de Braoses, then lords of Brecon, in 1276-77 it was a meeting point for Marcher lords in the wars with the Welsh, and in 1316 it was where Llywelyn Bren surrendered. Bren had been a loyal adherent of the de Clare earls of Gloucester, holding high office in Glamorgan. However, with the earl's death at Bannockburn with no male heirs, the earldom temporarily passed into the hands of the English crown. Edward II appointed officials who were anti-Welsh in sentiment and Bren was dismissed from his post. Provoked by this, and by the greed of Edward's favourites, who quickly swarmed over the earldom, Bren unsurprisingly rose in revolt. He received considerable support, but the Mortimer and de Bohun Marcher lords united against him and his revolt was soon suppressed.

The walk continues along the road, crossing a bridge over the Afon Llia and continuing to a road junction. Here you turn right and soon walk steadily uphill, eventually reaching a track off to the right to a car park at Blaen Llia. If this is where you started the walk, then walk down the track to your car, but if you started in Ystradfellte, continue along the road and after 450 yards you will reach, on the left, a wide gravelled area leading to a signposted track. Go to point 2 to continue following the directions for the walk.

Walk 5
Morlais & Pontsticill

6 miles, partly on the Taff Trail, together with minor roads and cross field paths, and those paths leading uphill to Morlais Castle, the latter in good condition and well walked. The climb to Morlais Castle is fairly steep in places, but much of the rest of the walk is fairly flat or with only gentle undulations. Includes the sites of two castles, one of them impressive, a church and its ruined forebear, Pontsticill dam and railway station.

You can start the walk from a number of places. You can park in a few spaces opposite what has been a car park on the road below Morlais Castle, just south of the narrow bridge over the Taf Fechan, at grid ref: 045 096, in which case start the walk at point 1. Or you can park at or near either of the pubs (the Butchers Arms and the Red Cow) in Pontsticill, in which case follow the walk from point 6, or there is some parking alongside the reservoir at the start of the road that leads to Pontsticill Station on the Mountain Railway at grid ref: 063 119, in which case start the walk from point 5.

❶ From where you've parked, walk down the road towards the Taf Fechan, taking the footpath off to the

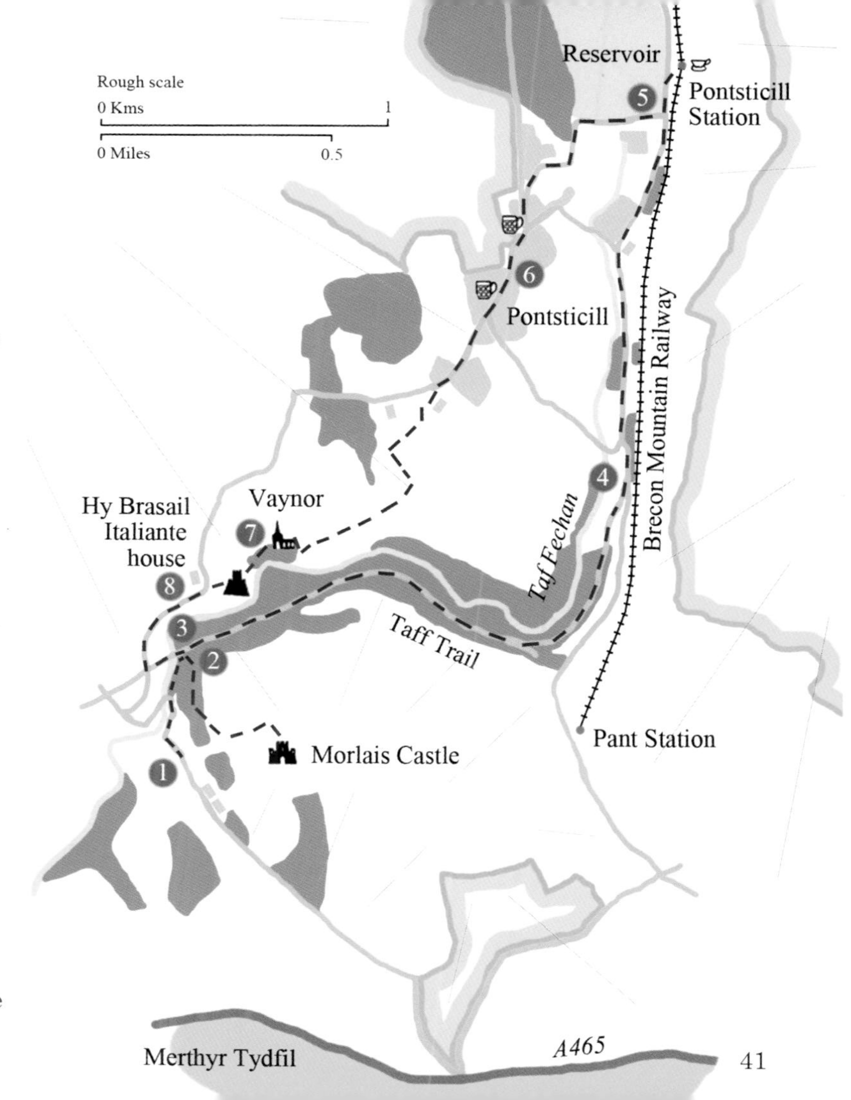

right just before you reach the narrow bridge across the river (though, in winter in particular, it is first worth going onto the bridge to see the water rushing through the mini gorge which it crosses). This path will lead alongside the river and immediately before you reach the arches to the old railway viaduct, turn right on a path that leads uphill to a junction of paths near the eastern end of the railway viaduct on your left.

If starting the walk at point 1, you have a choice here as to whether you visit the remains of Morlais Castle now or at the end of your walk, for the circular walk will bring you back to this point.

❷ To visit the castle, take the path off to the right that slants uphill, which will meet another path which roughly contours round the hillside. Turn right on this and after 150 yards, take the stony path off to the left that once again slants uphill. This will lead you out to a wide track near an old quarry which has cut deeply into the hillside. Cross this track and take the path on the other side which follows the lip of the quarry uphill. Once you are above the quarry you will be on open hillside and can bear right to reach the ruins of Morlais Castle. To continue the circular walk, you will need to return by the same series of paths to the point near the end of the old railway viaduct.

MORLAIS CASTLE

The castle owes its existence to the wars with Llywelyn ap Gruffydd in the aftermath of the barons' quarrels with Henry III, when Llywelyn was allied with Simon de Montfort. In 1268, the Marcher lord of Glamorgan, Gilbert de Clare, built the vast and militarily impressive castle of Caerphilly to assert his power and influence in the area. Despite Llywelyn's death in 1282, the area was not at peace and in 1287 Gilbert led an army northwards from Caerphilly, in part to secure the route to Brecon by clearing trees alongside the mountain road to make ambush less likely, but also with the aim of building another strong castle at Morlais, on the edge of his lordship. When complete, the castle consisted of a large northern keep, the remains of which collapsed during a storm in the early 1800s, to the south of which was an inner ward that contained the hall. The larger southern ward, entered by a gateway on the eastern side adjacent to a tower at the juncture of the two wards, had its own keep at the southern end. (The undercroft survives, exhibiting quality ashlar stonework, suggestive of how the rest of the castle may have appeared.) This ward had two further towers in its walls, one on the eastern wall between the keep and the entrance, and the other at the juncture of the southern and western walls. The ward held a number of buildings built against the walls and a cistern for holding water. Outside the walls, ditches were cut through the bedrock (quarrying to the west of the castle has served to markedly improve any ditch on this side). To the south of the castle, traces of worn rubble ramparts may suggest a lightly defended outer bailey, or could represent an Iron Age development of the site later largely obliterated by the castle. After the dispute with Humphrey de Bohun in the 1290s (for which see Vaynor Castle on p.50), the castle seems to have been neglected and does not appear in the records again. Gilbert de Clare died shortly after his squabble with de Bohun, and his heir, another Gilbert, died at Bannockburn in 1314, the male line dying with him and his estates being divided between three heiresses. No-one thought that maintaining a castle on a bleak, windswept hillside was worth the effort, especially with no local town and source of wealth to protect (the importance of Merthyr Tydfil lay in the future).

Above: Morlais Castle looking south, with the outline of the walls of the hall in the foreground and the southern keep beyond. Between the two is the outline of the wall that separated the inner and outer wards, with the entrance to the castle just beyond where this wall meets the curtain wall on the left.

Below: Morlais Castle looking north, showing the hollow marking the site of the well beyond which lies the outline of the wall that divided the outer and inner wards, with the remains of the northern keep beyond.

3 To continue the circular walk, at the junction of paths near the eastern end of the old railway viaduct, cross over the railings to join the tarmacked Taff Trail, which follows the old railway line, on which you turn right. Your route is now very clear for a while: you simply follow the Trail till you meet a road, but some way along look out for the entrance to the tunnel on your right which marks the route of a second railway line.

4 When the Taff Trail meets a road, turn left on the road and walk under the bridge that would have carried the railway, keeping right at the road junction almost immediately reached, and continue to follow the road along (this is still part of the Taff Trail). About half a mile along the road you take the

TAFF TRAIL AND RAILWAY

The Taff Vale Railway was Wales's first major railway, on which rolling stock was to be powered by steam engines. It was constructed initially to serve the Dowlais ironworks at Merthyr, which by 1830 were the largest in the world, but soon also transported coal to the docks in Cardiff. Construction of the railway began at Pontypridd in 1837, with Isambard Kingdom Brunel as its chief engineer. In 1841 the section between Merthyr Tydfil and Cardiff was opened, with 23 branch lines following to link other mining valleys to the docks. The railway so reduced transport costs that it became economically possible to export coal even to countries such as Argentina and India.

An idea developed to link the Dowlais ironworks and the coalmines in the area to the Midlands via a connection to the railway serving Hereford. This would require crossing the ridge of the Brecon Beacons. In 1859 Parliament authorised the Brecon and Merthyr Tydfil Junction Railway to construct a line from Dowlais to Talybont-on-Usk, whilst a separate line from Hereford to Brecon was approved. In 1860 the Brecon and Merthyr Tydfil Junction Railway gained additional powers to extend its line from Talybont to Brecon. Construction work began in January 1860 and by 1 January 1863 it was possible for a train to reach Brecon, with the line between Brecon and Pant fully operational from 1 May. (Pant is the next station south of Pontsticill, and is now part of the Brecon Mountain Railway.) Meanwhile, in 1862 the company gained approval for the line to run to Merthyr and connect with the Taff Vale Railway, the junction being formed at Pontsticill. It is part of this section of the railway network that forms part of this walk.

TAFF TRAIL AND RAILWAY (cont.)
In 1922 the Brecon and Merthyr Railway became part of the Great Western Railway, at a time when many of the ironworks around Merthyr and Dowlais were in decline. In 1933 pooling arrangements were made with the London Midland and Scottish Railway for handling mineral traffic, which resulted in a large reduction of traffic through the Brecon Beacons in favour of more efficient routes. Following the Second World War and nationalisation, traffic reduced further. The Merthyr to Pontsticill service was withdrawn on 13 November 1961 and closures elsewhere meant that by 31 December 1962 Brecon had no passenger train service. Goods and mineral traffic to Pontsticill ended in May 1964.

BRECON MOUNTAIN RAILWAY
In 1977, railway enthusiast Tony Hills purchased 5 miles of the abandoned trackbed of the former Brecon and Merthyr Railway at Pant and moved his existing collection of rolling stock there. Track was laid between Pant and Pontsticill in 1979-80, where the station house was renovated. Seven bridges were repaired or replaced. The first train ran between the stations in 1980. Between 1982 and 1996 a new station and workshop were built at Pant. In 1995 a further 1.5 miles of track was opened from Pontsticill to Dol-y-Gaer, and in 2014 the line was further extended to Torpantau, just short of the southern entrance of the Torpantau Tunnel, making a total distance of some 4.5 miles. By 2016, the original waiting room at Pontsticill was converted to a museum housing various stationary steam engines and three locomotives. The museum and café are open when the trains are running.

road off to the right (itself shortly after a driveway that leads off to the right) that heads slightly uphill. This will lead you past the Pontsticill waterworks below you to your left and up to the dam that holds back the Pontsticill Reservoir.
If you wish to visit Ponsticill Station, when you reach the dam, take the road ahead alongside the reservoir and you'll reach the entrance to the station in about 200 yards. There is a café here that is open for part of the year.

5 To continue the circular walk (or to start if you have parked here), turn along the dam and follow it to its far end, then stay on the road as it swings left, then right, then left again and leads you to a junction with another road. Here you turn left and walk into the village of Pontsticill, where there are two pubs, both on the right-hand side of the road, the Red Cow and the Butchers Arms.

6 Continue past these (or turn right on the road if starting from one of the pubs) and walk on past the public toilets on the right-hand side, then cross the road to the pavement on the other side to pass a small housing estate and garage block on the left, then take the bridleway off to the left that

PONTSTICILL RESERVOIR

Outbreaks of cholera in Merthyr Tydfil in 1832, 1849 and 1854 led to a demand for increased supplies of fresh water. This led to the construction of the Pentwyn Reservoir on the Taf Fechan river, which allowed water, albeit untreated, to reach, with the aid of steam-powered pumps, 11 standpipes and the ironworks. By 1880 increased demand led to Neuadd Reservoir, later Lower Neuadd Reservoir, being opened, located on the higher stretches of the Taf Fechan. Upper Neuadd Reservoir followed in 1902, as the settlements in the valleys expanded. Developments at Barry, Rhymney and Pontypridd demanded additional water and Pontsticill Reservoir (initially called the Taff Fechan Reservoir), planned in 1910 but with construction delayed by the First World War, was opened in 1927. This essentially extends the original Pentwyn reservoir, both reservoirs occupying a glacial valley scoured along the line of a geological fault named the Neath Disturbance. The 110ft-high dam is formed of earth, revetted with angled stone on its inner face. Reached on this walk at the far end of the dam is an outflow in the form of a circular convex-sided funnel with concrete ribs and a masonry lining. Nearby is a Gothic-style rock-faced octagonal valve tower with a steeply-pitched copper-clad roof.

starts down a tarmacked access lane (the bridleway's sign is on the right-hand side of the road) that initially leads to a white-painted house, passing through a gate alongside this house.

At the end of the tarmacked stretch, head through the metal field gate and continue down what is more a path than a bridleway, this soon bearing first left and then right to lead you to a novel stile into a field. The path follows the field boundary on your right to a metal footpath gate in the right-hand corner of the field. This may be padlocked, meaning you'll need to pass through the gappy fence to its left. Once in the next field, turn left and follow the hedgerow on your left and then continue along the bottom of the bank on your left, your target being a metal field gate in the field's far corner and to your right.

When you reach this gate, you want the path to its immediate right (there may be an old broken stile at its head, unless this has been repaired/replaced) which heads downhill between two fields. At the end of this path you will emerge in another field, the path now following the field boundary on your right. In due course this will lead towards a small field beyond which lies a church. Turn left just before this field and drop down the hillside a few yards to join a larger path on which you turn right. Go through the kissing gate to follow the path round to meet a lane. Turn left on this, reaching the church of St Gwynno's on your left.

VAYNOR CHURCHES

The first church, believed to have been built in the 700s or 800s and probably enlarged in the early 1100s, was burnt down in 1291 during the battle of Maesfaenor between Gilbert de Clare, earl of Gloucester, and Humphrey de Bohun, earl of Hereford (see under Vaynor Castle, p.50). The church was rebuilt in 1295. By 1867 it had become dilapidated and a new church, dedicated to St Gwynno, was built on a neighbouring site and completed by 1870. (St Gwynno, who lived around 487 to 507, is thought to have been an abbot, and was one of the many Celtic figures, subsequently deemed saints, who spread Christianity throughout the British Isles.) All that remains of the older church is its west end and a tower with battlemented parapets, clasping a pitched roof, on its east and west sides.

The architect of the new church was G.E. Robinson from Cardiff, the costs being met by Robert Thompson Crawshay, the Merthyr Tydfil ironmaster. It is constructed of multicoloured 'crazy paving' stonework with a roof of red tiles. By 1969 the tower was becoming unstable and the original spire was replaced by a strange-looking gabled 'cap'. In the 1980s the church was re-roofed with pantiles chosen to match the original as closely as possible. In the churchyard, Crawshay's slab tombstone, said to weigh 10 tons, has the inscription 'God forgive me', which has been taken by some as an apology for his closing of the Cyfarthfa Works, which made hundreds of his workforce destitute, or a plea for forgiveness for the way he behaved towards members of his own family.

THOMPSON CRAWSHAY
DIED MAY 10 1879
AGED 62 YEARS
GOD FORGIVE ME.

VAYNOR CASTLE

All that remains of the castle is a 3m high motte, which stands in a slight ditch on the edge of a gorge. Any sign of a possible bailey has disappeared due to subsequent ploughing, but the castle may have consisted of a single tower (like that at Camlais, see p.17), the motte covering its collapsed remains. The construction of Morlais Castle by Gilbert de Clare on the ridge opposite Vaynor angered Humphrey de Bohun, earl of Hereford and lord of Brecknock, who mistakenly believed that the land belonged to him. Royal officials sought to halt Gilbert's construction work, but he ignored their pleas. In 1290 both earls were summoned to a hearing, but Gilbert refused to turn up. Matters escalated and some of de Clare's men began making armed raids into de Bohun's territory. Technically the king could not interfere, for Marcher lords were free to make war on each other in the Marches or in Wales, but once de Bohun sought King Edward I's help, the king felt he could step in. De Bohun initially adhered to Edward's command to hold back, but with attacks by de Clare's men continuing (apart from killing some men, they carried off 1,070 head of cattle, 50 horses and bulls and countless sheep and pigs), he adopted military measures too. In 1291 men from the two earldoms are believed to have fought a battle at Maesfaenor, or Vaynor, during which the church was burned, de Bohun's men winning the day. De Clare refused to attend another summons in 1291, but eventually obeyed when Edward himself arrived at Abergavenny. Both earls were then found guilty (Edward was going to use this chance to clip the wings of Marcher lords in general) and summoned to Westminster for sentencing. This included imprisonment, fines and temporary confiscation of their estates, de Clare's sentence being the heavier. In 1294, another Welsh rising, this time by Morgan ap Maredudd of Machen, a local ruler whom de Clare had dispossessed, saw Caerphilly and Morlais attacked. At Caerphilly, the town was burned down but the castle was left unscathed, but it is possible that damage was inflicted on Morlais Castle, which may have been incomplete at the time.

7 Continue on the path you'll find at the end of the lane, almost immediately starting to pass above the ruins of the former church. Just before the path crosses a stream, there is a path to the left which leads into the grounds of the old church if you wish to visit it. The circular walk continues by crossing the stream (ignore the path that leads off to the right on the near side of the stream). After you have risen uphill and walked along the edge of a field on your left, look out for the motte of Vaynor Castle close to the path on the left, and through gaps in the hedge on the right for a startling Italianate house. Continue on the path to reach a road.

ITALIANATE HOUSE

In 1912 a solicitor, J.H. James, who lived in the Victorian house that survives as part of the existing building, added a wing with Italian pretensions. Two towers, one much smaller than the other, the larger apparently containing a monumental staircase, are linked by a room above an open loggia, the smaller tower having no rooms at all. One story tells that James, who was a solicitor in Merthyr, travelling there by train each working day, fell in love with an Italian lady (some say a Contessa, some say he met her whilst on holiday in Italy) and added the Italian wing to his house to encourage her to join him in his nest. If that was his plan, it failed, for James remained a bachelor all his life. He was a collector of porcelain and paintings, some of which can now be seen in Cyfarthfa Museum in Merthyr Tydfil, and it's possible that he used the extension to house his collection. Yet another story relates that he used the larger tower as an observatory. In 1948 the house was bought by a local butcher whose wife, of Irish ancestry, renamed the house 'Hy Brasail' after a mythical island off the Irish coast. In the stories associated with this island, it is always obscured by thick mist apart from one day every seven years. In 1674 a Captain Nisbet struck lucky and espied the island on its clear day and brought back reports that it was inhabited by a magician, who lived alone in a castle, and was populated by huge black rabbits.

8 Turn left on the road (or head right initially if you want a closer look at the Italianate house) and immediately after it crosses over the Taff Trail, take the steps on the right to join the trail. Turn right on the Trail and cross the old railway viaduct.

At the far end of the viaduct, cross the rails. If you parked below Morlais Castle and wish to return to your vehicle, turn right. If you wish to visit Morlais Castle, take the path ahead of you uphill and go to point 2, where 'the path off to the right' at the start of that point is the path you have taken ahead of you.

If you don't wish to visit Morlais Castle and parked either by the reservoir or in Ponsticill by the pubs, then continue ahead on the Taff Trail as set out in point 3.

Walk 6
Abergavenny

5.75 miles for the short version, 10.25 miles for the long version. On lanes and well maintained grassy paths in the main. If you tackle the long route then you have a long climb from the Usk to the top of the Sugar Loaf, which is steep in places; the shorter walk has only a bit of hill to climb. Includes the site of the Roman fort, the castle and the priory in the town, together with a church, chapel, vineyard and the Sugar Loaf, depending upon which route you choose.

The walk starts at the junction of the A40, Cross Street and Castle Street at the southern end of the high street.

❶ Walk up the narrow Castle Street, (the Angel Hotel is on the right corner). At the top, the car park ahead and to your right is on the site of the Roman fort of Gobannium, marked now by a ceramic plaque in the vegetation alongside the pavement in front of the car park.

Turn left at the top of Castle Street to reach the remains of Abergavenny Castle.

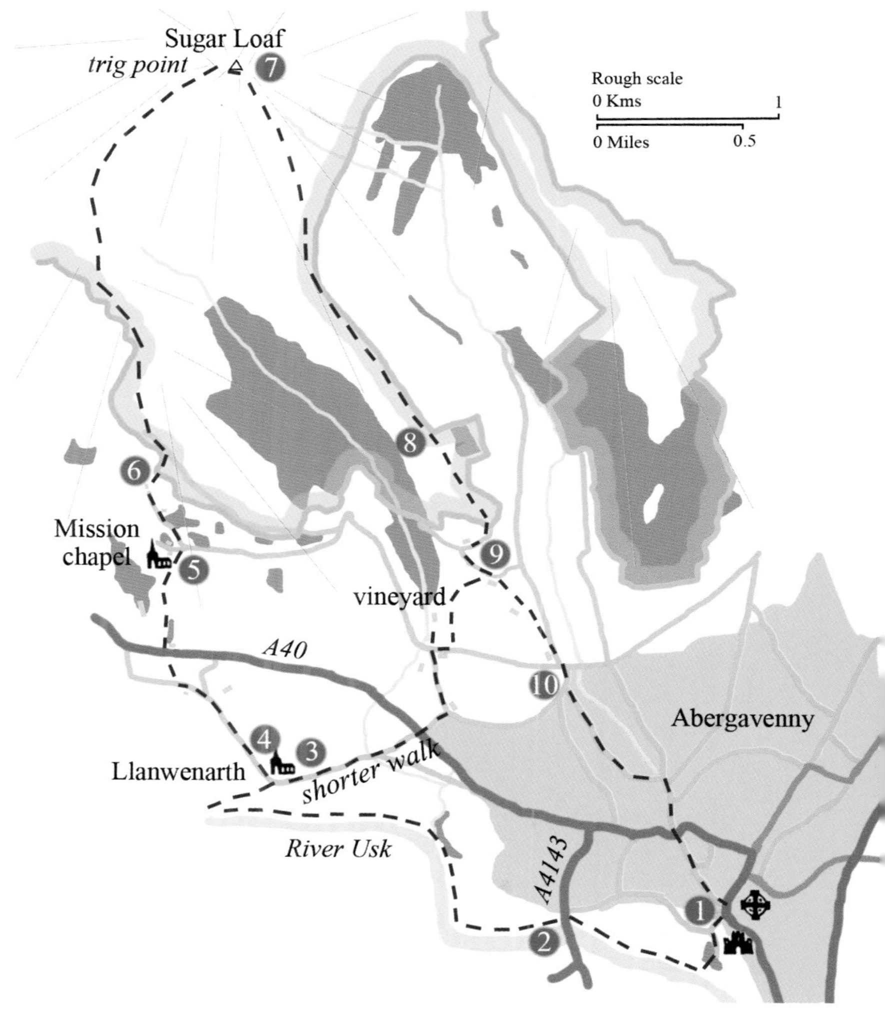

ABERGAVENNY

Whilst there would have been an earlier settlement in the vicinity, it was the Romans who appreciated the strategic nature of the site and built a fort, named Gobannium, which linked the forts at Usk and Caerleon with that at Brecon via Pen-y-gaer near Tretower (see p.122). The Normans also saw the site's potential and built a castle (see opposite page), and founded a priory (see p.66). In 1241 the defences were strengthened with the building of town walls that had four gateways, and over the years the town gained the right to hold two weekly markets and three annual fairs. Some of the settlement's prosperity came from the production of flannel and, in the 17th and 18th centuries, the making of periwigs from goat's hair.

With the Dissolution of the monasteries, the priory's endowments were used to found a grammar school. Around a hundred years later, in 1639, the town gained a charter of incorporation, giving it an economic boost, but the charter was annulled in 1688 when the town's chief officers refused to swear allegiance to William III. With Monmouth having been made the county town of Monmouthshire in 1535 following the Act of Union of England and Wales, Abergavenny's prosperity faltered, though it held important cattle and horse fairs. The arrival of the railways in 1854 brought some relief, and the town is now a service centre for a wide hinterland.

GOBANNIUM

A Roman fort, measuring approximately 120m by 110m, once occupied the flat ground above the confluence of the rivers Usk and Gavenny, now largely filled by a car park. Remains of the walls of the fort were discovered when foundations for a new post office and telephone exchange were being dug in the late 1960s. Excavations carried out in 1972-3 and in 1999 unearthed pottery remains which showed that the fort existed by 60AD, was rebuilt between 65 and 70AD, and was further repaired and modified sometime after 250AD. Not long afterwards, the military left the fort and a civilian settlement took its place. The site was occupied until at least the end of the 4th century.

ABERGAVENNY CASTLE

The first motte and bailey castle with timber defences was built around 1087, with rebuilding in stone starting a few years later. The castle became the centre of the Lordship of Abergavenny (usually spelled Bergavenny) and passed into the hands of the de Braose family, one of whom became known as the Ogre of Abergavenny due to a particularly brutal episode. In 1175 he invited Seisyll ap Dyfnwal, who was the Welsh claimant to lands in the area, and his leading adherents to a gathering at the castle on Christmas Day when he promised that they would also discuss their territorial differences, only to have them slaughtered. Angered by the news, Henry II, who broadly wanted good relations with the Welsh, sought to bring de Braose to heel, whilst the Welsh were out for revenge and attacked Abergavenny and Dingestow castles (the latter 4 miles west of Monmouth), causing considerable damage. As a result Abergavenny Castle was considerably strengthened from 1190, when the present keep, curtain walls and towers were constructed. Further periods of rebuilding followed, notably in the later 1230s after much of the castle had been destroyed in a rebellion led by Richard Marshal, earl of Pembroke, acting in concert with the Welsh. The last major addition was the barbican gatehouse, which was built around 1400, probably in response to the rising of Owain Glyndwr, who attacked and plundered the town in 1404.

During the Civil War the castle was garrisoned by the Royalists, who rendered it indefensible as their fortunes waned to prevent it being used by the Parliamentarian armies. In the following years, stone was taken from the resulting ruins for use in other buildings nearby. The building on the motte was built in 1818 as a hunting lodge for the marquess of Abergavenny and now houses a museum. In the Victorian era the castle grounds were laid out as a pleasure garden. The remains of the castle include the original motte formed around 1087 on which the lodge stands, the barbican, an impressive part of the curtain wall near the barbican, the outer walls of a circular and semi-circular tower probably built between 1295 and 1314 in the western corner of the wall, and other fragments of walling. Display boards explain much of the history of the castle.

Having seen what you want of the castle, leave by the same way you entered and turn left. By the tall remnants of the castle walls take the right-hand of two paths, the one that slants downhill, at times following a wall on its right. When this path divides, keep right, and keep ahead on the paved path. This will lead to a gate into the Castle Meadows. Keep to the path ahead which will bring you close to the river bank, where you turn right. Follow the path alongside the river through the meadows and it will bring you out onto a road near the old Usk bridge.

USK BRIDGE

The medieval bridge was widened in 1814, the widening taking place on the far side of the structure as one approaches it on this walk. By 1868 the bridge was joined by an iron railway bridge, again on its far side, which towered above it. This bridge was demolished after 1962, when the railway line was closed, though the bases of the bridge pillar supports can still be seen in the river bed when the water level is low enough.

2 Cross the road and turn left, to take the path off to the right just before the bridge. This will lead you down some steps back to the river bank, which the path once again follows. After a while the river bends to the right and further along the path crosses over a stile, then stays very close to the river, passing between it and a small wooded rise to your right, then turns left to cross a footbridge over a small tributary. Keep following the path along the river bank, in due course crossing another footbridge and then another stile. As you pass a group of trees on your right the church of Llanwenarth will come into view (see middle photo alongside). In due course you cross two more stiles in relatively quick succession, and

LLANWENARTH CHURCH

Local folklore tells that the first church here was built at the end of the 6th century or the beginning of the 7th and was dedicated to Gwen, the granddaughter of Brychan, the legendary founder and king of Brycheiniog. The partly curved outline of the churchyard certainly lends credence to a Celtic foundation. The first reference to the current building comes in 1254; the lower part of the tower probably dates from then. In the early 1300s the nave and chancel were largely rebuilt, and the tower was either raised in height or had its top parts rebuilt in 1631. Restoration in 1877 saw the rebuilding of the chancel arch and the south wall of the nave with two large windows: the stops to the external hood moulds (see photos opposite) were probably carved at this time, rather than being reused from an earlier feature.

We have never been able to gain access to the church, but there is supposed to be a rare example of a 'hanging cupboard', one suspended by a chain high above the floor to keep the Dole bread stored in it out of reach of mice and rats. The simple, rustic Norman font can be seen through the windows on the north side of the church should it not be possible to gain access.

The churchyard contains the remains of a 14th-century preaching cross, the upper part of the shaft and the steps having been restored.

once over the second your path turns right to follow the field boundary on your right away from the river. In the next corner of the field that you reach you will come to a stile which you cross, to take a small path between fields. Over two more stiles you'll emerge onto a lane, on which you turn right to visit Llanwenarth church.

At this point you need to decide whether you want to tackle the long walk up the Sugar Loaf, (for which see overleaf) or the gentler and much shorter walk back into Abergavenny: the longer walk turns right out of the churchyard, the shorter left.

SHORTER WALK

3 Having turned left out of the churchyard, follow the lane along, bearing left when the road forks in front of some houses, and follow it up to its junction with the A40. Cross this and take the lane on the far side (Pentre Road). Walk along this, and just past a white-painted house on the left, you come to another road junction.

If you want to visit Sugar Loaf Vineyard, turn left here and then immediately right up its drive.

SUGAR LOAF VINEYARD

The vineyard was established in 1992 and grows seven varieties of grapes (including Reichensteiner, Madeleine Angevine, Seyval Blanc and Regent) to produce red, white and sparkling wines. You can take a self-guided tour of the vineyard (between March and October), sample wines, and enjoy the café, which offers light lunches and other refreshments. There is also a shop offering other local produce.

To continue the walk, turn right and in about 100 yards, opposite the end of the grounds of the houses on the right, take the footpath off to the left up a bank and through a gate. The footpath will head uphill alongside part of the vineyard on your left, and then between fields to two metal footpath gates in quick succession. Go through these and enter a field. Here the path turns slightly right and heads uphill across the field, roughly bisecting a line between the large lone tree in the field and the field boundary on your left. As you ascend the hill you will soon see another small metal footpath gate in the hedge ahead of you, and this is your target.

Once through this gate you will be in another field. Look down the hedgerow on your right to the fence at the far end of the field, then follow this to the left and at its end you will see another small metal footpath gate: this is your next target. When you reach it, go through and follow the path which will lead to a steep stile which you cross and head up the bank on your left, turning right to follow the path through a patch of rough ground and then alongside a building to a stile that you cross to reach a lane.

Turn right on the lane and you will quickly come to a bend in the road at Home Farm (marked by a low line of buildings on your right, with two metal vents on top of the roof). You have now rejoined the longer route and need to head to point 9 on p.65 in the walk description.

LONGER WALK

4 Turn right along the lane on leaving the churchyard. When you reach a road junction, keep left. You will then pass a house called Pant-yr-Onen on the left. When you reach the next field gate on your right, enter the field by using the stile to the right of the gate. Cross the field towards the houses on the far side, aiming for a stile positioned where a short length of hedge meets a length of fencing.

Across the stile turn left along the A40, but almost immediately cross it to take the path just to the left of the hedges that mark the boundary of Grey Hall Cottage. This path passes between a fence to your left and a hedge to your right. Ignore the path that heads off to the left

over a stile and continue along the narrow alleyway to a gate at its far end that leads into a field. Follow the field boundary on your right up to another stile on the far side of the field, over which the path turns right and then left to cross another stile to enter the next field. You now have a stiff uphill climb! The path crosses a corner of this field, aiming for a single electricity pole standing just inside the field boundary on the left and to the left of a metal pylon. From this point the path follows the field boundary uphill on your left until you reach a stile which you cross to enter the next field. Once in this field the path continues to head steeply uphill, aiming for a point to the right of a cottage you can spot in the wood just above the field. There may well be a well-worn path to follow, which will lead you through a short section of bracken to a stile, which you cross to find yourself facing Llanwenarth Mission Chapel.

LLANWENARTH MISSION CHAPEL

This chapel was built in the early 1900s to serve the Baptist community living on Mynydd Llanwenarth (the hill you are on) and (Y) Graig, the adjoining hill to the west across a small stream that runs down to the Usk. Tithe maps of the first half of the 1800s show the south-facing slopes, well supplied with springs, to be dotted with cottages and small farms. Their occupants would have made a basic living from labouring work and what they could produce from the land, together with weaving, dressmaking and tailoring. Only a small number of these buildings survive today; the evidence of some of the others can be seen hidden in undergrowth and woodland, deserted when the landowner imposed rents, followed by the actions of bailiffs. The community may have begun in the latter part of the 1600s, the householders perhaps being Dissenters creating a self-supporting community, which may have led later generations to welcome Baptist teachings. In the late 1800s, the Baptist minister of the Frogmore Baptist Chapel in Abergavenny would come and visit members of his congregation who lived on these hills, and as a result of these visits, the Williams family started to offer their house as a venue for meetings. After members of the family moved to a larger house called Ty Deri which they built for themselves, they held meetings there before this chapel was built on a corner of their land.

5 Continue up the steps past the chapel to then pass through a gate onto some open ground. Cross this to join a lane on which you turn left. Don't take the track that almost immediately branches off to the left, but follow the lane as it bends right, to take the next, tarmacked, lane sharply left that immediately starts to ascend the hillside, passing a line of gnarled trees on your left. Follow the tarmacked lane to its end near a white-painted house on the left, to take the track to the right of the house and then the path to the right at the back of the house that leads directly up the hillside. This will lead to a gate out onto the open access land that surrounds the Sugar Loaf.

6 Continue straight up the hillside to meet a road, on which you turn left and walk along to a small car park. Walk through the car park, heading for the wide grass and earth track that heads off from above the car park and has a board containing a map just to its right. This track continues ahead, gently ascending the hillside. This will lead you to a wall near a 'corner' of the open access land, where you take the left-hand track (the right-hand one looks as if it will lead you to the summit more directly, but in fact heads down into a gully). In due course you will come to another piece of wall at another 'corner' of the open access land, and this time you take the right-hand track (in essence keeping straight ahead). Keep on this, crossing other tracks that you come to and this will lead you round the head of a gully (Cwm Trosnant) to your right. At the head of this gully there

is a choice of paths you can take to the summit of the Sugar Loaf. The photograph above shows the two paths; we suggest you take the left-hand one as it gives you a gentler approach overall.

THE SUGAR LOAF

The Welsh name for the Sugar Loaf seems to have been Mynydd Pen-y-fâl meaning mountain of the peak or summit. Like other hills in the Black Mountains, it is formed of Old Red Sandstone rock atop a mix of mudstones and sandstones. During the last ice age, the Usk Valley glacier divided to north and south of the Sugar Loaf as it travelled eastwards, the top of the hill probably remaining above it as it is free of glacial debris. The hill is owned by the National Trust, who manage its grazing, largely by Welsh mountain sheep. Some of the wooded slopes have been declared a Site of Special Scientific Interest.

7 To head back to Abergavenny from the summit, walk along from the trig point to the other end from which you approached the summit (if you followed our suggestion!) Looking down from here you will see a broad grassy path to the left of Cwm Trosnant that in due course keeps close to a field boundary to its left as it heads back towards Abergavenny along an outflung shoulder of the lower hill; this is your path. (The photograph on the left shows the path by which you want to leave the summit and the outflung shoulder of the hill along which the walk will lead you.) Start by taking the slightly stepped path to the left of this end of the summit and then swing round under the summit before dropping down the hillside on an earthen path. You will cross a stream, beyond which you keep to the path ahead at a crossroads of paths and

then left at the fork reached soon afterwards and straight ahead at the next junction almost immediately reached. This will lead you along a field boundary on your left (and the old field bank that would have been the original boundary).

8 When the field boundary on your left makes a right-angled turn away from the line of the path, keep straight ahead and the path soon starts to drop more steeply. Having passed close to a large tree on your left, it descends even more sharply and can become obscured in places by bracken. But the path is well walked; just keep going straight ahead downhill, crossing some smaller paths as you descend. Near the foot of the open access land the path bends slightly left to reach a metal footpath gate. Go through the gate and turn right on the path which will lead you down to a lane on which you turn right (essentially keeping straight ahead). You will pass through one gateway, or cross its adjacent stile, to reach a road junction where you turn left. Follow this down to Home Farm, marked by a low line of buildings on your right, with two metal vents on top of the roof, where the road bends to the left. Here the route of the shorter walk rejoins your route.

THE TWO ROUTES RECOMBINE

9 Don't turn left along the lane, but cross a stile just to the left of the entrance to Home Farm to enter a field.

Ahead you will see a fence marking another field; head to the right-hand corner of this to follow the fence on your left down to a stile. Cross this and follow the path between fence and hedgerow to a footpath gate, which you go through. You now briefly follow a path between two fields, passing through another gate to find yourself perched above a road. Keep to the path, which will lead you down onto the road on which you turn right (essentially keeping ahead). This soon passes a road off to the left and one off to the right.

10 Continue along the road and on the bend soon reached, bear left through the metal kissing gate. Continue down this road, Chapel Lane, which will become Avenue Road and bends to the left. At its end, turn right and walk down to the next junction: you will need to cross the road you're on to get to a pedestrian crossing across the A40. Once across it, walk through the pedestrianised town centre back to where the walk started, turning left at the crossroads here to reach the priory.

ABERGAVENNY PRIORY

A Benedictine monastery was founded in the 1090s by the first Norman lord of Abergavenny, Hamelin de Ballon or Balun, as a daughter monastery to that of St Vincent in Le Mans. By the latter part of the 1100s it had a complement of 13 monks, but by the beginning of the 1300s it was in decline, with just five monks. Not only that; they were charged with leaving the monastic enclosure, gambling, failing to fast and meeting women. Hearing of a forthcoming episcopal visitation, Prior Fulk Gastard, accused of perjury, stole the monastery's valuables and fled. A new prior was appointed, additional monks were recruited, the buildings were repaired and rebuilt, and the reformed monastery was made more independent of that of St Vincent in Le Mans. In 1403 the monastery was damaged during the Glyndwr wars, losing all its books and documents, and several monks departed. By the time of the Reformation, there were only four monks and the prior. The church was spared at this time, to become a parish church.

The church building largely dates from the rebuilding and repair carried out in the early 1300s. Between 1881 and 1896 it underwent a neo-Gothic renovation and partial expansion which saw the addition of a north aisle, the replacement of the west façade and the insertion of several new windows. The rest of the priory buildings lay to the south of the church. Of these, the eastern wing, with an eastern lancet window at the height of the dormitory and the original entrance portal, has survived. To the west of the church, the former monastery barn has also survived, though rebuilt, and it now hosts an exhibition about the history of the church.

Much of interest is contained within the church. There are carved oak stalls with misericords dating from the 14th or 15th century. A large wooden Jesse sculpture (middle left opposite) would have been part of a larger, originally painted sculpture standing some 20 or 30 feet tall and depicting the family tree of Christ as set out in the Bible (Jesse was King David's father). It dates back to the 1400s and is described by Tate Britain as one the finest medieval sculptures in the world. In 2016 a new stained-glass Jesse window designed by Helen Whittaker was installed; it includes the Jesse figure at its base. A large array of medieval tombs includes a monument to Eve de Braose, who died at the end of the 1200s; a wooden effigy of John de Hastings, Lord of Abergavenny, who died in 1324; a tomb thought to be that of Margaret de Hastings (often said to be John de Hastings' wife, but more likely to have been his half-sister), who is believed to have fallen to her death from the ramparts of Abergavenny Castle when trying to retrieve her pet red squirrel; and the tomb of Sir Lawrence de Hastings, who fought at the battles of Sluys and Crécy before dying of the Black Death. There are also monuments of Sir William ap Thomas, who fought at Agincourt in 1415, and Gwladys, his wife (bottom left opposite); and Sir Richard Herbert, who was executed after the battle of Edgecote during the Wars of the Roses in 1469, (bottom right opposite) and his illegitimate son of the same name, who spent his childhood as a companion to the future Henry VII at Raglan Castle and later helped Henry in his successful bid for the throne.

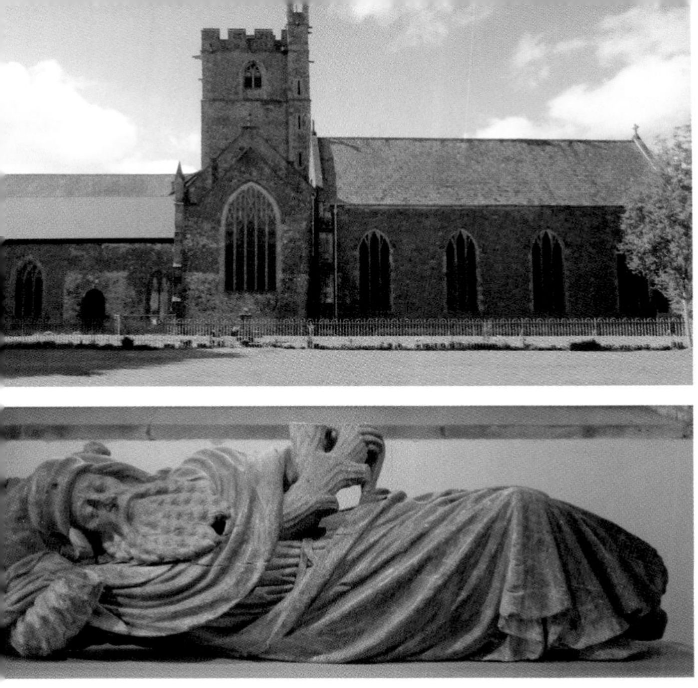

Walk 7
Llanvetherine & White Castle

3 miles, mainly on paths in fields, many of which are laid to grass. Several stiles. The ascent to and from White Castle is fairly gentle but still affords good views. Includes White Castle, a church and the remains of a mill.

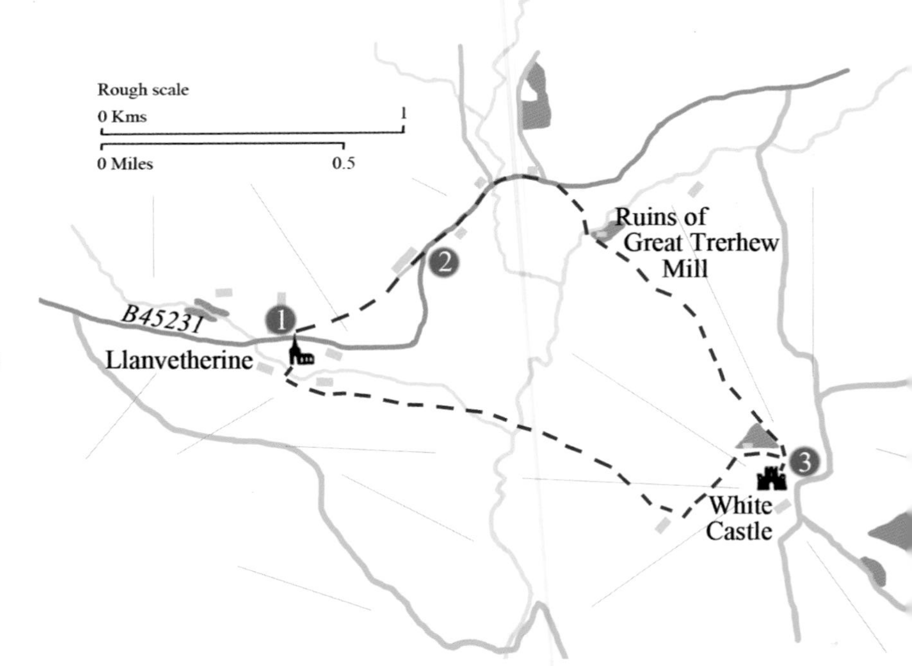

Park in the lay-by opposite Llanvetherine church on the B4521 Abergavenny to Skenfrith road (grid ref: 364 173). We suggest visiting Llanvetherine church on the way back, as the return path passes through the churchyard (see p.73).

1 Opposite the entrance gate to the churchyard (so on the side of the road that you have parked) is a stile into a field. Cross the stile and cross the small field to its top right corner, where you pass round the end of an overgrown hedge to a stile into the field on its far side. Cross this field, the path rising just slightly uphill, and note the array of Romany caravans and huts off to your left. Cross the stile on the far side to enter the next field, the path now following the old field boundary immediately

ahead of you: you'll probably need to follow it to its left or its right as seems best depending upon the state of cultivation – it is not a long stretch of field boundary and the two sides unite at the far end to leave the field down a tarmacked lane that leads back to the B road past some houses.

2 Turn left on the B road, passing two roads off to the left in fairly quick succession: there are some stretches of pavement and roadside verge you can use, though at times you will be walking on the road itself. Just past the second road, the road you're on becomes part of the Three Castles Way, which you now follow. After another hundred yards or so, cross a stile on the right-hand side of the road to enter a field. Follow the line of the sunken way on your right down to a bridge across the Tre-rhew Brook. On the far side you will see a sign that tells you about the mill.

GREAT TRERHEW MILL
A mill was first constructed here in the late 1100s or early 1200s, initially to serve the needs of White Castle. It had an overshot wheel, and information boards show the layout of the buildings (of which only low stone walls now survive), dam and millstreams. Use of the mill had ceased by the end of the 1800s, though the mill house remained occupied till the 1950s.

If you want to explore the ruins of the mill, take the path past the sign, but the circular walk continues up the steps to the right, crosses a stile and then turns left to follow the field boundary (and old sunken track that would have served the mill) up the hillside. Keep crossing stiles or heading through gateways up the hillside as you follow the field boundaries on your left, and in due course you will approach a wood on the crest of the hill. When you reach it, drop down the bank on your left and cross a stile onto a path that leads to a track alongside the wood.

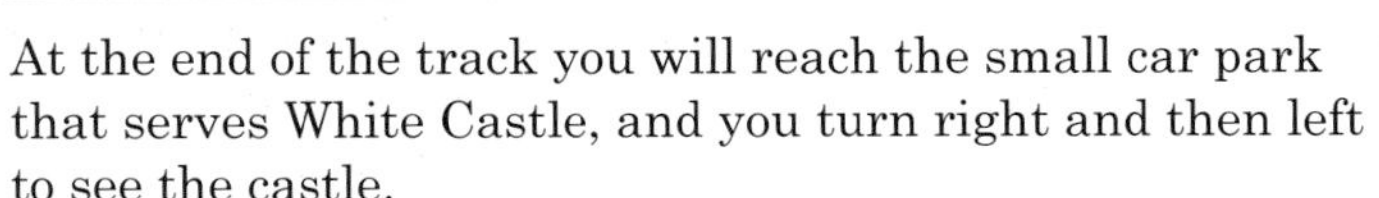

At the end of the track you will reach the small car park that serves White Castle, and you turn right and then left to see the castle.

3 Having seen what you want of the castle, leave it by the way you entered and turn left on a wide track that initially shadows the walls of the castle's bailey, also passing a cottage on the right. You are now following part of the course of Offa's Dyke Path, though the path is well off the course of any part of the potential dyke at this point. The track leads to a gate which you cross to enter a field, where you then turn right to follow the field boundary downhill.

WHITE CASTLE

The first structures at White Castle may have been commissioned by William fitz Osbern, earl of Hereford, who was responsible immediately after the Norman Conquest for securing the border south from Hereford. At that time the castle would have comprised a series of earthworks and timber defences, the original entrance being via a hornwork on the south side of the castle. In 1135, a major Welsh revolt took place and in response King Stephen brought together White Castle and its two neighbours, Grosmont and Skenfrith, subsequently referred to as the Three Castles, under a single lordship, with the intention of blocking Welsh incursions into England through the adjacent valleys. In 1184-86 a stone wall was built around what is now the inner ward, together with a stone keep.

In 1201, King John gave the lordship to Hubert de Burgh, then chamberlain to the king and subsequently justiciar to John and then Henry III. Over the succeeding decades, as political fortunes waxed and waned, the lordship passed to and fro between de Burgh, the de Braoses and the Crown. With de Burgh's death in 1243 the castles once again came into in royal hands, and in 1244 the then constable of the castle, Walerand Teutonicus, built a new hall, buttery and pantry. In 1254, the lordship was granted to Prince Edward, Henry III's eldest son and later Edward I, and it was most likely in the 1250s and '60s (though some think it might have been a decade or so earlier) that the castle was largely rebuilt. The keep was demolished, the inner ward saw the construction of a new gatehouse and four mural towers, whilst the northern outer ward was strengthened with a new wall and gatehouse, through which the entrance to the inner ward was made. The castle then included the usual chapel, hall and kitchen, but only ever seems to have been occupied by a garrison and its commander, never becoming a home for its baronial lord. In 1267 the lordship was transferred to Edward's younger brother, Edmund, earl of Lancaster and remained in the hands of the earldom, and later duchy, of Lancaster until 1825.

After the rebuilding of the 1200s, and then Edward I's conquest of north Wales, little work seems to have been done on the castle apart from the occasional repair. It was used as a base for local administration and also for mustering forces for wars in France and was briefly put into readiness during the wars with Owain Glyndwr. By the 1500s, however, it had been essentially abandoned to the elements.

Several information boards around the castle go into a more detailed history of parts of the building.

Just before you reach a building, the path turns right through a gate to follow the field boundary on your left and then, after a couple of hundred yards, passes through a gate in this field boundary, to then follow the field boundary on your right. After a few more hundred yards the path again passes through a gate on the right to enter a large field. Here the path initially follows the field boundary on your left but after a while bears half-right across the field, (there's a footpath sign in the hedgerow), aiming for a small gate. Go through this gate and cross a narrow field to a narrow footbridge across the River Trothy, then continue for about a hundred yards across the next field to an 'indented' corner of the field. Here Offa's Dyke Path swings right, but you keep ahead across the field to a small gate on the far side to then cross another bridge across a small stream. Over this, keep right to follow the field boundary on your right, in due course crossing a stile into another meadow. Further on you cross over another stile into a plantation of young trees which you cross to another stile and so return to the field that you were in just a moment before! Keep following the field boundary on your right to another stile by which you leave the field. Keep ahead across a gravelled track and then across a field with buildings to your right. At the far side of the field you cross a stile onto a dirt track-cum-path on which you turn right to reach the churchyard surrounding Llanvetherine church, and so return to your vehicle.

LLANVETHERINE CHURCH

The name of the settlement is derived from an anglicised form of the Welsh for 'the parish or land of Gwytherin(e)', a Celtic saint about whom little is known but who probably lived in the 6th century. The *Book of Llandaff* suggests that a church was first built here sometime between 850 and 916, but all traces of this have long disappeared. The oldest part of the existing church may be the lower part of the tower, the nave and chancel appearing to have been rebuilt in the 15th or 16th century. Further major repair work was carried out over following centuries. In the porch there is stoup for holy water, whilst the threshold to the door has a sword carved into it, now much worn away.

This is a church to which we have never gained access; the parish has a small, dispersed population and there are difficulties in recruiting people to unlock and relock the doors each day. If you are lucky enough to find it unlocked, we understand that there is an Arts and Crafts style screen which stands where a rood screen once stood, as evidenced by the door in the north side of the chancel, near the chancel arch. There is also a carved timber pulpit. The most interesting memorials would appear to be a worn figure of a priest, a bearded man holding a book and, either side of the east window, full length carvings in stone of the Revd David Price, who died in 1621, and his wife, Mary, who wears her wedding ring on the second finger of her right hand, as was then the custom. In the chancel, to the left of the altar, is a stone carved with a figure with one arm raised in blessing. It was found under the chancel during building work in 1750 and is said to represent St Gwytherin as it bears the inscription 'S. Vetterinus' (a derivative of the Latin name Victorinus which is considered to be equivalent to Gwytherin). Initially moved outside, it was brought back indoors to protect it from further deterioration. In the churchyard there are the remains of a preaching cross.

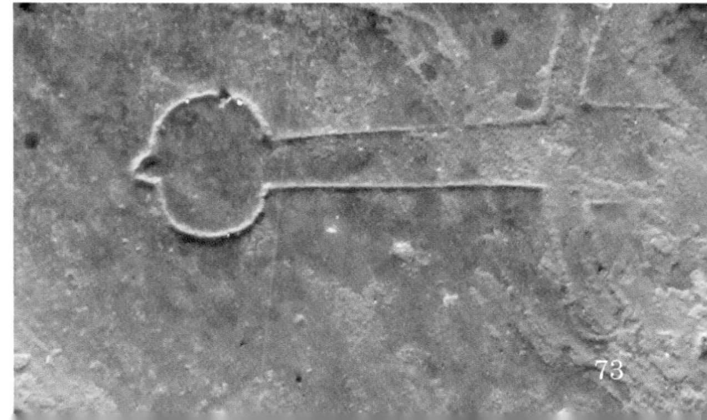

Walk 8 Llanvihangel Crucorney & The Skirrid

5.25 miles. Mainly on paths with some lanes and tracks. A few stiles. There is a fairly steep ascent and a particularly steep descent, though an alternative option is given. Includes buildings in and close to Llanvihangel Crucorney and the scant remains on the summit of the Skirrid. Llanvihangel Court is sometimes open for visitors; check www.llanvihangelcourt.com.

This walk starts from the Skirrid Inn in Llanvihangel Crucorney (grid ref: 326 206).

1 With the inn on your right walk along the road to Llanvihangel Crucorney church.

Having visited the church, take the tarmacked path opposite the church that starts between stone pillars and so reach the A465. Cross this and take the tarmacked lane up to Llanvihangel Court.

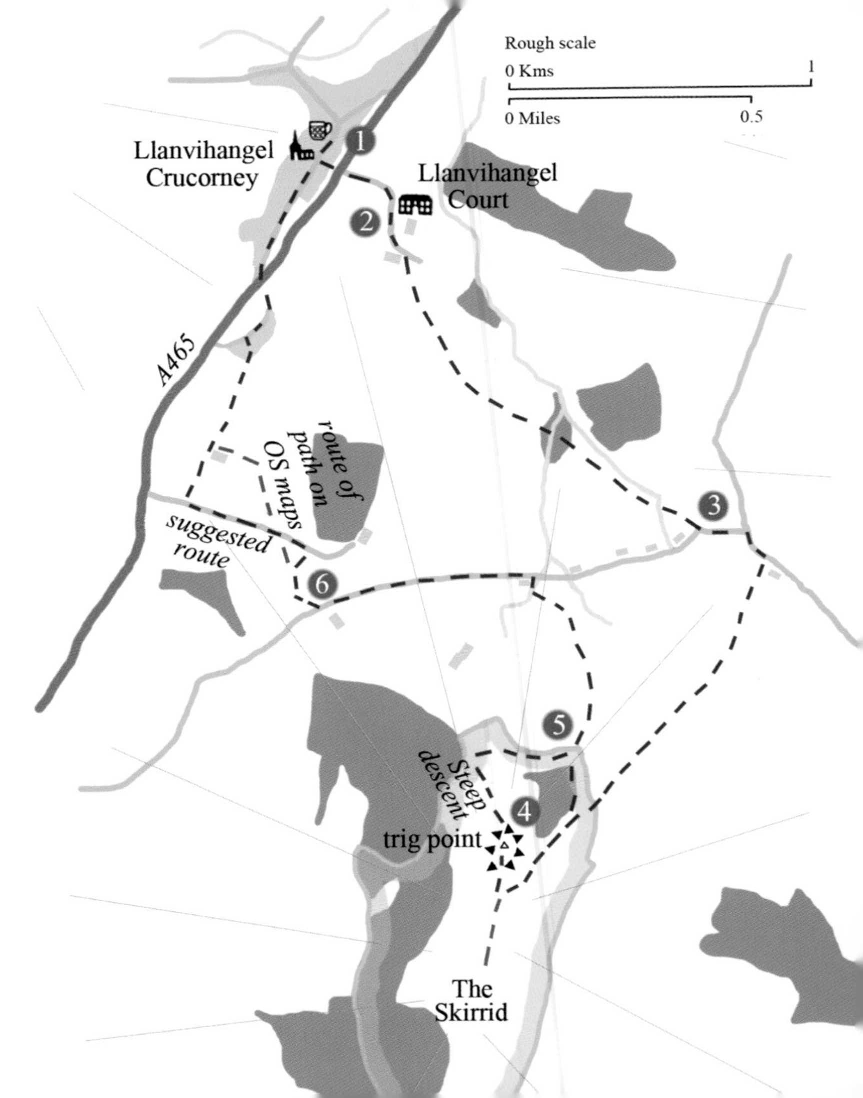

THE SKIRRID INN

The Skirrid is said to be the oldest surviving inn in Wales, dating back to the 12th century, though the present building dates to the 1500s. It was long used as a court room, serving as a venue for manor courts, church courts and travelling assizes. It is claimed that up to 180 of those found guilty were hung in the building or its forebear, and some believe that their spirits haunt the inn. Further details are given in framed newspaper articles displayed on the walls of the bar, along with some records from the inn. It is also said to have been visited by the *pwca*, a devilish sprite, and there used to be a custom that as the last customer left each night, a jug was left out which he could fill from a pot that held the devil's brew of ale that was kept above the fireplace.

LLANVIHANGEL CRUCORNEY CHURCH

Llanfihangel Crucorney is reputedly a corrupted form of the Welsh for 'The Church of St Michael at the corner of the rock', the rock being the Skirrid. The first church was erected on this site during Saxon times, but the earliest part of the existing building, the west end, dates to the early 12th century. The tower and chancel were probably added in the 13th or 14th century, the tower probably then heightened in the 16th century, a century that also saw the building of the porch. In 1835 the nave was rebuilt due to disrepair and the original oak roof was replaced, and in the late 19th century new windows were inserted. By 1974 the nave roof needed replacing again, having been damaged by an earth tremor, but only a partial replacement could be afforded, leaving some of the nave exposed to the elements until 2004, when the new roof was completed with the aid of the Heritage Lottery Fund. The reflooring of the nave in limestone slabs gives the church an unusual feel.

A window in the tower that looks into the nave is so aligned with one in the opposite outer wall of the tower that on the Feast of St Michael (29 September) the setting sun shines through both windows and illuminates the altar at the far end of the nave. (For more on this Feast Day and its local importance see under THE SKIRRID on p.80.)

In the nave is a very worn Elizabethan grave slab, brought inside the church to protect it from further weathering. The church's oldest dated memorial is that in the chancel to John Williams Parry, a local magistrate who died in 1633. Several of the memorials have been provided with notes about the person concerned, including those to Imogen Hall of Llanvihangel Court, who is commemorated by both a memorial on the north wall and the stained glass east window by Charles Eamer Kempe.

LLANVIHANGEL COURT

The first mention of Llanvihangel Court is during the reign of King Henry VI (1422-1471). In 1559 Rhys Morgan rebuilt the house, giving it an H-plan and the core features it retains to this day. In 1608 Rhys's son sold the house to Edward Somerset, 4th earl of Worcester. The Somersets held the property briefly, selling it in 1627 to Nicholas Arnold, MP for Monmouthshire, whose ancestors had obtained extensive lands at the Dissolution of the monasteries. Arnold was a noted breeder of horses and was probably responsible for the construction of the stables. His son, John, who inherited the property in 1655, was a staunch Protestant and such a hounder of Catholics that he was responsible for the arrest of several priests and the subsequent execution of at least one. During the period of Arnold tenure, the square Tudor windows on the north façade were replaced by longer ones, the front entrance was resited to make the central hall just that, and not a communal living room, and in 1673 a southern extension with a magnificent wooden staircase was added. John Arnold also carried out work to the gardens, laying out terraces and planting avenues of trees. He eventually fell foul of a reaction to his brand of Protestantism and was successfully sued for libel by more Catholic-leaning Tories, and fined the then huge sum of £10,000. Unable to pay, he was imprisoned for several years, but he eventually managed to regain his freedom, and was even re-elected as MP for Monmouthshire. After the death of his son and heir, his granddaughters sold the estate to the Harleys of Brampton Bryan in north Herefordshire, the family becoming earls of Oxford. The house subsequently passed through a number of owners, a Mr Bennett doing much to restore the house to its original state during the 1920s and '30s. Various outbuildings lie to the south of the house, including the stables, a large mid-17th century barn and a walled kitchen garden.

2 Continue on the lane round the court, its buildings and the brick wall alongside part of a walled garden, the lane becoming a track. Just past the last of the farm buildings on your right, go through the footpath gate on your right. The path crosses a corner of the field you are now in to pick up and follow the line of fencing on your left to reach a footpath gate into the next field. Keep following the fence on your left through the next two fields. In the third field, where there is no fence on your left, carry on ahead, aiming for a gate just to the right of a lone tree. Through this gate the path turns slightly left and heads towards some woodland; you will see a footpath gate into this as you near the wood. The path crosses a stream and carries on through the woods to leave them

by another footpath gate and enter a field. Cross this diagonally to the far left-hand corner, where a bridge and a footpath gate will lead you into the next field. The path shadows field boundaries on your left through the next two fields to lead you to a road, on which you turn left.

3 Follow the road along till it comes to a T-junction, where you turn right. Follow this road till it makes a bend to the left, where you go through a gate on the right and head towards a yard in front of a barn. However, before you reach the yard, the path goes through a gate on the right to follow the course of an old sunken lane to your right, quickly passing through another gate into a field. The path as walked on the ground now follows a different course to what is marked on OS maps, and sticks closer to several field boundaries. So, follow the fence on your right up to a gate into the next field, then once again follow the field boundary on your right to a stile into the next field. Continue following the field boundary on your right (it's useful to spot the location of paths on the Skirrid as you approach it across this field), at the end of the field passing to the left of a few trees and a small old quarry to reach a field gate into the remaining field between you and the steep slopes of the Skirrid. Through the gate into this last field, the path turns slightly left to cross the field; as you head uphill you should eventually be able to spot the marker post indicating the location of the stile over the fence on the field's far side. Once across the stile, follow the path left that slants up the slope, it soon making a zig-zag to the right and then back to the left. Keep following the path to the crest of the hill. Turn right along the summit path to reach the trig point and the two standing 'doorway' stones that mark the site of St Michael's Chapel.

THE SKIRRID, ST MICHAEL'S CHAPEL & HILLFORT

The hill is formed of old red sandstone atop mudstones, an unstable combination which has resulted in a landslip dated to the ice ages on its western side. The hill derives its anglicised name from the Welsh word *ysgyrd*, which means, appropriately, 'spilt' or 'shattered'.

According to legend, the split in the hill was caused by an earthquake or lightning strike which occurred at the time of the Crucifixion. This led to the belief that the hill's soil was particularly holy and fertile, and it was gathered for inclusion in the foundations of churches, for scattering on coffins and for use as a fertiliser. Pilgrimages used to be made to the summit, notably on Michaelmas Eve (28th September). The hill has belonged to the National Trust since 1939.

The summit is crowned by the scant remains of an Iron Age hillfort and those of a chapel dedicated to St Michael, a saint often associated with high places. The site of the chapel is now marked by low, well-spread, stony banks that define a rectangle some 7.5m east to west by some 4m north to south and marked with upright stones at the old doorway. These remains lie within a banked and scarped sub-oval enclosure, measuring about 14m by 10m. This in turn lies within the earthworks of the hillfort, which comprises two concentric banks standing about 0.8m high that can be seen to the south some 55 and 100m away respectively. A larger defensive bank, some 1.5m high and 2m wide, surrounds the whole; the bank is elongated and narrow in shape, measuring some 355m north to south, and 65m east to west. Some house platforms have been identified.

According to legend, the chapel owes its foundation to a prominent man of Abergavenny who had committed three murders. As a penance, he went on pilgrimage to Rome, and when he returned he went to the top of the hill to pray, and saw a vision of the archangel Michael. As a result he erected the chapel. For years afterwards, Catholics climbed the hill to pray, notably on Good Friday and the Feast of St Michael (29 September). In 1676 the pope, Clement X, pronounced an indulgence (valid for seven years) relieving from all temporal punishments for their sins anyone who, on St Michael's Feast Day, first went to confession and Holy Communion and then went to the chapel to pray for peace 'among Christian Princes', the rooting out of heresies and the exaltation of Mother Church. Services were held in the chapel till at least 1680.

Tales from the end of the 19th century tell of a 'cunning man' (one who was able to divine the future) who lived on the hill and who, in return for money left on a stone known as the Devil's Table, would offer advice and 'magic'.

In his book *The Southern Marches* (1952), H.J. Massingham, was clearly taken by the wider 'magic' of the mountain:

'I do not see how any sensitive person could fail to be drawn into the mysterious orbit of the Skirrid when he catches sight of it, as he will, from so many points of the compass among the Western Marches. Its hunched shoulders or bowed head overpeers the high places in so many different directions that I have seen it not far from Pandy, below where the Olchon and Escley mountain brooks join the Monnow, slowly emergent from a cloudburst, the vapours washing off it like the waves from the back of a risen sperm whale and looking so stricken and forlorn through the riot of the tempest that it appeared to be the high seat of grief and bereavement. Though it often changes from the various angles of vision, it is recognisable as the Holy Mountain.'

4 Your path down can either be to the left of the trig point as you approached it, this path being very steep and going close to the edge of the chasm between the two parts of the hill, or, for a more gentle route, you can backtrack and return by the same path that you came up the hill, but bear left near the foot of the hill on a path that runs around its foot. If taking the

steeper route, when, part way down, you will meet a path running round the hill. Cross it to follow the less distinct path that continues downhill. When you join a wide path along the foot of the hill, turn right and follow it till you reach a footpath sign in the fence on your left. (If you've taken the gentler option, this sign will be on your right.)

❺ Go through the gate here and then shadow the field boundary on your left (passing round a small depression in the field) to the far left-hand corner of the field. Cross a stile here and again follow the field boundary on your left to the far left-hand corner of this field. Here you will find another stile over which the path crosses a small field to another stile in the far right-hand corner. Over this the path turns right and heads through a narrow grassy plock to another stile that leads out onto a road. Turn left on the road and follow it along till you reach the entrance to Llwyn Franc farm on your left.

❻ Opposite this is a gate that leads onto a bridleway. Take this and follow the field boundary on your right, continuing to follow it when the boundary makes a sharp turn to the right. When you reach the corner of the field, cross the stile. From here the footpath technically curves through the field, but its route has long disappeared, along with some of the hedges it once followed. On occasions when we've walked it, the farmer has suggested a preferred route. To follow this, once over the stile, follow the field boundary on your right till it meets a tarmacked lane. Turn left on this and follow it downhill, turning right on the track that heads to a large new barn. Keep on this track, which passes to the left of the barn, and follow it along the hedgerow on your left to reach a gate out onto a short section of grass track that then meets a tarmacked lane near some houses.

Follow this along and round to the left to meet a road, on which you turn right. Follow this and it will lead to a short section of path out onto the A465. Cross this and take the road back into Llanvihangel Crucorney to return to the Skirrid Inn.

Walk 9 Cwmyoy & Patrishow

7 miles, on lanes, tracks and paths. A few stiles. Set in very undulating country, this walk involves four ascents and descents of hills and ridges. Includes the two very individual churches of Cwmyoy and Patrishow, a holy well that still receives offerings, a Tabernacle Chapel and a hillfort.

Park at Cwmyoy church (grid ref: 299 234). To reach the church, take the road from Llanvihangel Crucorney to Llanthony. It is best to take the second turning signposted to Cwmyoy, soon heading through a narrow gap between two recently restored stone buildings. When you reach a fork in the road with a white-painted house in the centre of the fork, take the road to the left. This twists uphill and you turn left again immediately past another white-painted house, following the churchyard wall to an area where there are some four parking spaces.

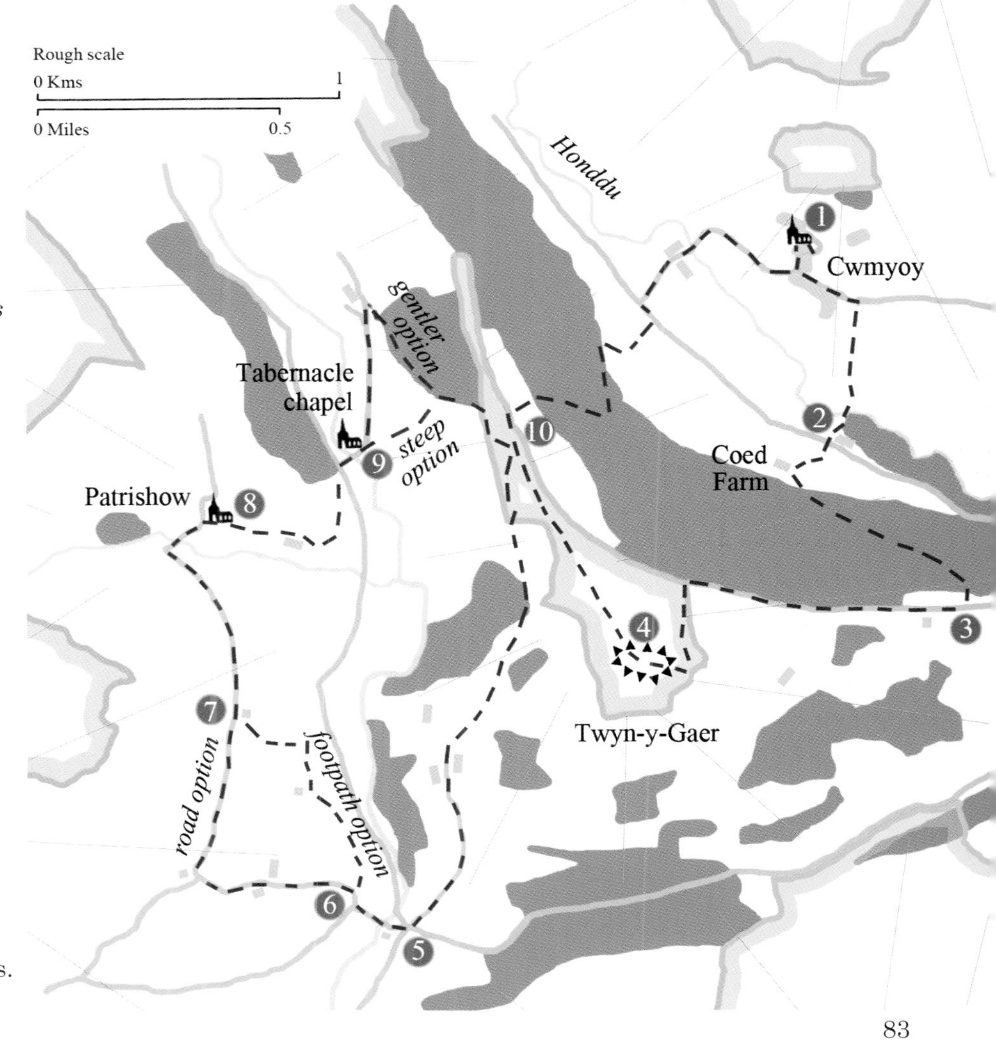

CWMYOY CHURCH

The church is distinctly tilted (the north-west corner of the tower leans at 5.2° to the perpendicular), the result of being built on loose ground formed from landslips, as suggested by the presence of the cliffs on the Darren above the church, the geological cause of which is explained on a board inside the church.

The church was begun in the 12th century, though most of the surviving structure dates to the 13th century, with many of the windows renewed in the 16th century. Inside is the Cwmyoy Cross, which would once have been erected at the wayside for veneration by pilgrims travelling from Llanthony Priory to St David's, the church then belonging to the priory. The cross carries a depiction of the Crucifixion, with Christ wearing a mitre. At the Reformation the cross was buried in the churchyard for safekeeping and it was only rediscovered when it was dug up in a garden in 1861. In 1967 it was stolen from the church, to be discovered in an antique shop in London, where it was recognised by the British Museum's Keeper of Sculpture.

Inside the church there is a fine collection of tombstones and memorials carved by the Brutes, a famous family of monumental masons. There are also moulded plaster decorations in the porch which might have originated in the plaster ceiling of the nave, which was replaced in 1887 when the church was restored.

The churchyard contains the grave of Heinrich Harkotter, a German prisoner of war held at the Llanthony PoW camp, who died in October 1918. A farmer before the war, he was working at a sawmill set up in the camp when he slipped and fell on a roller, to be cut by the rotating circular saw. Also buried here is Arthur Gill, a 500cc racing car driver of the early 1950s who subsequently farmed nearby.

❶ You can visit the church at the start or the end of the walk, but to start the walk go through the gate into the churchyard near where you've parked, and then bear left when you meet another path leading to the church. Note the memorial inscribed in the stones of this path to Mark Gibbons, in whose memory the path was laid.

When you leave the churchyard on this path, turn right on the road you drove up to park, noticing the old cider mill on the right-hand side and turning left when you reach the fork near the Royal Mail letterbox. Just past the barns on the right at the end of the village, look out for a stile on the right next to field gate and cross over this into a field (this is the second field past the barns). Walk downhill, following the field boundary on your right. At the end of the field cross the footbridge over the river, the path then turning slightly left and then right up a track to a gate into another field. Through the gate, shadow the field boundary on your left to leave the field by a stile to the immediate right of a cottage on the far side. This will lead you out onto a road.

❷ Turn left on the road and almost immediately right to walk up the track that leads to Coed Farm. Just in front of the farm the path turns left up a bank and slants across the hillside alongside some woodland to soon cross a stile into the woodland. Follow the path through the wood to reach a wide forestry track. Cross this to the footpath on the far side and take this, continuing up and across the hillside, to eventually emerge into a piece of bracken-covered land. Follow the path through this and it will soon lead you out onto a road.

❸ Turn right on the road and follow it along, the road becoming a track and after a while leading you to a gate out onto some open bracken-covered hillside. Through the gate, turn left and take the path that follows the fence on your left up the hillside. Near the top, the path swings left and then curls round the top, to then turn into Twyn-y-Gaer hillfort on the summit and enter it through its old 'inturned' entrance – you can see the banks to either side of the entrance passage.

TWYN-Y-GAER

Twyn-y-Gaer is a univallate hillfort, oblong in shape, enclosing an area of some 4.5 acres which is divided into three parts by two cross ditches. There is a single entrance on the eastern side. The top of the hill is formed of a band of sandstone which sits on a mixture of sandstone and mudstones. The latter are prone to causing landslips, which would have helped shape the slopes to the south. The site was excavated from the mid 1960s by Allan Probert, who identified six periods of occupation and use, beginning *c.*450BC. At this stage the fort began as a promontory fort with a palisaded outer enclosure for stock. In subsequent periods, commencing about 390BC, the earthworks were extended before contracting again to a small defended enclosure. During the second period the form of the eastern gate was found to be similar to designs found at Croft Ambrey and Midsummer Hill in Herefordshire. This, coupled with finds of Malvern ware pottery during the third period, a rare find in South Wales, suggests that the occupants of the hillfort had family or cultural ties with the people of what became Herefordshire.

In the fifth period the eastern gate was extended and rebuilt in a new style, suggesting a new cultural influence, perhaps due to a change in overlordship of the area. Certainly, Malvern ware is not found in the remains of the fifth and sixth periods of occupation, the pottery of that period being of a type known as Lydney-Llanmelin. The pottery, together with finds of beehive-shaped rotary stone querns and ironwork, points to the hillfort having become part of Silurian territory in the years leading up to the Roman invasion. Also found were glass beads made in what is now Somerset, and a form of coarse pottery used for storing salt, presumably imported from saltworks at Droitwich or in what is now Cheshire. The salt would have been used for storing meat, cooking, and fixing dyes. A find of weapons dating to the period when the gate was reconstructed in a new style could indicate that the hillfort was taken in warfare, even if the weapons were only a votive offering by the new Silurian chief.

4 Continue across the centre of the hillfort, reaching a cairn at the highest point. The path continues on, and turns slightly right to head downhill and follow the approximate crest of the slopes to either side. (The photo on the opposite page is taken on the hillfort rampart with the path you initially take seen passing through the bracken in the centre of the photo.) This path will eventually meet another path on the right-hand side of the common which has a wall (possibly rather obscured by bracken) on its far side. Here you turn sharp left away from the wall and take a narrower path through the bracken which will lead you downhill across the slope and bring you to a metal field gate beyond which lies a path. (If you find yourself facing a gate with a stile alongside,

turn left on the path this side of the stile and this will lead you to the required gate in about 100 yards.) Go through the gate and follow the path, which initially has the remnants of a stone wall to its right. The path continues for a while, eventually gaining a tarmacked surface and later becoming an actual road. Ignore all turnings to left or right and follow it down to a five-way road junction.

5 You want to take the right-hand of the two roads on the far side of the junction (signposted to Patrishow and Crickhowell), which quickly leads to a red-painted house on the banks of a river. Continue along the road, bearing right at the next junction.

6 You can either follow the roads from this junction, bearing right at the next road junction, to reach the holy well alongside a stream close to Patrishow Church, or

take to a path for part of the route. If the latter, you want to cross the stile on the right reached almost immediately past the junction mentioned at the end of the previous paragraph. Walk up and slightly across the field to a field gate in the fenceline near its crest. Here you will find a stile along with another field gate to its left. Cross the stile, then keep to the right of the group of trees immediately ahead to cross the next field to the old gateway (now just an opening) into the field beyond. Through this, follow the line of the track across the next field to near the ruins of Ty-mawr (see photo alongside). A few yards past the ruins, the path jinks left then right to cross to the far side of this next field. You will see a field gate as you approach the far side. Head slightly to its right where you will find, slightly hidden, another field gate and a stile. Cross the stile and turn left to follow the field boundary on your left to the top left-hand corner of this field. Cross the stile here and turn slightly right to cross this field, aiming just to the left of the cottage to the right of the far right-hand corner. Here you will find a substantial stone stile out onto a road, on which you turn right.

7 The two routes rejoin here. Follow the road and just after it makes a bend to left and then right to cross a stream, you can take the steps off to the right to visit an ancient holy well. (The photo opposite shows the well as you'll see it below you as you approach the site along the road.) Then return to the road and keep following it to shortly reach the lychgate to Patrishow church.

HOLY WELL
Known as Ffynnon Issui, or Issui's Well, it is named after Issui or Ishow, a 6th-century hermit. Legends say that he used the well to baptise people and that he was murdered by a passing traveller who sought shelter with him but took exception to Issui's attempt to convert him to Christianity. Stone steps lead down to the well, which is enclosed in a stone chamber. In the middle ages pilgrims came to the well in the hope of being cured of various diseases, a practice that continued until at least the 19th century, and may still. Niches allow pilgrims to place their offerings near the well, and offerings are left to this day.

PATRISHOW CHURCH

The church may be built on the site of St Issui's hermitage. The closed-off room on the west of the building is a hermit's cell and chapel, linked to the nave by a square grille, but this dates to between the 11th and 14th centuries, well after Issui's time. Issui's grave is said to lie under the altar, alongside which is a statue of the saint. The construction of the present building began in the 1050s, funded by pilgrims' donations. It was extensively rebuilt at times between the 13th and 16th centuries, the porch dating to the 15th century and the nave roof to the 16th century. The church escaped damage in the Reformation, and even avoided a Victorian restoration, being sympathetically repaired by the architect W.D. Caröe in 1908.

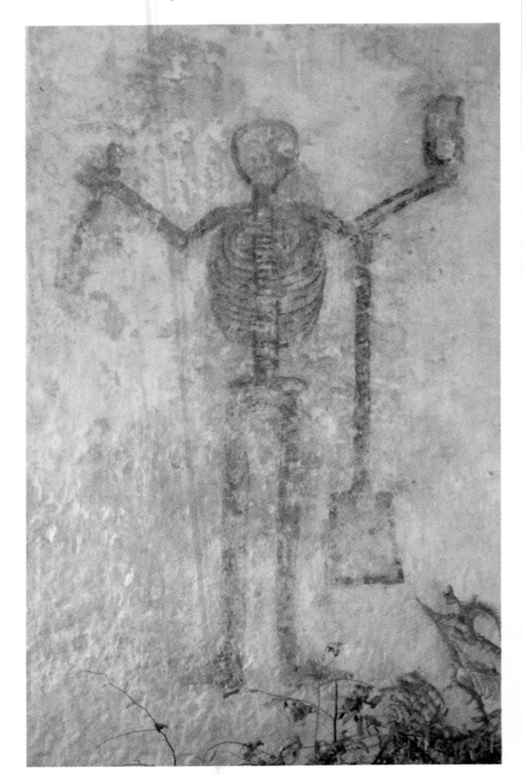

The church contains a round font dating from the first church (it carries an inscription dated 1055), pre-Reformation stone altars to the left and right of the chancel arch, a number of pre- and post-Reformation wall paintings, and, most visually impressive, a rood screen of *c.*1500. This was described in the early 19th century by Richard Fenton, an inveterate traveller, as 'the most perfect and elegant Rood loft now standing in the kingdom'. When the screen was erected, the two stone altars were already present, so the screen had to be designed around them. Above the middle rail height, however, the screen is regular in design with five bays to either side of a doorway. Some of the woodwork has been renewed over time. Forming the front of the parapet are 17 bays, each filled with a panel of lacy openwork. The bressumer on which these sit carries three trails of running ornament: a vine trail strung between two wyverns is uppermost, then comes one of a water-plant, and the lowest is composed of serrated leaves issuing from an undulating stem. There would once have been a tympanum filling the upper part of the chancel arch, but this has long since disappeared.

The wall paintings include a royal coat of arms, probably of James I, an assortment of Biblical texts, and a 17th- (or possibly 18th-) century depiction of Death: a skeleton holding an hourglass in one hand and a knife (or scythe?) in the other. A spade hangs off one arm.

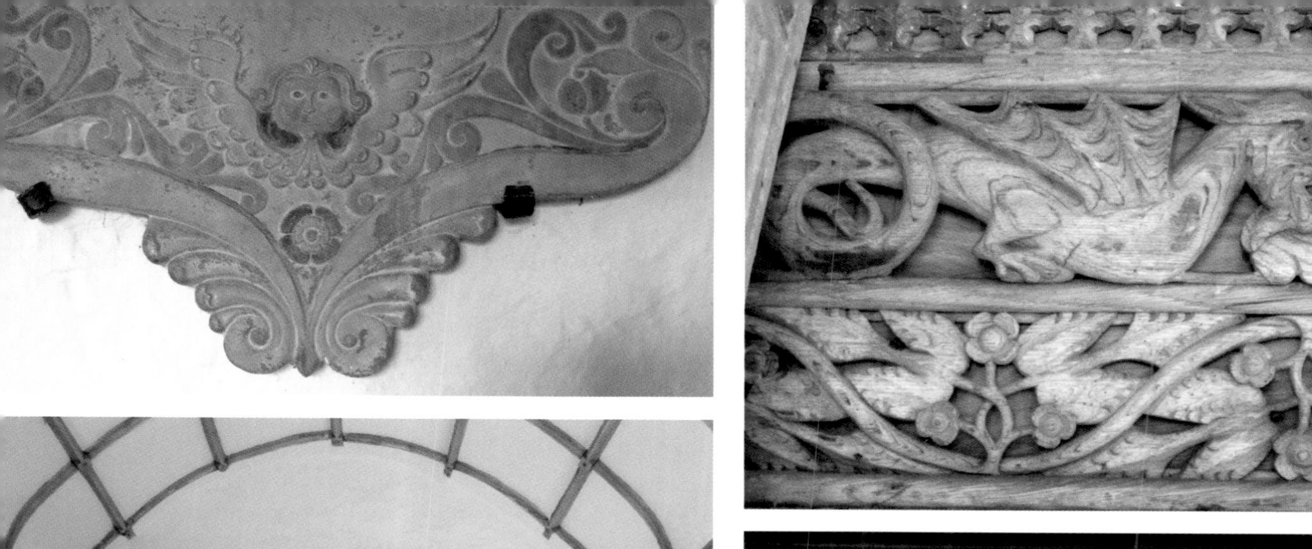

137
534
302
354

TABERNACLE BAPTIST CHAPEL
This was built in 1837 by Morgan Lewis, the minister of the Baptist chapel at Capel-y-ffin, who felt that other places of religious worship were needed in the sparsely populated terrain under his care. This chapel served the communities of Grwyne Fawr and Fforest Coalpit. A manse was subsequently added, though this has not been occupied for several years. The two buildings are considered to be relatively unaltered examples of a Baptist chapel and manse of their time. In recent years there has still been a strong congregation, with at least one service a month during the winter and more through the summer.

8 Having visited the church, turn left out of its door and walk along to the gate that leads into a field. The path soon joins an old track which runs slightly downhill to shadow the wall at the edge of a house and farm buildings. Your path then bears right round the corner of the fence that forms part of this boundary, to follow the fence on your right to a gate into a small thin field. Here the path bears left to the far end of the field to cross a stile. The path then turns right and follows the fence on your right to a gate into the next field below, where it swings left and gains more the appearance of a track as it passes through the ruins of Ty'n-y-pant Keep following the path down to a road, which you cross to take a tarmacked lane down and across the Grwyne Fawr river to reach the Tabernacle Chapel on your left.

9 Keep on past the chapel to a sharp bend in the road where you have a choice of routes. The shortest but steepest way is straight ahead of you across a stile. If you cross this, the path follows the fence on your right to the top of the field, where it turns left, then after 50 yards turns right into an extension of the field and so reaches a stile out onto a path on which you turn right. The longer (by about half a mile) but much gentler route is to stay on the road and follow it along to another Ty-mawr, bearing right when the road forks and right again on a grassy track at the point where the road swings left round a building set hard against the road. The track will lead to a gate, beyond which it becomes a path.

Whichever route you've taken, follow the path and it will lead you via a field gate onto the bracken-clad slopes around Twyn-y-Gaer. Head up the bank beyond the gate to reach, in about 15 yards, a track on which you turn right. Almost immediately you will reach a fork where you bear left to return to what should be a familiar junction of paths where you

will meet a wide track beyond which lies a stone wall, possibly obscured by bracken.

10 Turn left on the track and follow it for a few hundred yards till you come to a metal field gate on your right, which you go through (see photo above). Walk down the field, diverging slightly from the line of the fence that is initially on your right and continuing on that line across the field when the fence turns to the right. On the far side of the field you will find a gate that leads onto a path that slants right and downhill through the woodland. Follow this path and in due course it will meet a wide forestry track. Turn left and almost immediately right to take another path downhill and when this divides, turn left. This path will lead you down to a metal footpath gate which you go through and keep ahead, ignoring all paths to left and right. The path will reach a wooden footpath gate, through which you turn right. As you follow this path downhill, if you look through the few trees along the left-hand side of the path, you'll see the road heading away from you on which you drove to Cwmyoy church. Just to the right of this road's junction with the road that runs along the valley floor, you'll see some fence rails and a stile in the hedge on the far side of the field below you. This is the stile you need to head for, by turning left off the path at a suitable point and crossing the field.

Once over the stile, turn left on the valley bottom road, and then right on the road to Cwmyoy. You can follow the road you drove along to return to your car, or, just before reaching the white-painted house in the fork in the road, take the signposted path off to the left that leads directly uphill to enter the churchyard by an old kissing gate, and so return to your vehicle.

Walk 10
Llanthony

5 miles, on largely well-maintained tracks and some paths. Three stiles. There is a stiff climb onto the ridge above Llanthony, with a more gentle descent. The history is focused on the priory and the associated buildings, but the circular walk provides, in clear weather, stunning views in all directions, and is an enjoyable experience at all times of year.

Park in the car park near the priory remains (grid ref: 288 278). The priory and church can be visited before or after your walk. The hotel tends to be open at lunchtime between April and October on all days except Monday, and just at the weekend for the rest of the year, but for current information, see www.llanthonyprioryhotel.co.uk.

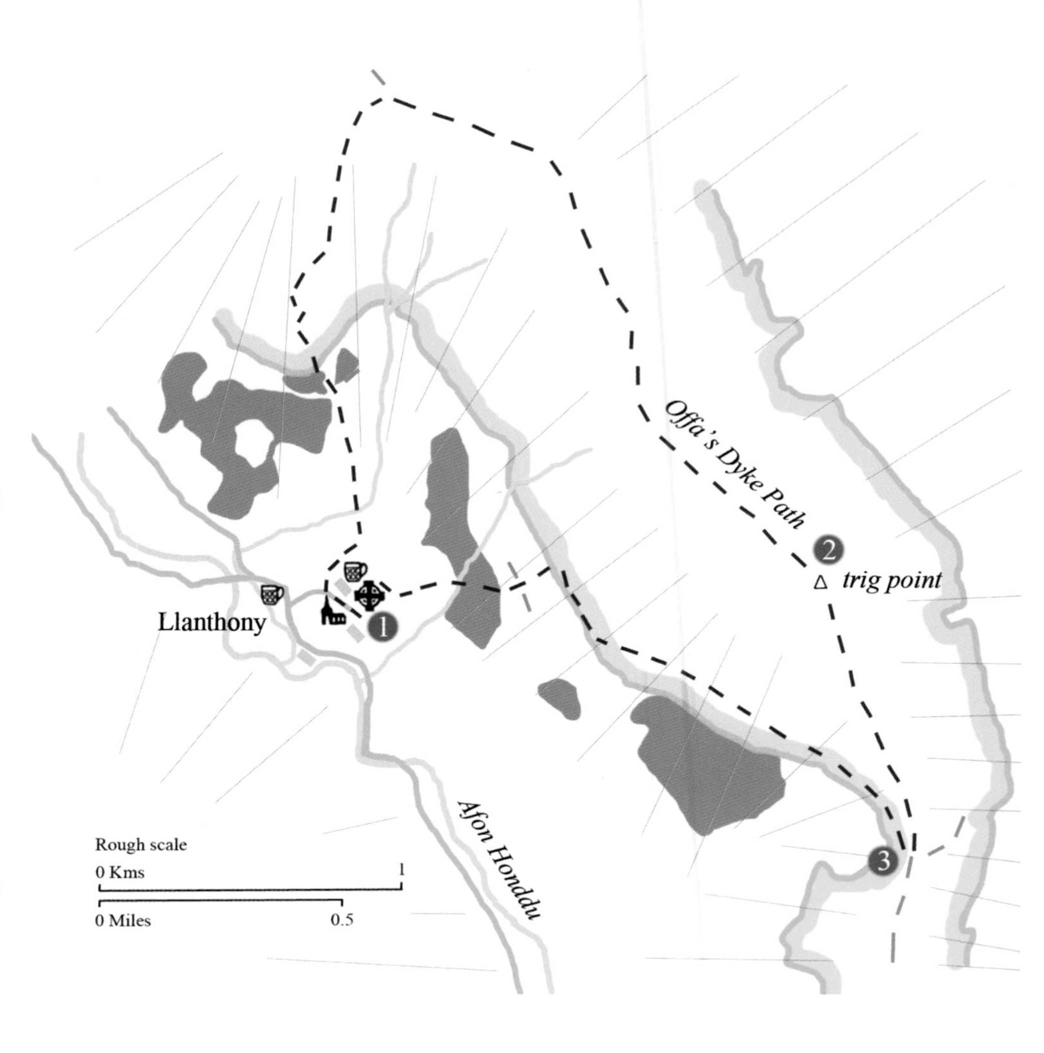

LLANTHONY PRIORY

William, a Norman knight, is said to have chosen this spot to build a hermitage and lead a religious life, having sought shelter in a chapel nearby when out hunting. As Giraldus Cambrensis, Gerald of Wales, the 12th-century traveller and chronicler, was to note, this was a site 'truly suited to the monastic life ... in a wilderness far removed from the bustle of mankind'. William was joined by Ersinius, a former chaplain to Queen Matilda, the wife of King Henry I, and then by others. William had been one of Hugh de Lacy's knights, and Hugh lent the new foundation his support, so that by 1118 a priory had been established, endowed with land granted by the de Lacy family. It quickly gained royal patronage and received many visitors, growing to a community of 40 Augustinian canons who helped clear some of the land for farming, as well as constructing an infirmary, a dovecot and fishponds. Welsh incursions in 1135 led to the site's abandonment for a while, the canons establishing Llanthony Secunda outside Gloucester. Of the first building at Llanthony Prima nothing now survives, the present remains dating to a rebuilding between 1180 and 1220. Given the preponderance of Norman round-headed arches at the east end and in the crossing, it is thought that the rebuilding started here, with the new Gothic style being adopted as the building work progressed westwards. The building would have been one of the medieval wonders of Wales; 18th-century travellers were still able to see the tracery of the east and west windows in place, one of their number, Sir Richard Colt Hoare, actually being present in 1803 when the west window fell. Excavations have revealed that there was a clock in the crossing tower, probably dating to the 14th century and of a primitive kind that had no dials but would have struck the hours. On the east sides of the transepts would have been chapels, now only indicated by footings. The west face of the church is the best place to gain an impression of its original appearance, which has been described as of 'lightness and elegance'. Of the priory's other buildings, many have formed the basis for the present hotel, parish church and farm buildings.

Following the disruption along the border caused by the wars with Owain Glyndwr in the early 1400s, many of the canons departed for Llanthony Secunda, and by the time of the Dissolution only four remained at the original priory. The site was sold for about £160 and left to decay. In 1799 the estate was bought by Colonel Sir Mark Wood, who converted some of the buildings into a domestic house. In 1807 he sold the estate to the poet Walter Savage Landor. Landor was taken by the country life, describing the joys of nightingales and glow-worms to his friend Robert Southey, and wanted to become a model country gentleman. A supporter of liberal and republican causes, Landor planted trees, imported sheep from Spain, improved the local roads and sought to improve the lot of the poor, but his impetuous character and contempt for authority created petty squabbles with neighbours, lawyers, the lord lieutenant and the bishop of St David's. After a few years, Landor gave up his project, left the country (heading initially to Jersey and then France) and abandoned the estate to his mother, a wealthy heiress who was one of his major creditors, the buildings continuing to deteriorate thereafter. Wood's house later became the Abbey Hotel.

LLANTHONY CHURCH

In the early 18th century, what had been the infirmary of the medieval priory was converted to become the Church of St David, to whom the original chapel in the valley had been dedicated.

1 From the car park, walk back along the road past the priory on your right and when the road bends left, keep ahead to go through a gate onto a wide, stony track. There are footpath signs here; you will initially be following the signs with mauve markers and those indicating the way to Hatterall Hill / Hatterall Ridge North.

Thus, follow the track into the next field quickly reached, then continue along it until you reach another footpath signpost. Here, take the path signed to the left to reach, after 50 yards, a gate into another field. Head up this field to reach a gate into the next field and then on up the next field, bearing slightly left, heading to the left of a line of

WHINBERRIES

The picking of whinberries (also known as whimberries, bilberries, blaeberries and wortleberries, depending on the area of the British Isles you're from) was once a family affair, the berries providing both a source of food and, more importantly, income, for the berries were packed up and sold on, often through a local middleman, for use as a dye or in making preserves. Children would often be absent from school for several days during the picking season, joined by their parents and elders on their days or evenings off. Whinberries are apparently good for the eyes: eating them is said to improve night vision (RAF pilots would eat whinberry preserves before night missions) and can help combat eye disorders such as glaucoma and myopia by improving the microcirculation and regeneration of retinal purple. Dried whinberry fruit and whinberry tea have been used as a treatment for diarrhoea and as a relief for nausea and indigestion, whilst the leaves and berries are used in the homeopathic treatment of diabetes.

conifers. At the far end of this field you no longer follow the signs carrying mauve markers, but cross the stile into a strip of woodland and carry on uphill, soon crossing another stile. From here your path is essentially straight up the hillside, crossing another stile onto open access land, though it does zig and zag a little to make the gradient less severe than would otherwise be the case.

Keep on the main path as it starts to level out as it nears the crest of the ridge, gaining a gravelled surface near the 'summit'. When you reach Offa's Dyke Path, which follows the eastern ridge of the Black Mountains at this point, turn right and walk along the ridge.

❷ In due course you'll come to a trig point. From here, the path drops down towards a point where the ridge narrows before rising and broadening

once more. As you reach this narrow part you'll come to a low, rounded stone marker on the left-hand side of the path, which shows Offa's Dyke Path continuing ahead, and a path to the left that leads to Longtown. (The photograph on the left shows this stone marker just ahead.)

3 Take the path to the right, which turns somewhat back on yourself and starts to head downhill, soon picking up the line of an old drystone wall on your left for a while. Keep following this path (part of the Beacons Way) downhill and after a little over three-quarters of a mile, the path will bear right and follow a metal fence on your left as it roughly follows the contours of the hillside. In a short time you will reach a footpath sign with a wooden

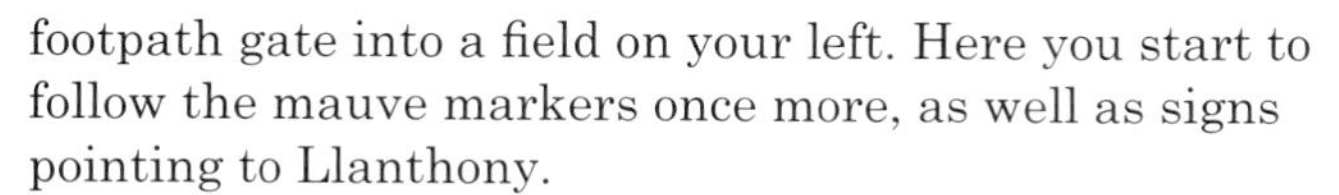

footpath gate into a field on your left. Here you start to follow the mauve markers once more, as well as signs pointing to Llanthony.

Go through the gate and follow the field boundary on your left (ignoring another footpath off to your left) and then walk down the hollowed path at the end of the field to reach a gate into some woodland. Go through this gate

and follow the wide track that slants downhill to the right through the woodland, to reach a gate out into a field above the priory. Head straight down this field, aiming for the priory, to reach another gate that will lead you to a path alongside a stone wall marking the edge of the current priory precinct and so back to where you started the walk.

Walk 11
Crickhowell

9.25 miles, on a mixture of lanes, tracks and paths, all in generally good order. A few stiles. There is a steady climb to reach Crug Hywel hillfort, followed by a descent that is steep in places, and a gentler ridge to cross. Includes two interesting churches, the hillfort of Crug Hywel and another enigmatic earthwork, along with Crickhowell itself. (The Dragon's Head Inn in Llangenny is open Wed to Sun evenings, and Sat/Sun lunchtimes. They will open at other lunchtimes for groups of 6 or more with advance warning. Phone 01873 810350. For the Red Lion at Llanbedr, phone 01873 810754.)

You may wish to park in the main car park in Crickhowell (which is a pay and display), or along Llanbedr Road as indicated

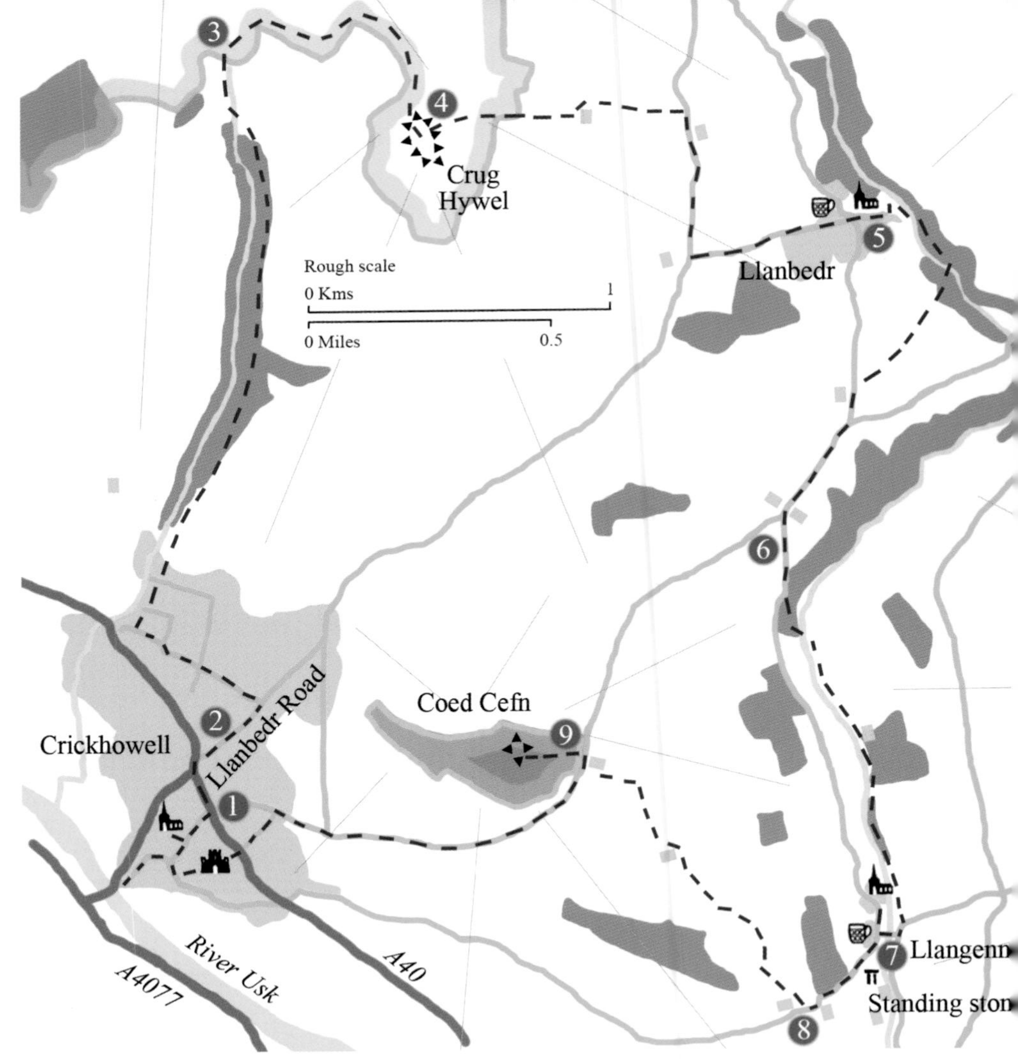

CRICKHOWELL

The town may take its name from the hillfort known as Crug Hywel ('the mound of Hywel') perched above it on the flanks of the Black Mountains, Crickhowell being the anglicised version of the name, though it might be that Crug Hywel is in fact a relatively modern name given to the hillfort. In any event, in 1263 the town was referred to as Crickhoel.

It is possible that the original site chosen for a castle and town in this vicinity was at Maescelyn, 1.5km to the north-west of the present town, where a small motte still stands and is said to have been built by 1121. Adjacent to it was a chapel of which nothing now remains. The establishment of Crickhowell seems to have been later, but its castle must have taken shape by 1281, when the town was granted a right of murage for the construction of town walls and also confirmation of rights for the holding of markets and fairs. Whether any town walls were ever built is open to question, as no trace of them has been found. A Norman borough was gradually laid out in the vicinity of the castle and stretching down to the river, the market place presumably occupying the existing triangular area of ground at the northern end of the High Street where it meets the main Brecon to Abergavenny road. Burgage plots were certainly laid out either side of the High Street, those on its eastern side being relatively few as they abutted the castle walls.

The castle was uninhabitable by 1550, and its decline seems to have mirrored that of the town. By 1610 Crickhowell was no longer listed as a market town and in 1675 it was said to comprise only around a hundred houses and one inn. Somehow it picked itself up and by the early 1800s once more had a market and appears to have been thriving, Richard Fenton on his travels describing it as 'the most cheerful looking town I ever saw'. In Church Street a pair of stone-built towers (known as the Ivy Tower) were long thought to be an outer gateway to the castle, but investigations in the 1990s suggest that they were actually a folly built in the 18th or 19th century, behind which traces of a house constructed in the 15th or 16th century were found.

There are several historic buildings in the town, most of them dating from the 1600s or later, such as the Dragon Inn in the High Street. It is claimed that parts of the Bear Hotel date back to the 1400s, however, during which the original White Hart Inn (now the Red Indigo Indian restaurant) on the western edge of town was also built. A mill was built to the west of the town on the Cwmbeth brook, and medieval open fields lay to the town's north and west.

PORTH MAWR
Porth Mawr was built on the site of Cwrt-y-Carw, a late-medieval house which was demolished after a fire gutted it in 1810. The cream-painted gatehouse survived and dates to the 1400s. It is uncertain whether the tall adjacent boundary walls also date to the 1400s or are a rebuild from after the time of the fire.

on the accompanying map. The walk is described as starting from the drinking fountain in the centre of the town, at the junction of the A40 and Bridge Street (in effect the High Street). (The fountain was built *c.*1900 in memory of Henry Lucas, a local doctor, on what had been the site of a market hall.) If you have parked in Llanbedr Road, then start the walk from point 2.

❶ Walk along the A40 heading west (in the direction of Brecon, and with the Bear Hotel almost immediately on your right). Go past the petrol station and the cream-painted Porth Mawr (Big Gate) and turn right up Llanbedr Road, following it as it bends round to the left.

❷ Follow Llanbedr Road to its junction with Oakfield Drive, where you turn left. Walk along this, staying with it as it bends slightly right and then turns left at the junction with Cwmbeth Close. Look out for the tarmacked path that leads off to the right just before the last two houses on the right-hand side of the street. Take this path, then cross the end of the road you reach and head up a few steps onto a similar path that will lead you to another road. Cross this and turn left on the lane on its far side to immediately go through a footpath gate on your right into a yard near some buildings. Cross the yard to the field beyond, the path then showing itself as a well-walked route up the left-hand side of the field to a footpath gate at the top. Go through this, the path now shadowing a sunken stream valley to your left. The path continues along the edge of a couple more fields, passing through two more gates, then enters woodland above the stream where it becomes a broad path, often following

the remnants of a wall. After a while the path heads through a gate and enters a field. Here it turns left to cross the stream, then immediately right to continue following the stream but with it now on your right. After a while the path crisscrosses the stream, heads between two stone walls, then goes through a gate to enter an old sheepfold (a stone enclosure where sheep could be penned), emerging through a gate onto the open hillside.

3 The path now turns right and weaves around the lower slopes of the open hillside. Keep straight on where another path goes off to the right after a couple of hundred yards. If not spotted already, the rocky outcrop that has the hillfort of Crug Hywel on its summit will now be standing clear before you (assuming you're not attempting the walk in low cloud or fog!) and the path will eventually swing you to the right along the little ridge that connects it to the main mass of the Black Mountains. Clamber up to the summit and explore the banks and remnants of stone walling that make up Crug Hywel.

CRUG HYWEL

This hillfort occupies a spur of ground that protrudes from the flanks of the Black Mountains. Roughly triangular in shape, it is surrounded by two ditches and associated banks. The inner bank shows signs of once having supported a stone wall, as footings survive in several places, the wall itself now showing as loose stone on the western and north-eastern sides and as a turf and stone bank on the southern and south-eastern sides that reaches to c.1.7m high towards the entrance. This is on the eastern side, where the outer rampart turns inwards to form a passage leading to a gateway in the inner rampart. Some oval shallow depressions that abut the rear of the perimeter wall have been identified as platforms on which huts would have been built. Other vague depressions, notably in the southern half of the hillfort, might be other hut platforms.

4 In your explorations of the hillfort, when standing near the entrance on its eastern side take a look south-east towards the pointed peak of the Sugar Loaf and down into the valley between you and it (it is the view shown on the cover of this book and also top left on this page). When looking in that direction, you should see a grassy path heading almost straight down the hillside from the hillfort. That is the path you will need to take to continue this walk. It takes a line that goes just to the left of two stone buildings that sit alongside each other on the downslope. Beyond and slightly to the right of

the two stone buildings you'll see a village (Llanbedr) with a church, and further to the right, between it and Crickhowell, a wooded hilltop: both village and wooded hilltop lie on your route back into Crickhowell.

Follow the grassy path down the hillside, and in due course leave the open hillside by a stile and then follow the field boundary on your left down to the two stone buildings, crossing out onto their access lane by a stile. The public path takes a dog leg route through the field below these buildings (which form a bunkhouse) but the easier way is to walk down the steep access lane to the road below. When you reach the road, turn right, and then left at the next junction to walk into Llanbedr where you will find the Red Lion pub and the village church next to each other.

LLANBEDR AND ITS CHURCH & PUB

The pre-1600 full name of the parish was Llanbedr Ystradwy (or Ystrad Yw), 'St Peter's church in the vale of Yews'. The first record of a church here is dated 1060, but there is likely to have been an earlier forerunner. There was probably a small settlement around the church, though the first map of the settlement, which dates to 1760, only shows the rectory and eight other dwellings, well spaced out, of which only two or three survive. The buildings of 1760 included a mill beside the Grwyne Fechan. In the 18th and early 19th centuries the village was home to the Brutes, a family of four generations of masons whose distinctive memorial stones, often featuring the head of an angel above outstretched wings, are to be found in many local churches, including on the outside south wall here (see also pages 84 and 93).

The south aisle and chapel date to the late 15th or early 16th century, though the nave, chancel and tower are probably earlier. The church was restored in 1868 and 1883, and partially rebuilt in 1897. The stencil decoration appears to have been carried out in the early 1500s, shortly before the Reformation.

The church is home to several intriguing tapestries, about which there is an information leaflet. These were created in 2016 and depict a parish map and some parish stories.

The rectory (now Llanbedr House) was built in part of the churchyard, making the latter an irregular shape. Both Llanbedr House and the Red Lion date to the 1700s.

5 The walk continues ahead at the crossroads near the pub, taking the no-through road round the churchyard, which becomes a stony/earthen track beyond the houses on the far side of the church, and drops down to cross the river below by a stone bridge.

Cross the bridge and turn right along the far bank, following it along for a short while till

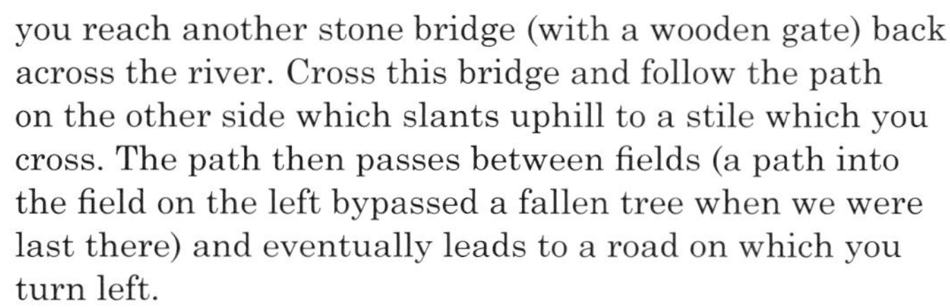

you reach another stone bridge (with a wooden gate) back across the river. Cross this bridge and follow the path on the other side which slants uphill to a stile which you cross. The path then passes between fields (a path into the field on the left bypassed a fallen tree when we were last there) and eventually leads to a road on which you turn left.

6 At the next road junction you have a choice. To shorten the walk (which would mean missing out on some lovely walking by a river and an interesting church), bear right at the road junction (signposted to Crickhowell) and continue along the road till you reach its crest and Coed Cefn (wood) on your right, then go to point 9 on p.114.

To do the full walk, turn left at this junction (signposted to Llangenny and Glangrwnwy). After walking along a straight stretch of road you'll come to a footpath on the left (just after a couple of gateways). Cross the stile and walk down the path to a bridge over the river. Cross the bridge and the stile on the other side, then turn right to follow the path by the river – over one stile to keep following the path, then over another to a gravel lane. Turn right on the lane and then bear right to cross a stile by a field gateway and enter another field by the river. Keep following the river, the path soon passing to the left of trees on the river bank before entering woodland; cross a stile and keep going, then go up steep steps to go over a stone wall.

Here you'll find yourself on a road; turn right along it, then right again to cross the bridge into Llangenny, where you'll see the Dragon's Head Inn straight ahead of you.

7 To visit Llangenny church you need to turn right here and walk along the road for about 200 yards. Then retrace your steps to this point, bearing right by the old inn. As you walk past the inn, now on your right, look to your left across a field to a small enclosure this side of a small white-painted building with a steeply pitched slate roof. In the enclosure you should be able to see a standing stone, a 1.2m tall rectangular block of grey limestone. It goes under two names, the Golden Grove stone and the Druid's Altar, the latter being the name of both the steep hill immediately to the west and the house that you pass on the left as you continue to follow the road and near the top of the hill. This Grade II listed house was built as a single storey cottage in the 1700s which, in the late 1800s, had a second storey and a crosswing added by the Cwrt y Gollen Estate.

8 Shortly after the road levels off and starts to head downhill you want to take the bridleway off to the right, this leaving the road just before you reach the refurbished stone buildings of Penmoel Cottage. The bridleway passes through two gates in quick succession, then the path goes through another gate and up the strip between two field boundaries. At the top there's a gate and stile into the next field.

Once in this field, bear right to follow a line of trees marching across the field, keeping them to your left. At the far end of the line of trees, follow the path that enters the wood ahead through a footpath gate. The path slants uphill through the wood to leave it by another gate. The path then heads left along the edge of the field you find yourself in, to rise uphill to a field gate. Through the gate a path leads one way and a bridleway another, and it is the bridleway you want.

LLANGENNY CHURCH

It is unclear whether Llangenny began its life as a chapelry of Llangattock, only becoming its own parish when the settlement is recorded in Edward VI's reign (1547-1553), or whether a 'Lann Cetguinn' mentioned in the 12th century refers to this settlement. In any event, an estate map of 1800 shows only three dwellings in the vicinity of the church, suggesting that any medieval settlement here was small.

The church does have a medieval core, but was extended, probably in the late 1400s or early 1500s, with the addition of a new nave and chancel. The original nave then became the present north aisle, though somewhat narrower than the original structure. New windows were also inserted into this 'new' north aisle. The building was restored in 1864 and again in 1894, in which year the north and west walls of the north chapel were rebuilt and a new bell-cote was added, and it was perhaps as part of one of these restorations that the roofs were raised. The font dates to the 1100s, and there are a series of Victorian scroll-texts above doorways.

Ffynnon Ceneu (St Ceneu's Spring) lies on the east side of the river, near Pendarren House, below which you pass on the walk. In the past the water from the spring was believed to have healing properties, and there was a tradition that whichever of a newly married couple first reached the spring and drank the water would rule the home roost. In due course an oratory was built nearby. In the 1790s the farmer of the land was clearing rubble from what was reputed to be the site of the oratory when he unearthed an early medieval four-sided iron bell, a style often used in chapels and oratories. The bell, which would originally have been cased with bell-metal, is now housed in the National Museum of Wales.

The bridge was erected in the late 1700s, and Church Cottages (beside the churchyard) also date to the 1700s.

COED CEFN

Known variously as Llangenny Camp and Coed Cefn enclosure, the earthwork comprises a single bank with an outer ditch enclosing an almost rectangular area, part of which has been quarried away. Stone walling may once have stood on the southern bank. Various suggestions have been made as to what the site represents: a particularly small and unusually shaped hillfort, an Iron Age farmstead (though they weren't usually located near the crest of hills) or the remnants of a Roman look-out post? The ancient broadleaf woodland in which the enclosure sits is managed by the Woodland Trust, the wood being renowned for its display of bluebells in spring.

This heads half-left up and across the hill, aiming for a group of pine trees on the skyline. Once you can see the white-painted house on the far side of this field, ensure that you're heading to the right of the house and its surrounding stone wall to cross a tall stone stile alongside a gate and land on a wide track which soon gains a tarmacked surface. Follow this around a couple of bends and it will lead you out onto a road. You can just turn left here and head back down into Crickhowell, or, for a small extra diversion, you can explore the earthwork in Coed Cefn. To do this, turn right on the road to reach, in about a hundred yards, the car park at the crest of the road.

9 Go through the car park signed for Coed Cefn and take the track on its far side, bearing left when it splits and then right to head up the hill to its summit. Here you will find some enigmatic earthworks, and the wood is known for its bluebells in the spring. When you've seen enough, return to the road and turn right to head down into Crickhowell.

When you reach the edge of Crickhowell, if you just want to return to the centre you can carry on across the mini-roundabout and then take the no-through road which will lead you back to the fountain. Or you can turn left at the roundabout and head down Greenhill Way. When you reach the A40, turn right and walk along to the pedestrian crossing. Cross this and go through the gate along the path to the castle (with the remains of two towers on your left and of the motte and other stonework to your right), and then keep following the path to the other side of the parkland. At the far side, turn right onto Castle Road/High Street.

At the road junction, if you want to see the Usk and Crickhowell bridge, you can turn left and follow the road downhill. Take the path off to the left at the bottom just after the last house to reach a little seating area with

CRICKHOWELL CASTLE

The castle, originally known as Alisby's castle, the derivation of the name being unknown, stands on a spur where the Cwmbeth Brook converges on the Usk, the ground dropping sharply to the river just to the south of the bailey. Little is known of its history, and there is no firm date as to when the first structure was built. In 1272 it was rebuilt in stone by Sir Grimbald Pauncefote, who had married Sybil Turberville, the heiress of the Turberville family, who are thought to have been the builders of the initial earth and timber castle. In 1322 the castle fell to Edward II in his war with several of the Marcher lords.

A shell keep appears to have stood on the motte, entrance to which was gained by a twin-towered gatehouse, only a fragment of one tower now remaining and standing three storeys high. Corbels and the crease of an earlier roof near the top of the inside of the remaining fragment show that this was heightened at some point from its original two storeys.

To the west of the motte stood the bailey which would have been flanked by a stone wall, as evidenced by the remains of the conjoined round and square tower. Usually round towers post-date square towers, but it would appear that the square tower abuts the drum of the round tower and is therefore later. From architectural details similar to those in other castles, the round tower would appear to have been built in the late 1200s, the square tower following not much later. Prints produced by the Buck brothers in the 1740s show a number of D-shaped towers along the curtain wall.

The castle was refortified by the English during the wars against Owain Glyndwr, but it was nevertheless taken in 1403, after which it fell into ruin, the keep certainly having been uninhabitable by the 1550s.

benches, then return up the road to the road junction, now bearing left. This will lead you along the High Street. Look out for a narrow lane off to the left leading to a lychgate into the churchyard, and take this if you want to visit the church. Otherwise you will soon reach the drinking fountain at the end of the road. (Go back to point 1 if you need to find your way back to Llanbedr Road if that is where you parked).

CRICKHOWELL BRIDGE

A crossing of the Usk by bridge, ford or ferry was probably in existence somewhere along the river between Crickhowell and Maescelyn at the time when the castle mottes were built, explaining their location. A bridge seems to have been built here by 1558, the present structure being in the style of bridges built at that date or slightly later, though the present structure dates from a rebuild carried out in 1706. It was widened in 1810 and has since seen other repairs.

CRICKHOWELL CHURCH

The core of St Edmund's church was built prior to 1303 by Lady Sibyl Pauncefote, and seems to have replaced the chapel at Maescelyn mentioned in the notes on the town. The aisles were added later, possibly in the 1400s, and the broach spire later still, after the Reformation. The church was much restored during the 1800s, most of the fittings dating to this century. From earlier days, the effigies of Grimbald and Sybil Pauncefote remain (in the chancel), as does the font (dated 1668) and other memorials.

Walk 12
Tretower & Pen-y-Gaer

4.75 miles. On lanes, tracks and some field edge paths, all in good order. Very few stiles. A walk that involves little uphill walking. Includes Tretower Court and castle (seen from the outside, which you can visit, for times go to: https://cadw.gov.wales/visit/places-to-visit/tretower-court-and-castle), the site of Pen-y-gaer Roman fort and Cwmdu church. You could arrange the walk so as to be able to have a break at the Farmers Arms pub in Cwmdu (check opening times at www.the-farmers-arms.com).

Park near the entrance to Tretower Court and castle (grid ref: 186 213).

❶ The walk starts at the entrance to Tretower Court,where you may wish to inspect one of the stones that form a pillar of the archway to the left of the door. You may be able decipher the letter 'V', which is recorded as having once commenced the word *Valente* and have come from the site of the Roman fort at Pen-y-gaer, through which the walk passes.

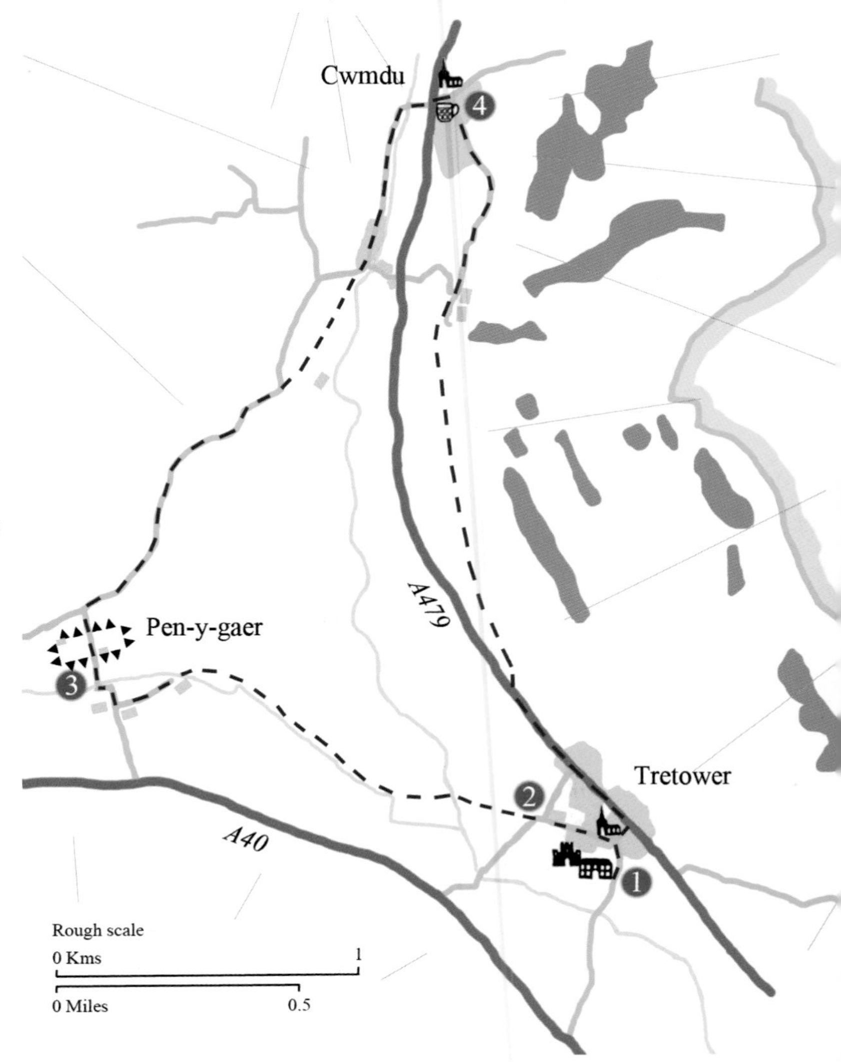

TRETOWER COURT

Tretower Court was built over a number of years, the north range dating largely to the early 14th century, the west range to the 15th, and the gatehouse and wall-walks on the south and east having been added later in the 15th century. There followed various modifications, culminating in a major repair and upgrading programme carried out in the early 17th century. The initial house would have consisted of a central ground-floor hall open to the roof, with a private living room or solar and a bedchamber on the upper floor at the west end, together with a separate apartment, also on the upper floor, at the east end.

Around 1540 Roger Vaughan, who had been given Tretower by his half-brother Sir William Herbert, refurbished the existing building, inserting a floor across the central hall, which had previously been open to the roof (a common adaptation at this time), turning the whole range into a two-storey structure. The ground floor now provided storerooms, with living accommodation for the family above. He then more than doubled the size of his house by adding a long west range. This range included a new ground-floor hall open to the roof, a new solar, and other rooms on the upper floor. Roger's son, Thomas, added the battlemented wall-walk and gatehouse to enclose the courtyard on its eastern and southern sides.

When the Vaughans ceased to live at Tretower, the house became a tenanted farm. The living rooms at the end of the west range which had been refurbished during the 17th-century renovations became the farmhouse, with the rest of the ranges adapted to become barns and sheds. The Court was bought for the nation in 1934 and has undergone periods of restoration, the most recent in 2010. It is in the care of Cadw.

TRETOWER CHURCH

The present church is Victorian and replaced an earlier building that may originally have been a chapel attached to the castle. It later became a chapel of ease, the parochial church being that at Cwmdu. (A chapel of ease was a chapel that was built in a part of a widely spread parish distant from the parish church, to make it easier for people to attend church.) The building had fallen into disrepair by 1870, but the Victorian church which replaced it, designed by the architect J.L. Pearson when he was the architect for the Glanusk Estate, seems to have been of the same size and shape. The village hall behind the church was built using the same pattern of stonework at the same time.

TRETOWER CASTLE

The initial castle, as was usually the case, was an earthen motte with a timber tower along with a bailey protected by a wooden palisade; it was constructed by a Norman by the name of Picard. The lands of the lordship were expanded under his son and it was probably this expansion that allowed the building of a shell keep in the mid 1100s. From the positioning of its chimneys, this building appears to have been quite innovative in design and it is comparatively rich in Romanesque ornamentation. The castle was severely damaged when Richard Marshal, earl of Pembroke, rose in revolt along with the Welsh in 1233. Soon afterwards Roger Picard, then head of the family, began a rebuilding campaign which involved the construction of the large round keep within the damaged shell keep, to which it was linked by a bridge at wall-walk level. He also oversaw the construction of a triangular-shaped bailey which had the keep at one point and a circular tower at each of the other points, along with a gatehouse in the wall opposite the keep. Roger's son, another Roger, appears to have retained the castle during the 1260s and beyond, despite having sworn allegiance to Llywelyn ap Gruffydd and also supporting Simon de Montfort. In 1308 the Picard family died out and the castle passed to the Bluets of Raglan, who commenced the construction of Tretower Court as a manor house. The castle, however, was still defensible as it was put into repair against Owain Glyndwr, a wooden four-storey storehouse and possible garrison quarters being built between the circular keep and the earlier shell keep.

With your back to this gateway, turn left and walk towards the church, turning left at the road junction this side of the church and passing the white-painted Ty Llys farmhouse on your left. A second stone believed to have come from Pen-y-gaer is some six courses up from ground level at the left-hand end of the front façade of the house, immediately adjacent to the unpainted garden wall. The full inscription when recorded was *Peregrini Fec*, 'made by Peregrinus'.

There are good views to be had of the castle along the next stretch of the road. Keep going along the road and immediately past a converted chapel and then a road off to the right, and where the road you're on bends left, keep ahead, to go through the left-hand of two field gates.

2 Follow the field boundary on your right to the far end of the field. Here you cross over the concrete farm bridge over the wide Clarach Brook and go through the field gate into the next field. Again follow the field boundary on your right to the far end of the field. Here, go through a field gate on your right into another field and immediately left through another field gate into a third field and then through a small metal gate to take a path through a narrow stretch of young woodland. Leave the woodland via a stile at its far end, and walk through another narrow stretch of woodland, leaving it at the end via a small metal gate. Follow the stream on your left across a short stretch of field to a field gate and stile onto a bridleway, on which you turn left. Follow this until it emerges onto a gravelled track near a house, the track soon becoming a tarmacked lane. Keep ahead on this, passing an interesting array of gates and doorways on your left, to a junction with another lane. Here, turn right and walk up the lane, looking out for signs of Pen-y-gaer Roman fort and its civilian settlement or *vicus* as soon as you cross Ewyn Brook. The photograph below shows the view across the *vicus*, thought to have extended for 60m to the west of the road.

PEN-Y-GAER ROMAN FORT

The visible remains consist of a rectangular platform defined by scarped slopes, measuring some 130m east-west by 90-100m north-south, and enclosing an area of about 1.2 hectares. Limited excavations carried out in 1966 suggest that the fort underwent three periods of construction, beginning with its foundation around 70 or 80AD, presumably during the military operations conducted by the then governor of Britain, Julius Frontinus, when a rampart of stone and soil was erected some 25 feet wide fronted by a timber revetment and backed by a stone kerb. Under the Emperor Trajan (*c*.98-117AD) the rampart was topped with a stone wall some 3 feet wide. Shortly afterwards this work was replaced by a wider wall outside of which a ditch was dug some 10 feet wide and 3.5 feet deep. The remains of stone and timber buildings found within the confines of the fort all date to this final phase. However, it was soon after this work was completed that the fort was abandoned under Trajan's successor, Hadrian, in *c*.130AD. Aerial photographs have suggested that a barracks block existed in the western part of the fort, perhaps allowing for a garrison of infantry numbering some 500 men. It seems that a civilian settlement or *vicus* grew up to the south of the fort, as a strip settlement along the road along which you approach it; you may be able to discern the scarped platform indicating the site of one building. The buildings here may well have been of timber-framing erected on shallow foundation walls and with tiled roofs. Evidence of smithing and glass-making has been found. The *vicus* probably extended to the other side of the road too, but no recent archaeological work has been carried out here. A cremation burial has been recorded some 350m west of the fort, and aerial photos have suggested a circular feature to the east that is thought could be the remains of a tomb or shrine. Finds of 4th-century coins suggest that later use was made of the fort.

3 Continue on the lane through the site of the fort, with Pen-y-gaer farm (thought to be on the site of the *principia* or headquarters of the fort) on your right and Greenhill Farm (in the north-west corner of the site) on your left, then descend to another road junction. Turn right and follow the road till it bends left and there's a gravelled track to the right (with black and white arrowed warning signs for motorists indicating a sharp bend) that leads to Lower Mill. Cross the stile adjacent to the field gate to the left of the track and enter a field, which you cross diagonally to its far corner, aiming to the right of a group of white-painted buildings on the far side of the field. Cross the stile here and turn right on the road, keeping ahead at the junction soon reached. Follow this road, and after a quarter of a mile or so it will cross the Rhiangoll river to meet the A479 near the Farmers Arms, a community owned pub. Cross the A479 and walk uphill to reach Cwmdu church.

CWMDU CHURCH

The church largely dates to the 1400s, though it may well contain masonry from an earlier church, as a church is thought to be have been founded here in the 1000s. It was extensively rebuilt in two stages, in 1831-33 and 1907. In 1830, a pillar stone found about a mile away and measuring some 5 feet tall and 1 foot wide of late 6th- or early 7th-century date with Latin and Ogham inscriptions was built into a buttress on the south side of the church, between the main porch and that used in those days by the priest. The Latin inscription reads *Catacus hic jacit filius Tegernacus* ('Here lies Cattoc the son of Teyrnoc'.) Fragments of other carved stones, one dated to between the 7th and 9th centuries, and one to the 11th century or later, with possible later inscriptions, can be glimpsed in the priest's porch.

4 With your back to the church's lychgate, walk ahead along the road (i.e. turn right if you've come up from the Farmers Arms and don't wish to visit the church). Follow the road till it makes a hairpin turn to the right by Penrheol Cnappa Cottage on the left. Continue ahead along the tarmac for some 20 yards and then again keep ahead, this time on a wide track. Keep to the track, which becomes more of a path later on, then briefly a wide track just before it meets the A479. Turn left and in some 200 yards you'll reach a roadside pavement in Tretower. Carry on along the main road and take the third road off to the right, which will lead you straight down to the church and Tretower Court.

Walk 13
Talybont-on-Usk

5.75 miles on well-made tracks and a variety of paths. Few stiles. One steep climb, but otherwise quite gentle. Incorporates routes of early industrial transport from canals to tramroads and railways, along with an Iron Age hillfort, views of Talybont Reservoir and encounters with the poetry and life of Henry Vaughan. There are two pubs and a café near where the walk starts.

Park in Talybont, somewhere along the road near the village shop and café, from where the walk starts (grid ref: 114 226).

❶ With your back to the shop entrance, turn right and walk along the road, soon crossing it to walk up the sloped path this side of a road junction and the white-painted lifting bridge to join the canal towpath of the Monmouthshire and Brecon Canal.

Turn left along the canal and after crossing the aqueduct above the Caerfanel river, walk up the path on your left and turn right onto the Taff Trail, as per the signpost. The trail will lead you across the bridge (no.143) over the canal and then turn right onto a track which soon crosses the route of the Brecon and Merthyr Railway. (Talybont was at the start of what was known as the

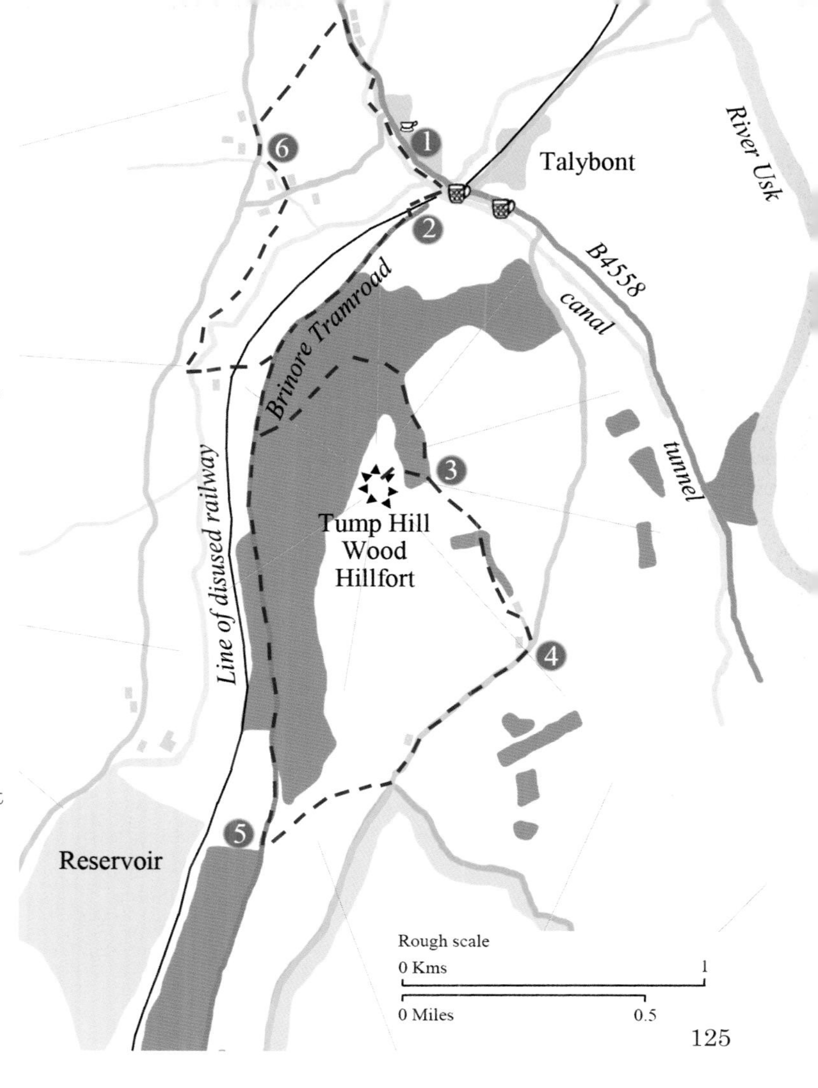

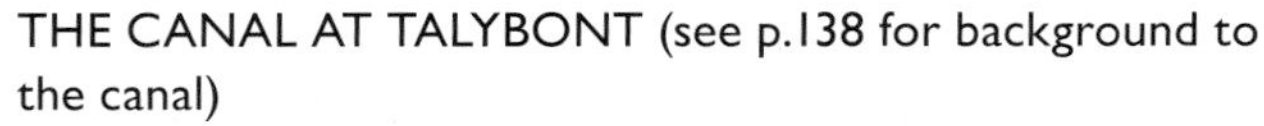

THE CANAL AT TALYBONT (see p.138 for background to the canal)
A wooden drawbridge first carried the road over the canal here, and was only replaced by a fixed bridge after navigation on the canal ceased in the 1930s. Before the canal reopened to boats in 1970, a steel drawbridge with an electric operating mechanism was installed, since replaced by the structure present today. There are four other drawbridges along the canal to the west. They are of a less elaborate design as they simply allow farmers to access fields and originally saved the canal company the cost of building stone bridges. The steep embankment required by the canal here has caused problems, for example in December 1994, when a breach caused local flooding, after which it was rebuilt with a concrete lining.

Seven Mile Bank which had an unusually steep 1 in 38 gradient. Longer trains needed an additional engine, which was kept at Talybont station for the purpose, at least until *c.*1900. In the early days, downhill trains often made 'wild runs' down the Bank. In 1878 the drivers lost control of a train that comprised 36 carriages and three engines. It came off the line once it had crossed the canal at Talybont, killing two of the drivers and two of the stokers, and strewing wreckage widely. For more on the train line see pages 45 and 46.)

❷ Keep on the Taff Trail as it turns right onto the line of the Brinore tramroad (for which there is a stone marker on the right). Some 60 yards along you'll reach the entrance to the Henry Vaughan Garden on the right. This displays some of the herbs that Vaughan will have

BRINORE TRAMROAD

The Brinore Tramroad was built in 1814-15. A clause in the Brecknock and Abergavenny Canal Act of 1793 allowed the canal company to construct tramroads to workings within 8 miles of the canal, or for landowners of such workings to obtain wayleaves to do so. The company declined to build this tramroad, so £12,800 was raised by public subscription to construct it to limestone quarries at Trefil, the stone being used to create lime used for improving the quality of acidic agricultural land. One of the tramroad's sponsors, Benjamin Hall, then obtained permission to extend the tramroad to serve the Rhymney Iron Works and the collieries at Bryn Oer (the original Welsh name from which the anglicised 'Brinore' developed) in the Rhymney Valley, so that coal from the collieries could be transported to the canal for transhipment to mid Wales.

The engineer was George Overton. Cast-iron tramplates or rails were fixed to cast-iron tie bars which then rested on stone sleeper blocks (many of which are still visible – the photograph above shows one of them). The gauge was 3 feet 6 inches (c.1.06m), the trackbed itself being 9 feet (2.7m) wide. It was a single track tramway with 13 passing places about half a mile apart, the only places where the tramplates were spiked into the stone sleeper blocks. The whole was gently inclined to aid the haulage of the filled trams. The boundaries of the tramway were largely marked by hawthorn hedges, which the tramroad company had to keep in repair, together with the drainage ditches on either side. The tramroad fell into disuse around 1860-70 due to the spread of the railways. Interestingly, there is no evidence that the Brinore Tramroad Company has ever been legally dissolved, so the present ownership of the tramroad is unclear. Public access, however, is not in doubt.

used in his treatments, and also has some picnic benches and bug hotels (one of these is pictured above). For some information on Henry Vaughan himself see p.134.

After about a further half a mile along the trail you'll see a footpath leading off downhill to the right through a metal footpath gate: make a mental note of this, for it is a path you'll be taking later in the walk. For the moment, keep ahead and look out for a path off to the left that you'll reach in a further few hundred yards. Take this path, which initially angles sharply back on the line of the tramroad, and follow it uphill, ignoring smaller paths to right and left, and a wider forestry track off to the

right. The path passes through tall conifer plantations and just after it levels out meets a fence in front of which it turns right and goes through a footpath gate into more thinly planted woodland. Here the path shadows the field boundary on your left and in due course reaches a field gate out into a field beyond.

Before you go through the gate you can choose to use a permissive path to visit the hillfort at the top of the hill, by turning about, retracing your route for a few steps and then taking the path-cum-track that forks left and circles up the hillside through the woods and out into grassland. If you continue to the top of the hill, you can see

TUMP HILL WOOD HILLFORT

This Iron Age hillfort is roughly oval in shape, measuring some 170m north-south and 130m east-west, and encloses an area of about 1.5 acres. Its entrance is on the south-east side. There are two banks separated by a ditch that surround the whole fort, the inner bank being the larger of the two. At the northern end is a short section of outer ditch with a further low bank beyond, as is likewise the case to the south-east.

Most Iron Age hillforts in what became Breconshire are quite small, as with this hillfort, and are not located in overtly strong defensive locations even if sited on a hilltop. Their location would often give good views across a swathe of countryside, however, so providing the opportunity to spot impending danger. They may have been occupied by an extended family group, the defences giving a degree of security and a chance to corral livestock. There are concentrations of such hillforts along the Usk Valley and along the Wye Valley near Builth, suggesting that access to better quality land was also a factor in their location.

the largely univallate hillfort and also gain glimpses of Talybont Reservoir to the south. Then retrace your steps to the field gate.

3 Continue the circular walk by going through the gate. Ahead of you, you will see two paths crossing the field, one on the right shadowing the field boundary on your right and one on the left slanting slightly downhill. Take the left-hand path and head to an internal corner of the field to then turn slightly right and follow the field boundary on your left. Pass a field gate in this boundary and keep ahead to another field gate at the end of the field. Go through this and keep following the track, which follows a field boundary on your left, to another gate as you approach the buildings of Upper Wenallt farm. Go through this gate and follow the track along to a further gate, through which you drop down to join the tarmacked farm drive; turn right on this and walk down to meet a road.

4 Turn right on the road and follow it along, passing Pantywenallt on your right and later crossing a cattle grid. Once over this, cross the stile on your immediate right and enter a large field. Cross this field, aiming for the centre of the saddle in the summit ridge on the far side of the valley in front of you. As you cross the field you'll see a stile in the far fence. Cross this and head across the next field to its far right-hand corner, passing first to the left of three large oak trees that stand in this

part of the field, and then through a line of trees which mark a small stream which you cross. Keep going ahead, and in the far corner of the field you'll come to a stile which you cross to rejoin the old tramroad.

5 Turn right and walk along this. In due course you will cross a wide forestry track, staying on the line of the tramroad which also becomes the Taff Trail at this point. In due course you'll pass the start of the path off to the right that you took up the hillside and then come to the path off to the left that you hopefully spotted and memorised earlier in the walk and which you now need to take. Go through the kissing gate and down this path, which follows a field boundary on your left. At the bottom of the field turn left and go through another kissing gate, the path being well waymarked, to join a track on which

TALYBONT RESERVOIR

In the early 1900s expanding industrialisation led to a rapid growth in population in Newport that in turn increased demand for a steady supply of clean drinking water. In due course the valley of the Afon Caerfanell to the south-west of Talybont was chosen as the source of this water. By 1926 a water treatment works had been built, supplied by an intake weir that could extract water directly from the river without the need to build a dam. However, it was soon realised that surveys of the site hadn't discovered that in dry years the river partially disappeared into the post-glacial gravels in the valley bottom. In 1931 a dam was therefore constructed, comprising an earth embankment and puddled clay core, the underlying rock being sealed, and a new water treatment works was constructed about a quarter of a mile downstream as the original site was found to have insufficient solid rock for the foundations. In 1939 water started to be supplied to Newport. To create the reservoir, 17 farms and homes were acquired to give the water company complete control of the catchment area, adding to the problem of rural depopulation. Now owned by Welsh Water, a £10 million upgrade to the plant and pipes within the dam was carried out in 2019.

you turn left. Follow this track for a few yards, then bear right and downhill, turning right to pass under the line of the old railway.

Cross the track on the far side of the old railway to go through a kissing gate and then down some steps to another kissing gate through which you enter a field. The path crosses this to head down to a footbridge across the Caerfanell. Once over the footbridge, turn right and walk along the riverbank. You will eventually reach a footpath gate with an adjacent tall post – if you pull on the handle on the post, a panel will appear, bearing a quotation, in Welsh and English, from the poetry of Henry Vaughan.

HENRY VAUGHAN

The poet Henry Vaughan, descended from the Vaughans of Tretower Court (see p.119), was one of a pair of twins born in 1621 in the parish of Llansantffraed, across the River Usk from Talybont, where he lived for most of his life. Aged 17 he was sent to Oxford to continue his education, begun under the Revd Matthew Herbert, rector of Llangattock, who had a reputation as a schoolmaster. He left Oxford without taking a degree and by 1640 had moved to London to study law. At the outbreak of the Civil War he returned to Breconshire and took up arms for the king, becoming a lieutenant in a troop of cavalry. He is recorded as fighting near Chester in 1645. He published a small collection of poetry in 1647, but the publication of a second volume was delayed by the second Civil War in 1648. He fell under the spell of the poetry of George Herbert and in 1650 published his first collection of the devotional poetry for which he is generally remembered. By the end of the Civil War he had also started to practise medicine, though how or where he received his training is unclear. He died in 1695 and is buried in the churchyard at Llansantffraed.

Go through the gate and continue along the river bank, eventually reaching a kissing gate. Through this, the path starts by following the river bank, then bears left to cross the field to a stone stile to the left a large ash tree (if still standing; it may have succumbed to ash die back) and a white-painted cottage. Cross the stile and then a similar one a few yards to the right on the other side of the road. Now follow the path ahead, following the stream on your left (and ignoring a bridge across it), to reach a kissing gate out onto another road.

6 Turn right on the road and as you approach a white-painted house on the left adjacent to the road, go through a kissing gate on the right to enter a large field. Cross this field diagonally to its far corner, where you will find a stile. Cross this and head towards the left-hand end of the houses ahead, to reach another stile. Cross this and the small field you enter to another stile and footbridge out onto a road. Turn right on the road and once you have crossed the canal, take the path on the left to join the canal towpath, where you will find another pillar with some of Henry Vaughan's poetry.

Turn left on the towpath, and you will soon be back at the lifting bridge near to which you parked.

Walk 14
Pencelli

5.75 miles on a canal towpath, roads, lanes and paths through fields. Few stiles. Most of the walk is on the level with one small ridge to cross. Takes in the site of Pencelli Castle, two churches and a length of canal with an aqueduct over the River Usk. If you time the walk right you can avail yourself of the Royal Oak inn in the village at the end of your walk (check opening times at: www.theroyaloakpencelli.com).

The best place to park is in a large lay-by just south of Pencelli (i.e. on the Talybont side) almost opposite the entrance drive to Pencelli Castle Caravan & Camping Park (grid ref: 095 247).

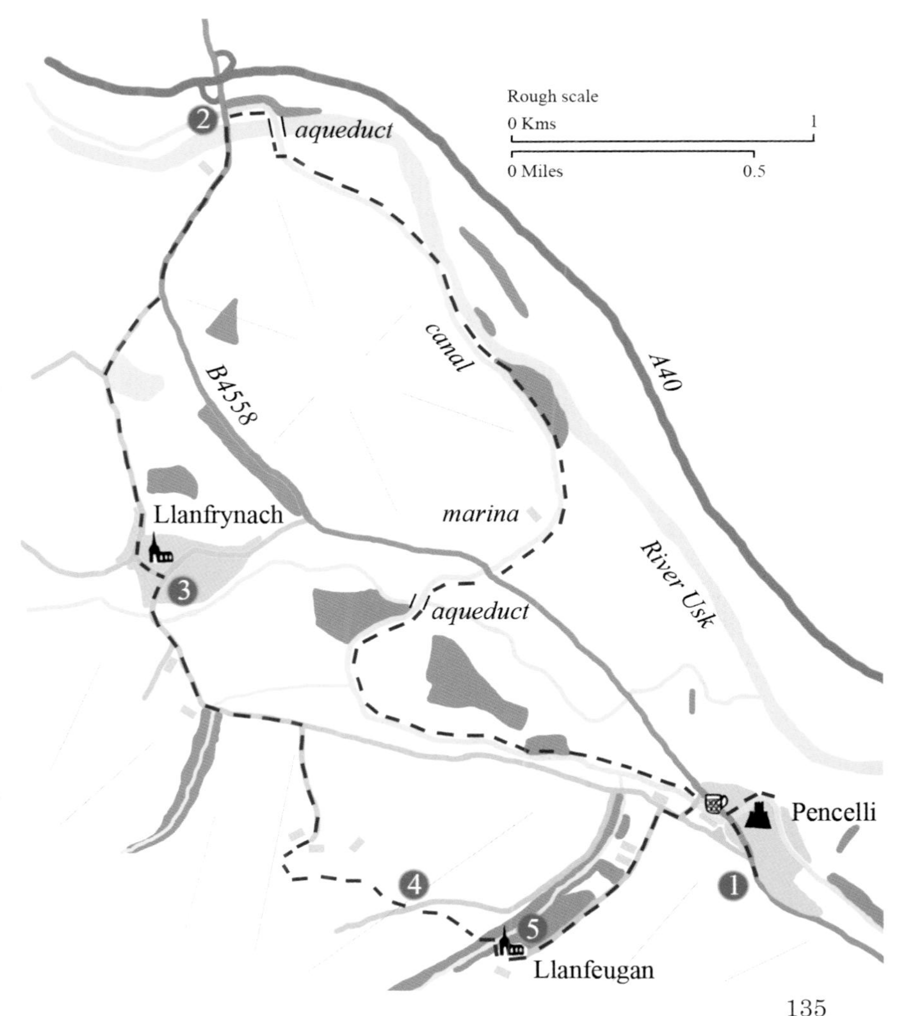

❶ Turn left out of the lay-by and walk towards Pencelli, looking out for Pencelli Tower House, set back from the road on your right. (The house was built from the stone previously used in the construction of Pencelli Castle.) Cross the bridge over the canal, and drop down the steps on the left to the canal towpath. Initially turn left to head under the road and wander a short

PENCELLI CASTLE

The name 'Pencelli' means 'the head or end of a grove'. The castle that once stood high above what is now a bend on the Monmouthshire and Brecon Canal was built by one of the Baskerville family, who had their base at Eardisley in north-west Herefordshire. It was probably initially an earth and timber structure built in the late 11th or early 12th century, when Bernard de Neufmarché was making inroads into this part of Wales. The castle clearly passed into Welsh hands, probably during the unsettled times when King John was seizing the lands of the de Braoses, for in 1215 it is recorded as being captured by the English. It appears to have passed to and fro between English and Welsh lords in the 1200s before it came into the possession of the Mortimers (by marriage) in 1247, and it was this family who were probably responsible for improving the fortifications, perhaps being the first to construct them in stone after the defeat of Llywelyn ap Gruffydd who, with his allies, had controlled much of this area between 1262 and 1276. The castle was never at the centre of a Marcher lordship, but functioned more as the heart of a manor.

The castle now consists of a series of earthworks with few masonry remains. A survey of the site suggests that a rectangular keep stood in the northern corner, now marked by a mound of what is presumed to mainly comprise collapsed masonry. From the evidence of a drawing made by the Buck brothers in 1741, a twin-towered gatehouse was built as an entrance in the curtain wall. The earthworks suggest there were two baileys. In 1494 or '95 the castle was acquired by Sir Richard Herbert of Montgomery. It must still have been in reasonable repair, for he used it as a residence during the reign of Henry VII, who died in 1509. However, by 1583 the castle had been superseded by the farmhouse which is built within the curtilage of its walls, its builders clearly using stone and architectural details from the castle in its construction. Though the Buck brothers' illustration shows substantial standing remains built in stone, these seem to have all but vanished by the early 1800s. Unusually for a Norman castle it is not paired with a church to form the basis of a settlement, the local church being that of Llanfeugan (visited later in the walk), but nevertheless a settlement grew in the shadow of the castle to the north-west, laid out on a grid plan, since disrupted by the arrival of the canal. The settlement was known as Castro in 1675. The only building of any age is the Royal Oak, which is thought to date from the 1700s. Pencelly Court, which lies to the west of the planned settlement, carries a datestone of 1691.

way along the canal so you can see the setting of the large castle motte on your right, around which the canal has to swing; this is easier seen in the winter due to tree cover. Then about turn and return under the road – and follow the canal towpath!

In about 2.5 miles you come to a junction of routes at bridge no. 162. You want to follow the footpath signs for Brecon, which means crossing the bridge over the canal, then taking the path on your right to join the towpath now on the other bank of the canal. About halfway between the bridge and the Brynich Aqueduct ahead of you, look out for an old trunk plug used to

BRECKNOCK AND ABERGAVENNY CANAL / MONMOUTHSHIRE AND BRECON CANAL
The Act of Parliament allowing construction of the canal (the Brecknock & Abergavenny Canal Company Act) was passed in 1793, construction of the canal commencing in 1797 at Gilwern near Abergavenny, where an aqueduct was needed. The canal was completed from Gilwern to Brecon three years later, and a section was then constructed from Gilwern to a wharf at Govilon, closer to Abergavenny, which was completed in 1805. By 1812 a junction with the Monmouthshire Canal had been made, enabling barges to travel between Brecon and the coast. The wharves at Brecon were enlarged between 1809 and 1812 and largely used for handling coal and lime, a horse-drawn tramway taking coal as far as Kington in Herefordshire. The companies running the two canals amalgamated in 1865 to become the Monmouthshire and Brecon Canal. With the coming of the railways, and notably after 1880 when larger train engines were introduced and the canal was taken over by the Great Western Railway, traffic on the northern sections of the canal was much reduced, though it continued to be used till *c.*1933.

drain the canal, now on the edge of the footpath. Keep on the towpath along the aqueduct (built by the engineer Thomas Dadford at the end of the 1700s) across the Usk and stay on it till you reach a road. (The photographs alongside show the view looking each way along the River Usk from the canal aqueduct.)

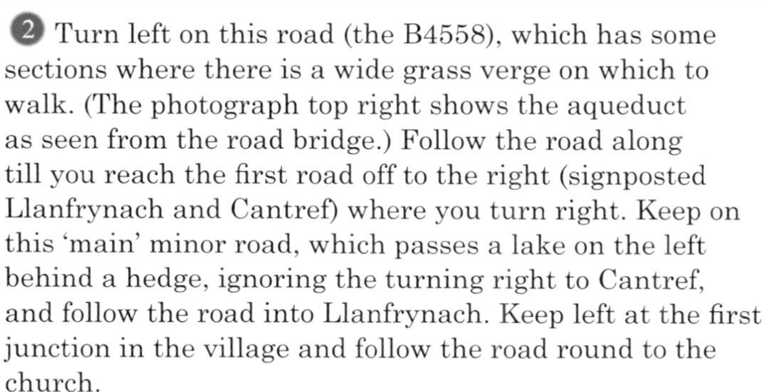

2 Turn left on this road (the B4558), which has some sections where there is a wide grass verge on which to walk. (The photograph top right shows the aqueduct as seen from the road bridge.) Follow the road along till you reach the first road off to the right (signposted Llanfrynach and Cantref) where you turn right. Keep on this 'main' minor road, which passes a lake on the left behind a hedge, ignoring the turning right to Cantref, and follow the road into Llanfrynach. Keep left at the first junction in the village and follow the road round to the church.

LLANFRYNACH CHURCH

The earliest reference to a church here is in 1291, but the large curvilinear churchyard, the dedication to St Brynach and the presence of a pre-Conquest pillar stone suggest a much earlier original foundation. The earliest part of the current building is probably the core of the tower, which could date to any time between the 13th and 15th centuries. In 1809 the church was described as 'low and narrow, not ceiled, and but indifferently lighted' and in 1855-6 it was rebuilt, a larger opening being made into the tower at the same time. The interior is notable for its scheme of Victorian decoration, painted with the use of stencils. Included are a Te Deum, the Ten Commandments, Sanctus and a frieze of floral designs in the chancel. On the chancel's east wall, there are two large angels with a foliage background. The pre-Conquest pillar stone can be found against the north wall at the west end of the church and shows a figure with upraised arms above a Maltese cross and a small bird. Two other carved stones of this date disappeared during the restoration, one of them, at least, built into the foundations of the new church. There are several memorials to the members of the de Winton family, who owned much land in the area; having made money from their bank business, they were generous benefactors to the churches here and in Brecon.

❸ On the bend by the main entrance to the churchyard, take the road opposite that is signed as part of the cyclists' Taff Trail. (The first house on the left is called Jay Cottage, as a check that you have the right road.) This will soon lead you over the Nant Menasgin. Keep on the main minor road (ignoring Tregaer road off to the right) and further on follow it round the bend to the left, then take the narrow lane off to the right after a further few hundred yards.

Follow this uphill to the farmyard of Pentwyn, keeping to the right of the house and the stone barn to follow a track between fields. This will presently reach a gateway across the line of the track. Here, you need to turn left up a grassy track reached just before this gateway. Keep an eye out for the first field gate on your left, for the path you want goes through this to then follow the field boundary on your left to a stile on the far side of the field. Cross this and then cross the next field on the diagonal to its far corner. Here you cross a stile out onto a road.

❹ Cross the road and go over the stile on the far side. The path crosses a corner of this field, aiming for the left of a white house on the far side of the valley and heading to a stile in the field boundary. Once over this, the path gradually closes in on the line of a small gully on your right. Cross the gully to pick up a path that runs down through the trees and which soon passes to the right of a large boulder, as well as to the right of some derelict buildings that stand on the edge of the field. This path will lead you along the edge of a stream to a bridge which crosses it, and then up some steps to a gravelled area in front of a house. Almost immediately you'll come to a stone stile on your left, which you cross to enter the churchyard of Llanfeugan church.

LLANFEUGAN CHURCH

The location, on a spur between a stream and its tributary, and its dedication to St Meugan, suggest that there may have been a Celtic church on the site, perhaps dating from the 600s, but no hard evidence has been found. Meugan is a better known Celtic saint than many. He was the grandson of Meurig ab Tewdrig, king of Morganwg, and is believed to have served under both St Illtud and St Dyfrig, the latter being the patron of a college on the banks of the River Wye which he perhaps also founded. There are churches dedicated to him in various parts of Wales and he was buried on Bardsey Island. In the churchyard stand 12 yews, at least one of which is thought to be over 2,000 years old, suggestiing that this may have been a pagan site that was 'Christianised'.

There has been much discussion as to which parts of the church were built when, but the style and records suggest that a church was built here around 1272, funded by Roger (III) Mortimer at the time he was working on the defences at Pencelli Castle. In the 1300s the church seems to have undergone major repair as well as being extended – either the north aisle being added to the nave, or a new nave being constructed to the south of the old, turning the old nave into a north aisle, with windows and doors being reused. It may be that the stone used came from the valley to the church's north, accounting for its steep-sided character at this point. Subsequently the tower was added and new windows were provided for the south wall of the church, whilst the east end was also rebuilt. Unresolved queries as to the structure of the church include why the westernmost bay of the arcade is of different design to the others, and the significance of reused dressings in its build. The photograph shows the westernmost bay of the nave, with two different forms of arch support.

A rood loft was taken out during alterations carried out around 1813, and a gallery spanning the nave was constructed around this time, and discovered later to have been in part built from elements of the rood loft. In 1891 the north and east walls of the chancel were rebuilt, the gallery taken out and dumped in the churchyard where it and earlier timbers from the roof loft were left to rot. A doorway and head-beam were finally rescued and assembled to stand in the north aisle (now also the Lady Chapel). On the rear of the timbers several white roses of the house of York have been painted, suggesting that the rood screen was erected in the reign of Edward IV or Richard III. It seemed that the locals used the churchyard for play: the west wall of the tower was used to play handball, the play area being between the top of the projecting base and a string course some three feet higher, the ground area then being kept free of graves. It is thought that further west there was once a cockpit.

5 Leave the churchyard by its main path and gate (or its adjacent stone stile) and turn left on the lane. Follow this downhill, ignoring a turn to the right quickly reached, till it meets another road. Turn right on this and left across a bridge over the canal. You can then either keep ahead to the road and turn right to reach the Royal Oak and then your car, or turn right along the canal towpath to do likewise, reaching the pub through its garden if you so wish.

Walk 15
Llangasty-Talyllyn & Llangorse Lake

5.25 miles on minor roads, tracks and good quality paths in the main, though those close to Llangorse Lake can be very wet in winter. A few stiles. Much of the walk is fairly level, but there is a long gentle ascent to Allt yr Esgair hillfort with options for a steep or gentle descent. Includes Llangasty church, part of the lake shore and a hillfort with wide views.

Park near the church at Llangasty-Talyllyn, or just beyond it in the small car park at the lakeshore (grid ref: 134 262).

You may want to visit the church at the start or end of your walk.

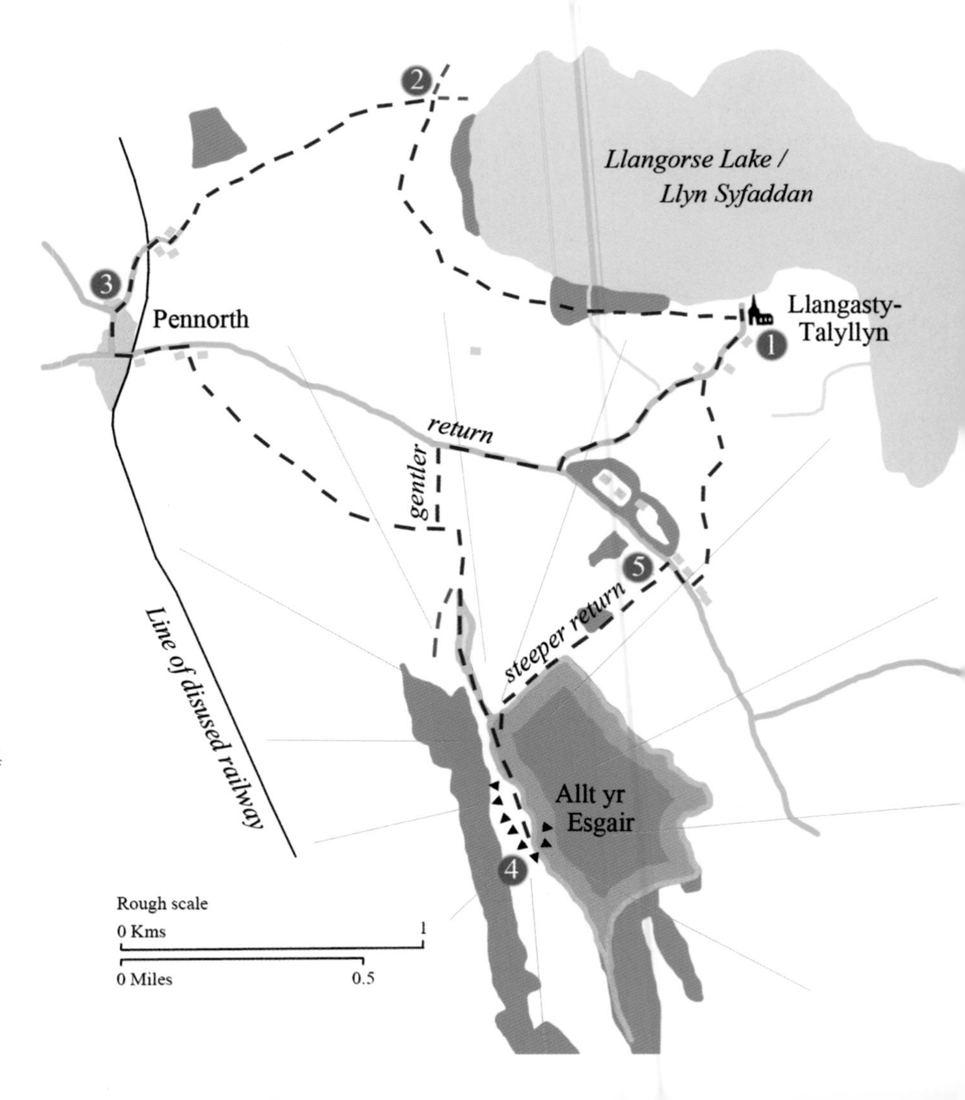

LLANGASTY-TALYLLYN CHURCH

As its name suggests, this is the church of St Gastyn (also known as Casten and Casteu) situated at the end or edge of a lake. The church is the only one in Britain dedicated to this Breton saint and the name is suggestive of a Celtic origin. The curving west side of the churchyard is also indicative of a Celtic foundation, supported by surveys which show a now buried curving ditch on the east side. Other parts of the churchyard appear to have been lost to other uses over time, making an original circular churchyard a possibility. There is no evidence that a settlement ever formed in its vicinity. A survey carried out in 1998 did discover some signs of human activity to the east of the church, but not enough to suggest that there was ever a Celtic monastery here. This all suggests that the local saint was a hermit, living in a timber building near where the church now stands. This might have been in the early 400s.

Described in 1838 as a 'dark, ancient and decaying edifice', the medieval church that had been built on the site was completely rebuilt in the mid-1800s with the possible exception of the lower courses of the tower. The architect was J.L. Pearson, employed by Robert Raikes, a banker who had bought the adjoining Treberfydd Estate in 1840. When at university, Raikes had been strongly influenced by the Oxford Movement, a High Church movement within the Church of England, and the design shows an almost complete Tractarian interior, built in the gothic revival style and adorned with ornate, decorative touches such as castle-like towers, parapets, tracery and pointed windows and arched entries, all likely to be rather more elaborate than what was there before.

Nothing is known about the structure it replaced, though one document suggests that it was of mid-16th century date, with a tower added in 1670. The fixtures and fittings all date to the rebuild, with the exception of some fragments of the medieval screen which were utilised in the new chancel screen. Three bells were also saved. The present interior is noted for its altar steps made of Devonshire marble, and the painted and gilded walls and roof timbers. Raikes was also responsible for the construction of the neighbouring school (now a private house) and of Treberfydd House. The house and its gardens are open to the public sometimes; to find out when, phone 07748 155484 or email info@treberfydd.com.

❶ The walk starts on a footpath that leaves the lane between the church and the lakeshore, on the left if heading from the church to the lake, or right if heading from the lake to the church! This path is well waymarked and roughly parallel to the lake shore, though sometimes on the landward side of woodland. In the first field, for example, stay on the bank and pass to the left of the thicket, then go through a kissing gate. Keep following the path through the fields and passing through gates and some woodland, often on raised walkways across boggier ground (but not everywhere!) (Through one gate, where the path turns left through a second gate, you may first wish to go straight ahead and visit a thatched bird hide on the lake shore.)

LLANGORSE LAKE

The lake's current name is relatively recent. In ancient times it was known as Llyn Syfaddon/Syfaddan, and more recently it was called Brycheiniog Mere. It sits in a glacially-scoured rock basin, has a perimeter of some 3 miles, and is very shallow, with a maximum depth of 7.5m. It has plenty of plant life, such as pondweeds, creating a varied habitat for wildlife (including the rare blue-tailed damselfly). This has led to its being declared a Site of Special Scientific Interest (SSSI), and the Llangasty Nature Reserve serves to protect an area round the lake's edge. In the 12th century Gerald of Wales mentioned the waterfowl here in his *Description of Wales*. Some 40m from the lake's northern shore (not passed on this walk) is a small island measuring some 50 x 55m. This was first identified as an artificial crannog in 1876, and has since been dated to *c*.890AD, though its foundation may go back earlier. It was created by sinking large planks of wood deep into the lake's bed and behind them building up the island in layers of stone, soil and brushwood as a platform on which to build a series of circular buildings. Archaeologists investigated it between 1989 and 1993, finding some remains of high quality textiles and a bronze hinge from an 8th- or 9th-century Christian reliquary, similar to those found in Ireland, together with fragments of pottery and animal bone. It may be that the place was destroyed in 916, for in that year Æthelflæd, daughter of Alfred the Great, who ruled Mercia between 911 and her death in 918, sent an army into Brycheiniog to avenge the murder of the Mercian abbot Ecbryht and his companions. Reports tell of the burning of a Brycheiniog royal fort on the lake and the seizure of Brycheiniog's queen and 33 others. Two dugout canoes have been found in the mud of the northern edge of the lake, one in 1925 (measuring 25 feet long) and the other in 1990. The latter was radio-carbon dated to between 754 and 874AD. Much folklore relates to the lake, including the story that it is the site of the now submerged Roman city of Loventium. Down the years people have claimed to have seen the foundations of buildings during droughts and have interpreted sounds heard in stormy conditions as church bells ringing out from below the waters.

Keep following the path, and at the end of the third field after the hide there's a carving of a damselfly with a button to press for audio information about local wildlife. After crossing three more fields you'll come to a field in which you pass two ancient oaks standing alone on your left and a wood on your right, the lower parts of the trees being submerged in water at wetter times of year.

❷ At the end of this field you'll come to gate with a length of walling to its right. Don't go through the gate! Instead, turn left and follow the field boundary on your right, initially round a very small old quarry (the path is supposed to be close to the fenceline all the way, but it is somewhat awkward to adhere to that route at this point) and so up to a collection of gates in the far right-hand corner of the field. Go through the gate (hopefully marked by a yellow-topped waymarking pole) that leads out onto a track and follow it along to Ty-Gwyn Farm, appropriately painted white (*gwyn* is Welsh for white). The path goes through a gate just to the right of the house and enters the farmyard. Keep ahead to the barn in front of you and then turn right and walk round the barns, turning left to leave the farmyard by a tarmacked lane. You almost immediately cross the course of the old Brecon, Hay and Hereford railway. Follow the lane down to a junction with a road.

BRECON, HAY AND HEREFORD RAILWAY

Work on the line between Hereford and Brecon was begun on 1 October 1868 by the Mid Wales Railway Company, which was taken over by the Midland Railway Company exactly a year later. The nearest station to this part of the line was Llangorse Lake Halt, where the single track had a platform and small passenger shelter on one side of the line. As it was a 'halt', the train would only stop there by request. The Midland Railway used the line as a link in a through route from Birmingham to Swansea, so that they could compete with the Great Western Railway. They ran the line essentially for the transport of goods, with local passenger traffic as an incidental service. Through passenger traffic was never a priority, and indeed trains for such traffic were discontinued between Hereford and Swansea in 1931. The line was never a huge commercial success, and as road traffic burgeoned, the line became economically unviable. The line was closed to passengers on 30 December 1962, and to freight in 1964.

3 Turn left on the road and at a T-junction soon reached again turn left. Go past the chapel on your right and take the bridleway off to the right between a house called Moorlands and a bungalow called Mercia. Follow this bridleway up the shoulder of the hill; you'll have good views to either side at different points along its course. (The bridleway follows the route of the Roman road that ran between the forts at Brecon Gaer via Pen-y-gaer near Tretower to Gobannium [Abergavenny].) After a while the bridleway will fork, one fork dropping away downhill

to the left, but you stay to the right and continue uphill. (Make a mental note of this point, for you may choose to return to your vehicle this way if you want the gentler descent option.) Keep following the path up the shoulder of the hill, and where the bridleway again forks, keep left. As you approach the top, just after you go through a small gate there's a stile immediately in the wall to your left; this will be your route down the hillside if you prefer the steeper option. Keep going till you reach the top of the hill, passing through the earthworks of a hillfort.

ALLT YR ESGAIR HILLFORT

This hillfort has steep natural defences on all sides, the gentlest being the way you've approached it on this walk. It measures some 566m by 115m and although the understanding of the remaining earthworks has been complicated by damage caused by forestry and quarrying, it would seem to have been built in two phases. At the southern end there appears to be what is left of an earlier bank and ditch beyond the earthworks that currently form this end of the hillfort, or perhaps this was a subsequent annexe to the hillfort. The top of the ridge is capped by a cairn of unknown date and purpose. Turf-covered banks following the line of the ridge cover the rumps of stone walls of later date than the hillfort. Highland cattle were introduced onto the hill a few years ago with the aim of clearing the vegetation and restoring the terrain to open pasture; this has essentially been achieved.

(4) Having taken in the views to your heart's content and explored, you need to make a choice as to your route of descent. One gives you a steep descent and is largely on paths, the other is a more gentle descent but involves more road.

Dealing with the latter, gentler, descent option first, return down the hillside to the split in the bridleway mentioned in point 3. Turn right and follow this down to the road, on which you turn right. At the first junction you come to, turn left (it will carry a brown sign pointing to the church) and follow the road down to where you parked.

For the steeper descent option, return to the stile in the wall mentioned above, now on your right, go over it and follow what might be a slightly indistinct path that broadly shadows the wall on your left. This will lead you to a stile across a fence. Cross this and then turn right, picking a route through the bracken, staying fairly close to the fence on your right. Keep following the field boundary on your right down the bracken-clad hillside (there is a path immediately alongside the fence, but if you find this slippery, just walk down the field), then cross into another field, again following the field boundary on your right. This will lead you to a stile that takes you out onto a wide gravelled track. Keep ahead on this down the hillside to reach a road.

(5) Turn right on the road, and about a hundred yards past a converted barn on the roadside and two small barns set back from the road, take the signposted foot-path off to the left (by a telegraph pole). Follow this between two hedgerows down to a stile on the left which you cross to enter a field. Initially turn right and walk alongside the bank on your left, then turn left and cross the field to the right-hand of two gates on its far side. Through the gate, the path diagonally crosses the field to the far corner, where there's another gate. Go through this and follow the boundary on your left to a stile at the end of the field. Cross the stile and follow the hedge on your right to another stile, which leads out onto a road. Turn right on the road to return to where you parked.

Walk 16
Mynydd Troed & Mynydd Llangorse

6.5 miles for the full figure of eight, though you could choose to do a shorter walk by undertaking only one loop. All on paths, some of which are broad and in good condition, some of which (on the lower ground) can become muddy and hard going in winter. No stiles. There is a fairly steep ascent up Mynydd Llangorse, and an equally steep descent, with the rest of the walk undulating. Includes an enigmatic earthwork, the merest hump indicating the site of a once extant castle, and several Neolithic and Bronze Age burial sites. If the historical remains sound slight, they are, but their settings are worth the exploration!

There is space for about 4 cars at the crest of the pass between the two hills, on the minor roads that pass between Llangorse to the west and Waun Fach on the A479 to the east (grid ref: 161 283).

The walk is a figure of eight centred on where you parked, so you can choose to do the tougher loop first or last, or just choose one loop. The description starts with the easier, northern loop, the southern loop staring at point 3.

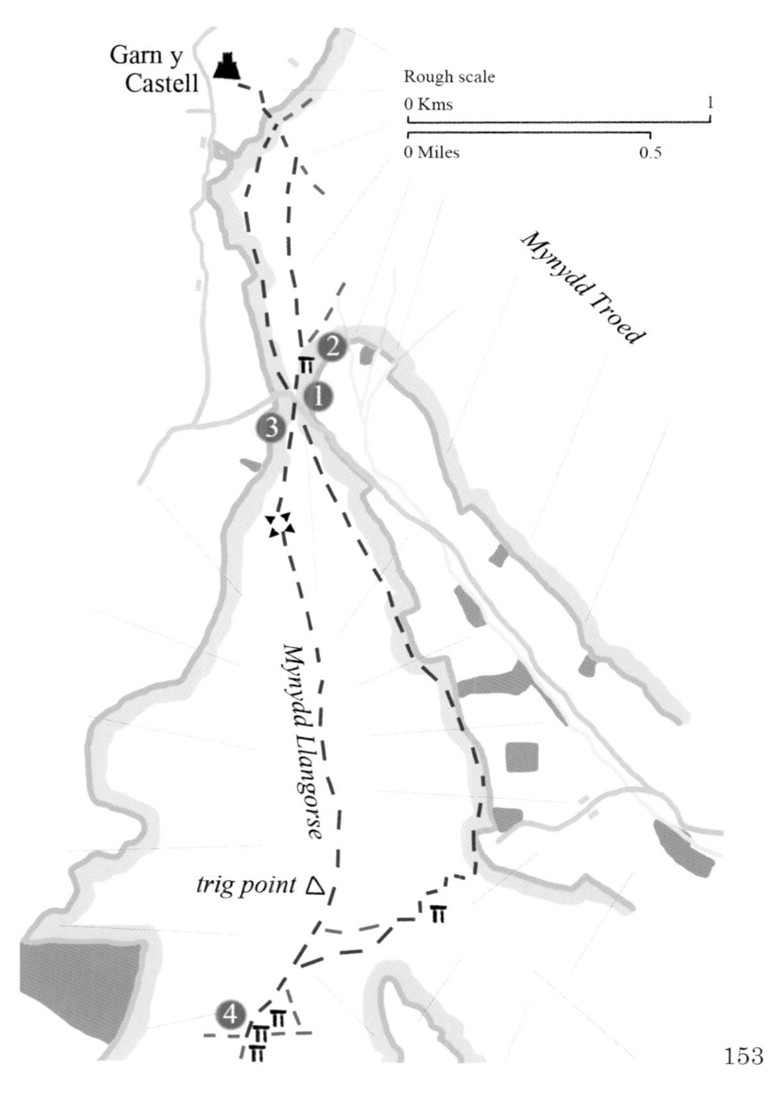

MYNYDD TROED

According to legends circulating in the 11th century, in the early 5th century the area around Talgarth and Mynydd Troed formed a small kingdom known as Garth Matrum, Matrum referring to a mountain spur supposed to be Mynydd Troed itself. Its king was Teuderic, who claimed descent from a Roman nobleman and was the grandfather of the legendary Brychan. In turn, Brychan is believed to have been the founder of the kingdom of Brycheiniog, which grew from that of Garth Matrum.

MYNYDD TROED CAIRN

This Neolithic long barrow measures about 25m by 15m and up to about 1m in height, the northern end being slightly square in shape, whilst that at the south is more rounded. First recorded in 1921, it was partially excavated in 1966 when two trenches were dug into the sides of the tomb to recover buried soils for environmental assessment. A stone revetment wall was found on both sides; that on the west had collapsed but that on the right stood 22 courses (0.43m) high. Some Neolithic pottery was found, together with flakes of stone indicating the making of stone tools. The large hollow now formed in the cairn marks the site of one burial chamber that was found, and it is thought that there were two others.

1 Go through the gate on the north side of the parking area (there is no gate or fence on the southern side!) and take the path straight ahead that aims roughly for the top of Mynydd Troed. After some 75 yards take a path off to the right. You'll soon reach a place where a lone gorse bush stands on some pitted and relatively bracken-free ground, as seen in the photo alongside. This is the remains of the Mynydd Troed cairn or burial chamber.

2 Continue along the path heading uphill from the cairn and when this meets other paths, cross the one that heads up to the summit of Mynydd Troed and continue along the one that circles round its lower slopes. After about a third of a mile this path will meet a larger path on which you turn left and follow it as it slants downhill to meet another path nearer the edge of the open access land. At this point you should see a little gate leading off the open access land that stands adjacent to a section of stone walling (as seen in the photo below). Go through this gate and follow the shady path alongside the field boundary on your right, which curves first left and then right. Just before you reach another small gate on the line of the path, the low level 'hump' in the field to your right is what is left of Garn y Castell.

GARN Y CASTELL

The two farms of Upper and Lower Trewalkin, which lie about a mile to the north of the castle site, once formed a township founded in the aftermath of the original Norman conquest of the area. The farms take their name from Walkelin Visdelon, whose father, Humphrey, accompanied Bernard de Neufmarché in his conquest of Brycheiniog and who was probably the founder of the castle. It would have had good views across the lands further into Wales. It is thought that the castle subsequently became known as Waynard's Castle, which was referred to in the early 1100s. The castle was probably a ringwork and from the rise in the ground caused by the remains of the ground where it once stood (since ploughed out) seems to have encircled the top of a mound some 40m in diameter. However, by 1144 the Visdelons appear to have forfeited the manor and castle, for it had been returned to the earls of Brecon and Hereford, who were then feudal overlords, and they in turn granted it to the Benedictine monks of Brecon priory. They sought to assart more of the ground around the township, (assarting was clearing woods to create fields), causing various disputes and leading to the small rectilinear fields seen to the north of the site today. The castle probably quickly fell into decay under its new holders.

Return back up the path to the open access land and then join the path you crossed near the foot of the slope and turn right, following it along to return to the suggested car parking area. The photograph above shows the site of Mynydd Troed cairn on the lower slopes of the far hillside, clearly visible as an island in the snow.

3 To do the southern loop, on the unfenced side of the road, take the path that heads straight up the hillside to reach the rocky outcrops that initially mark your horizon as you climb: this is the location of a possible promontory hillfort or cross-ridge dyke.

POSSIBLE PROMONTORY HILLFORT

This possible promontory hillfort, (pictured below), measures some 60m long by 30m wide at its broadest, and is marked by an indistinct ditch between banks of earth rubble that stand to c.1.2m high in places running east-west across the ridge. The track on which you reach the hillfort cuts across the eastern part of the banks. It's possible that the pair of banks and associated ditch might have been reused as a cross-ridge dyke in the 8th or 9th centuries, or even that that is all the structure ever was. Such dykes were constructed as boundary markers, sometimes delineating the limit of hunting grounds belonging to the local lord.

Carry on walking up the ridge and shortly after you reach the crest, take the right-hand fork which broadly follows the crest and in due course drops slightly downhill to reach a trig point. Keep ahead from the trig point, the path descending to meet another path on which you turn right. A couple of hundred yards along this path there is a boundary stone some 20 yards off to the right, (it can be reached down a small path), one of a number now largely buried in bracken that at one time marked the boundary between two estates. Keep on the main path and you'll soon come to a junction of paths in the saddle in the hill. Near a footpath fingerpost and a small stone cairn lie three Bronze Age burial cairns.

4 From the cairns, (seen in the photograph above), return back up the path, but after about 120 yards, take the slightly smaller path off to the right which roughly follows the contour of the hill's slope. In due course this will meet a larger path on which you turn right and almost immediately left onto another path that passes immediately alongside another burial cairn atop which sits a modern stone cairn (see photo alongside). Keep on this path, which soon descends the hill slope on a slightly zig-zag course, before turning left. Ignore the path off to the right at this point and keep ahead on the path which slants down into the valley and then follows it gently uphill back to where we suggested you park. En route the path forks a couple of times, and we suggest taking the higher left-hand path on each occasion, but all should bring you back to the start point.

Walk 17
Castell Dinas

4.75 miles. A beautiful walk on lanes and tracks and a few paths across fields. A few stiles on the last part of the walk. The walk is fairly flat to begin with, but you take an angled ascent onto the ridge above Castell Dinas and have an undulating return, some of it steepish in places. Includes the site of a Neolithic chambered tomb, and the combined site of an Iron Age hillfort and Norman castle.

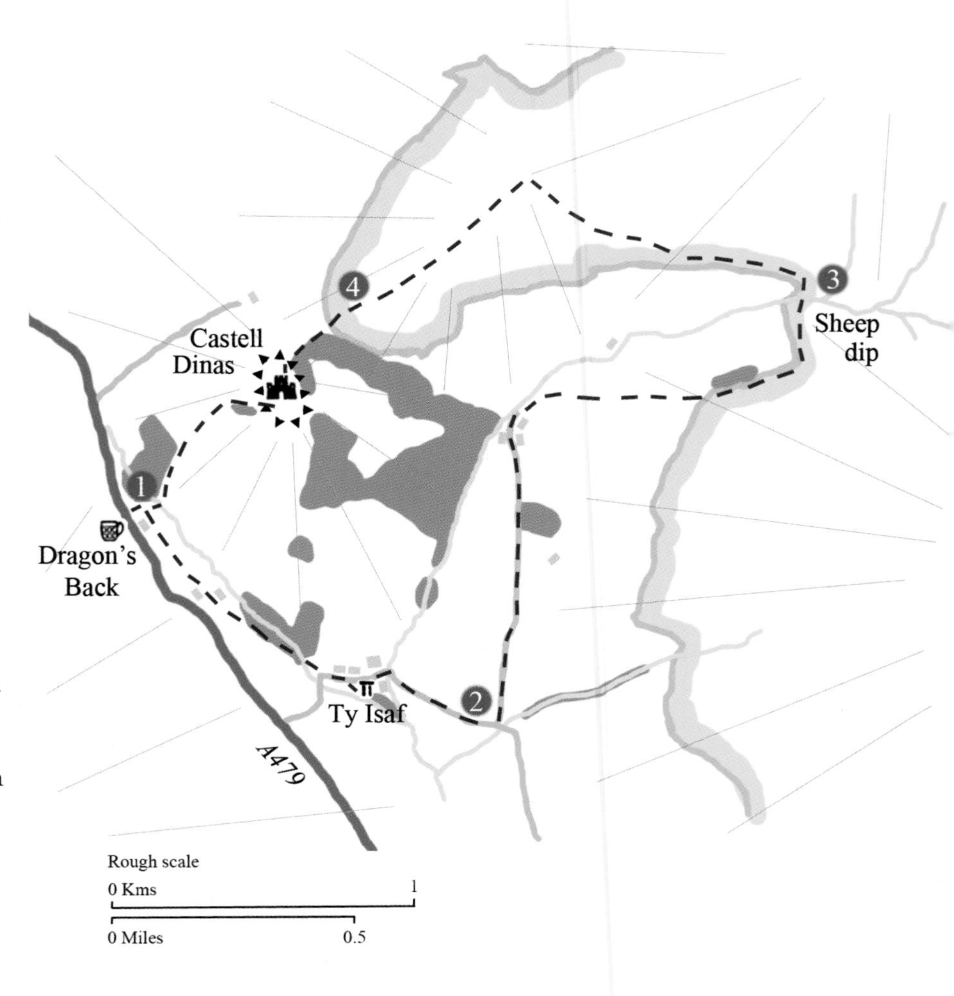

It is best to park in the Dragon's Back's car park (for a small charge) (grid ref: 173 296). If coming from Talgarth this is just over the crest of the hill on the left-hand side of the road just before you reach the Dragon's Back; if coming from Tretower, then you pass the Dragon's Back and the car park is immediately on the right.

❶ Walk up to the Talgarth end of the car park (i.e. away from the Dragon's Back), where there is a footpath sign and you can drop down some steps onto a track. Turn right on this and follow it for about two-thirds of a mile until it reaches a road (en route it does a small kink left and right where it passes Lower Panteg). Turn left on the road. After 75 yards, take the track off to the right and as you reach the point where the track is hedged on both sides, you can see the remains of Ty Isaf Neolithic burial chamber on your left. Then return to the road, turn right and follow it past Cwmfforest stables and keep going till you reach a junction with another road.

❷ Here turn left and follow the road for about two-thirds of a mile into the cluster of buildings that form Rhyd-y-car farm. Just past the farmhouse on your

TY ISAF

This Neolithic chambered tomb was excavated in 1938 and shown to have a number of chambers, passages and a false portal set between horns, creating a façade. The only remains left today are a number of orthostats (large stones erected standing upright) that formed part of the walls of the chambers and an outline of the extent of the mound. The plan shows the overall layout of the monument, the large southern chamber believed to have been the initial burial chamber, with those to the north and the false entrance added later. As a result of the excavations the bones of up to 33 individuals were recovered. The style of burial in each of the three chambers was different. That to the north-west contained crushed bones from 17 individuals along with leaf-shaped arrowheads, a polished stone axe and some undecorated pottery. The almost complete remains of just one individual were found in the north-eastern chamber, along with some pottery bowls, though two more articulated skeletons were found in the passage. In the southern 'cairn' two more articulated skeletons were found in the passage and a number of crushed bones together with undecorated pottery in the chamber. To the south of this, a small Bronze Age cremation urn was found in another chamber, along with some burnt wooden boxes that may also originally have contained some remains. Pottery was also found outside the burial mound. The different burial arrangements and the presence of a Bronze Age burial suggest that the monument was in use for the burial of the dead over a lengthy period.

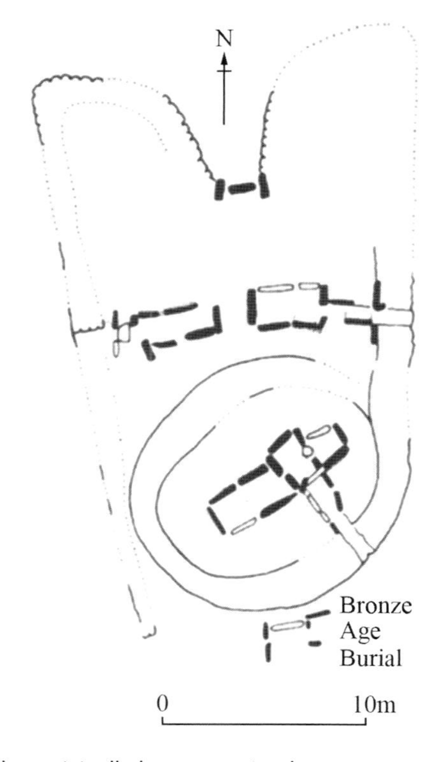

right, take the track off to the right that slants uphill between the stream and the farmhouse. Keep on this track, which runs between fields, and it will eventually lead you through a gate out onto the open hillside.

Here, turn left on the track that lies just ahead of you, and when that forks almost immediately, keep left and follow the path that stays close to a fence on your left.

Just past a small wood on your left, the path turns left and heads downhill, aiming for the stone walls that once enclosed a yard used for dipping sheep in the adjacent stream.

SHEEP DIP

These days wool is washed and cleaned once it has been shorn, using modern detergents and methods, but for centuries sheep were washed before shearing. The building of a permanent sheep dip represented a one-off input of labour which would save crucial time during the annual labour-intensive period of shearing. It was important to remove at least some of the grease from the wool, otherwise the yarn could not be readily combed and spun, reducing its value. Washing in a river or stream was preferable to using a pool, as the flow of water carried the grease and other detritus away. The stream might be dammed to create a pool in which at least a few sheep could be floated at a time, each sheep needing to be swung to and fro in the water. The labourer would then squeeze as much water out of the fleece as possible, using his forearms and drawing the fleece back along the body of the sheep in the process, before releasing the sheep onto a clean patch of ground where it could dry out. Ideally this patch of ground would be reached by a gently sloping 'beach' near the outflow from the pool to make releasing the sheep an easy process. When well organized, the average rate of washing permitted four men, with one or two boys to drive the sheep, to wash about 750 sheep a day.

③ Your route crosses the stream to the right of this pen, and then swings round behind it. Follow the field boundaries on your left and you should be able to see your route ahead: a grassy track that gradually diverges from the field boundaries and then gently, initially, climbs the hillside. Follow this track and it will swing slightly right this side of a gully in the hillside and so lead you out onto a ridge that juts out from the flanks of the Black Mountains.

Once on the ridge, turn left and follow it along towards the site of Castell Dinas, but take your time as this is the best vantage point from which to see the castle.

CASTELL DINAS

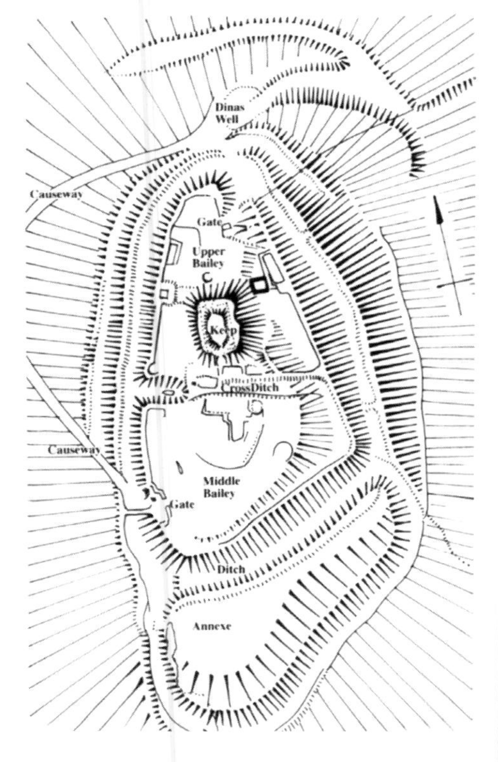

The Iron Age multivallate hillfort that crowns the hilltop was reused by the Normans as the basis for a castle that became the seat of the lordship of Dinas. The Norman castle was probably founded during the 1070s, when William fitz Osbern, earl of Hereford, was campaigning in the area. It was soon eclipsed by the more strategically sited castle at Brecon, which was begun after Bernard de Neufmarché's victory near the town in 1093. At over 450 metres above sea level, Castell Dinas is the highest castle site in mainland Britain, but overlooks the lowest pass between south and north Brecknockshire, making it a site of strategic importance. The oval-shaped hillfort encompasses some 22 acres and at some point was divided into two by the construction of an earthwork bank, the Normans selecting the northern portion as the site of their castle. This included a rectangular keep measuring some 30 x 12m which included the main communal hall of the castle, whilst a curtain wall was erected on the hillfort's ramparts with square towers at intervals along its length. A gatehouse was constructed on the northern side.

In 1125, Castell Dinas passed to William de Braose, the then earl of Hereford. When the de Braoses fell out with King John, the king passed the castle to Peter Fitz Herbert and it became, for a while, the centre of the lordship of Blaenllynfi; some rebuilding may have been done at this point. Fitz Herbert was able to retain the site even after the de Braoses' estates were restored to the family, but in 1233 it was seized by Richard Marshal, earl of Pembroke during his rebellion against Henry III. It was subsequently returned to the Fitz Herberts and underwent further rebuilding, then passing to Walerand de Teys and in 1263 being captured by Llywelyn ap Gruffydd when in alliance with Simon de Montfort. Five years later it was once more returned to the Fitz Herberts. The castle remained garrisoned until 1326, though little seems to have been spent on its repair and by 1337 its gatehouse was described as 'weak and ruinous'. What remained seems to have been destroyed in the wars between Owain Glyndwr and Henry IV, and John Leland, who visited the site *c.*1540, described it as an abandoned ruin. The remains include part of the gatehouse, of which three sides stand up to 1m high. One mound halfway along the western side and another at the northern end of the enclosure are thought to be the collapsed remains of towers along the curtain wall.

❹ If you look down into the dip between the ridge and the hill on which the castle sits you should see a stile in the fence that runs across the dip, and this is your target. Once over the stile, follow the path up into the castle.

Having explored all you want, follow the slight track through the castle site to the far side from which you approached it. At the field boundary, turn right, then bear left down the hillside, your target being a stile to the right of a small conifer wood. Once over this stile, another follows in quick succession, and then you follow the fence on your right downhill, passing over a stile into the next field and so down to a stream in the valley bottom. Cross this and a stile on the far side, then follow the field boundary on your right up to another stile. Over this you will find yourself on the track just below where you parked, so turn right on it and then left up the steps to return to your vehicle.

Walk 18
Talgarth & Penywyrlod

4.25 miles. On lanes and field paths with several stiles. The walk is set in undulating countryside. Includes a large Neolithic tomb, a religious college, a couple of castle mounds (one very difficult to see) as well as the centre of Talgarth.

It is best to park in the free car park on the edge of Talgarth, so from the roundabout on the recently built bypass turn towards the town, and then immediately left into the car park (grid ref: 153 337).

1 From the car park entrance turn left and walk into town. Cross the bridge and on the right is Talgarth Mill and on the left, the building that houses the Tourist Information Centre, which was once Talgarth's castle.

Recross the bridge and turn left up Bell Street (on the corner of which is Talgarth's museum, housed in the old post office), to then turn right up a no-through road. This

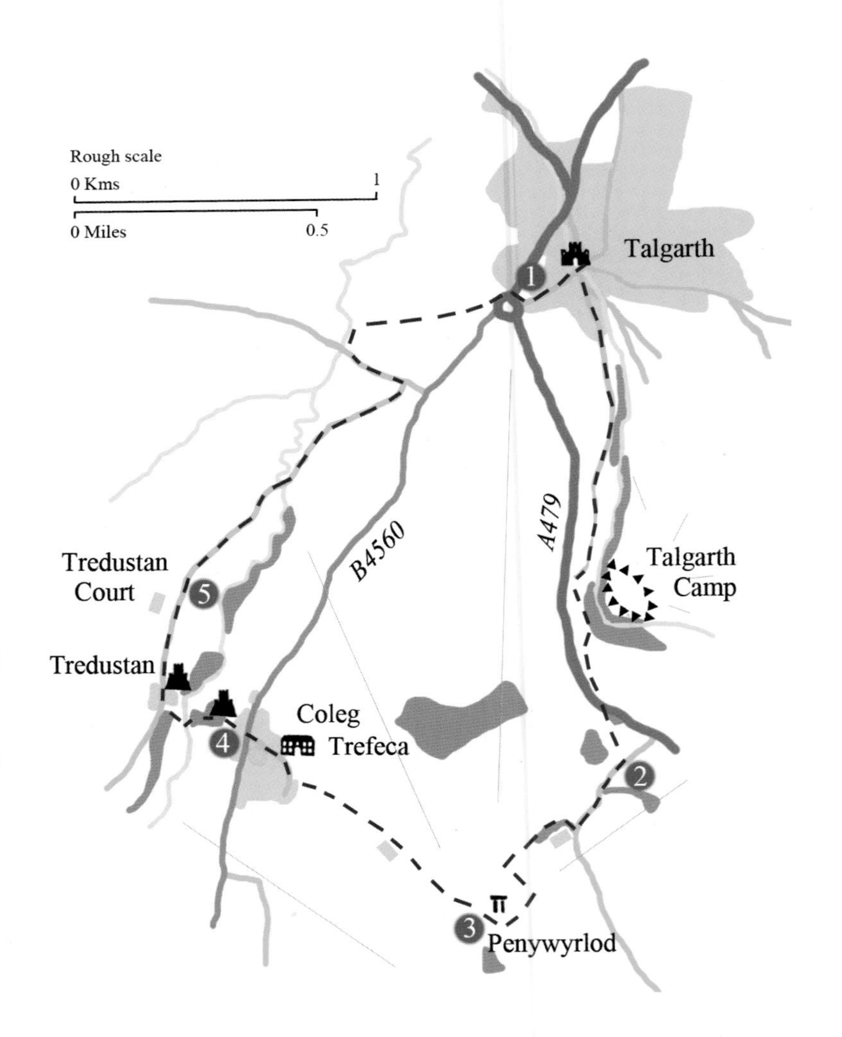

TALGARTH

Talgarth is believed to have been the site of the palace of Brychan, king of Brycheiniog in the 5th century AD, following on from the possible siting of a Roman fort in the area near the junction of two or even three possible Roman routes, if not fully constructed roads. With the coming of the Normans, the Marcher lordship of Brecknock was created and a castle was built to the south of the town at Castell Dinas (see p.164) to control the pass through the Black Mountains. When the lordship of Brecknock was split in the early 1200s, Talgarth became the main town of the small lordship of Blaenllynfi, the lordship being merged back into of Brecknock just over a century later.

In 1735 the area became important in the history of the Welsh Methodist revival after Howel Harris, a schoolmaster, went to pray in the church at Llangasty-Talyllyn (see p.145), where he had a profound religious experience. Harris became a fervent Methodist and went on to found the nearby Trefecca College (see p.172). Also converted to Methodism was William Williams Pantycelyn, who listened to Harris preaching in Talgarth churchyard and went on to become one of Wales's most prominent writers of hymns.

More recently Talgarth was home to a large mental asylum, later renamed a hospital, which opened in 1903, designed for up to 352 patients from Radnorshire and Breconshire, who were often given what would now be seen as controversial treatment. Numbers had risen to 496 patients by 1955. The hospital closed at the end of the 1990s once an improved system of care in the community had been established for people affected by mental illness. The construction of the asylum supported the development of the local railway line, which had been completed in the 1890s and was built on top of the tramway that had connected Brecon to Hay via Talgarth. Whilst stone for much of the construction of the asylum was quarried locally, many of the fixtures and fittings, together with the roof slates and many other materials, came from elsewhere in the UK, which led to the development of a large goods yard. The railway was also used to bring coal to supply the hospital's large boilers, the coal being ferried from the yard by the hospital's own steam-powered lorry.

TALGARTH MILL

This is a former corn mill with an overshot wheel and two pairs of stones. Its first definite mention is in 1309 in an inquisition following the death of Griffith de la Pole. From that date it seems to have been in fairly continuous operation, if at a low level during plague years, until it ceased operation in 1946. Following a lottery grant in 2010 which allowed for the mill's restoration, it is now run as a community enterprise, milling flour from locally grown wheat three or four days a week; it has a shop and café. Tours can be arranged (phone 01874 711352 or email admin@talgarthmill.com).

TALGARTH CASTLE

Orderic Vitalis, a Benedictine monk who chronicled English and Norman history in the late 1000s and early 1100s, says that Talgarth was once the caput of Brecknock, in other words the centre of the lordship before Brecon replaced it. Whether or not this was the case, it was certainly an early town in this part of Wales, and sat on the Roman road that ran between Abergavenny and Brecon, which may have been the cause of its foundation. Neither details of the construction nor written records give any definite clue as to when the stone tower that stands by the bridge was constructed. Architecturally it could date to any time from the late 11th century. There is a record of the existence of a castle in 1155, but not what it was like. There was once a projecting latrine which has been compared to one built in the keep at Longtown Castle in Herefordshire, which has been dated to between 1216 and 1228. In 1282 Reginald fitz Peter, then the lord of Talgarth, was holding a court in Talgarth twice a year, and it would seem likely that this would have been in the upper floor of the stone tower, giving an end date for when the tower is likely to have been built. Even so, this leaves any time between the late 1000s and early 1200s as a possible date of construction. The tower is some 10m square, with walls circa 2m thick. Clearly built to control the river crossing at this point, the tower is of three storeys with a later pyramidical roof added in place of the parapet that would once have crowned the structure. Entrance would have been from the side now occupied by Talgarth's square, machicolation remaining above the original doorway, which was later blocked. It still retains stone stairs within the thickness of the walls, and a garderobe on the first floor was later converted into a cell.

is the old course of the A479, which you will be following for a while, and it is interesting to see how quickly nature is reclaiming it following the construction of the bypass in 2007. To the left of the old road, perched above the wooded banks and impossible to see from this walk (it is not crossed by any public paths) is Talgarth Camp, a large promontory hillfort. Two banks of stone and earth form the defences across the promontory, with some evidence of scarping on the slope above the river. The fort is undated and there have been minimal archaeological investigations. In due course the road turns into a gravelled path between fences, and from that point, keep your eye open for a stile in the fence on your right.

When you reach the stile, cross it and then the new bypass and turn right on the far side to walk behind the low crash barrier. After about 15 yards, the path turns left into the small coppice and leads alongside a hedge on your right to a stile. Cross this and walk up the field boundary that runs uphill to a gate at the top. Go through this and turn right on the road.

2 Follow the road up to Penywyrlod farm. Here the road bends left, but you turn right just in front of the farm onto a wide patch of grassy ground and walk down to a gate into a field. Through the gate, follow the field boundary on your left to the next corner of the field where some steps and boarded walkway will lead you up to a stile. Cross this and follow the field boundary on your left alongside

a wood to reach another stile at its end. Cross this and follow the field boundary over to your right uphill. In the top corner of this field you'll come to another stile which you cross to follow the hedge on your right. You will then cross an open 'gateway', just beyond which is a

PENYWYRLOD LONG BARROW

The mound was long obscured by trees and was only recognised as a long barrow in 1972, when part of the eastern corner was quarried for stone to be used as hardcore. The quarrying destroyed one chamber and partially destroyed another, but also revealed a false portal (a dummy entrance), a central chamber and substantial revetment walling (that is, walling behind which soil was packed) on the north-eastern side of the mound and in part of the forecourt area. An archaeological excavation was then undertaken, and this suggested that the original mound measured 52m long by 22.5m wide, the excavation revealing the central chamber, three side chambers and a north-eastern horn round a forecourt area. The central chamber was possibly entered from the north-eastern side and included two orthostats which might have provided some of the support for either a large capstone or a number of smaller stones. The north-eastern side chamber was almost completely destroyed by quarrying, a single orthostat remaining which might have defined two separate chambers to either side, one measuring 2m x 1.2m and the other 1.6m x 1m. This latter was entered by a passage bordered by two revetment walls. One of the other side chambers was thoroughly investigated and measured 2.85m by 1m x 1.3m high, its walls formed of large stone orthostats dug into the ground, and was sealed off by a large slab. The third side chamber was only partially investigated but was found to include an entrance reached between revetment walls.

It was discovered that the horns of the forecourt curved in to a depth of about 6m, ending at the remains of a false portal probably formed by two parallel stone slabs 1.5m apart, between which a low threshold would have supported a dry-stone wall blocking the 'entrance' which would have been capped by another large stone. As for the cairn covering the chambers, this was shown to have two lines of revetment wall built towards its outer edge to ensure stability, these acting to prevent the soil and stones that formed the cairn from slipping sideways and 'spreading' the cairn. One wall was solidly built and stood about 1.4m high, at least near the forecourt, while a slighter wall built some 1.5m further out from the centre of the cairn stood just some 0.3-0.5m high.

A substantial amount of disarticulated human bone was recovered from the central chamber and the one investigated side chamber, piled in such a way that the chambers resembled ossuaries rather than places of rest for specific individuals. Also found was a flint knife, a possible bone flute, a large range of animal bone, and several fragments of pottery which had a thick rolled rim and was decorated with oblique incisions, twisted cord impressions and multiple rows of circular stabs. This was identified as Abingdon ware, dated to between 3000 and 2500BC.

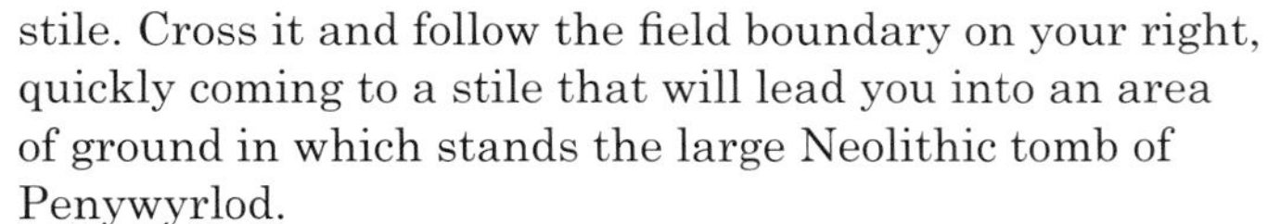

stile. Cross it and follow the field boundary on your right, quickly coming to a stile that will lead you into an area of ground in which stands the large Neolithic tomb of Penywyrlod.

3 Having seen what you want, recross the stile and turn right to continue following the fence on your right downhill. When you reach the corner of the field, turn left and within some tens of yards you'll come to a stile on your right which you cross. Follow the field boundary down on your right and through a gate into the next field. At the bottom of this, cross over a stile and soon you'll enter the grassy farmyard of Cefn-Mawr Farm.

Keep following the hedge on your right and at the far end of this patch of ground you will come to a stile. Cross this and follow the path through the scrub woodland for a short way to reach another stile which you cross to enter

TREFECCA COLLEGE

The house that forms the original base of Trefecca College, which was built around 1700, was the home of Howell Harris (1714-73), the founder of the Methodist movement in Wales. In 1752 Harris established Teulu Trefeca ('the Trefeca Family'), a Christian community, in his house, then called Trevecka Fach. In 1768, Selina, countess of Huntingdon, a friend of Harris, wished to establish a theological seminary, and chose Harris's home as its base so that Harris could keep a watchful eye on it. (Selina was an ardent Methodist who also financed what became known as Countess of Huntingdon Chapels, which were established across the country.) Thus was born Trefecca College, some of its first intake comprising six students expelled from St Edmund Hall in Oxford due to their Methodist inclinations. In 1772 Harris's home was extended to provide extra capacity, perhaps with Harris acting as his own architect, to create what William Williams Pantycelyn called 'a castellated monastery' built in the Strawberry Hill Gothic style. Apart from their religious training, members of the college worked at over 60 trades, the most important being agriculture and weaving, the college renting a neighbouring farm. There was also a printing press that was used to publish over 100 religious books. Many of the students were despatched on long preaching assignments around Britain as part of their studies.

Harris died in 1773, and not many years later the college began to falter. In 1792 it moved to Cheshunt in Hertfordshire, and after a gap of a number of years, in 1842 Trefecca became home to a Calvinistic Methodist college, supported by the Welsh Calvinistic Methodist Connexion. In 1872, a Harris Memorial Chapel was added. The building is now Coleg Trefeca, a lay training centre for the Presbyterian Church of Wales. Some of the rooms retain their plaster ceilings from the time the building was lived in by Howell Harris, together with associated wooden panelling and fireplaces. There is a small museum, open by appointment, that focuses on the life of Harris and of Teulu Trefeca.

a field. Again follow the hedge on your right, passing through a gateway between fields and then two gates that form a little yard to the right of a barn. Once through these, cross the stile on your right and turn left on the track. Follow this, it gaining a tarmacked surface and passing the cream-painted Trefecca College on your right.

4 At the road junction beyond the college turn right and immediately left down a track. Follow this past a shrouded castle motte on your right to the Afon Llynfi. About 20 yards before the river, the path turns left and wiggles through a bramble patch to reach a footbridge across the river. Once over the bridge, keep ahead up the bank on the far side of the 'field' and so to a gate out onto a road. Turn right on this, and after you pass the barn on your right keep an eye out for the prominent castle mound of Tredustan Castle. Tredustan Court, a large 17th-century stone-built house will be seen on your left about 150 yards beyond Tredustan Castle.

TREDUSTAN CASTLE

The name, which derives from the village or settlement of Durstan, who was presumably the builder of the castle, may refer to a Turstan Bret who is recorded as being in Brycheiniog in the late 12th century. The motte, measuring some 14m across and 5m high, has been cut into by farm buildings. The bailey may have lain to the east.

5 Keep on the road and in due course it will cross the Afon Llynfi and then come to a T-junction with another road. Turn left here and after a few hundred yards you will see a stone bridge ahead of you, but you want to turn off the road before you reach it. About 150 yards before the bridge there's a metal field gate and a wooden stile on the right. Cross the stile and take the signposted footpath up a grassy track which follows a stream on its left. This track will soon cross the stream and then it turns right. Continue following it to reach a stile and a stone bridge which you cross to enter a field. Follow the field boundary on your right to a stile and gate into the next field. Cross this field on the diagonal to a small gate to the right of a small barn. Go through the gate out onto a lane, which you follow down to Talgarth's bypass. Turn left and then cross the road, and so return to the car park where you parked.

Walk 19
Llanfilo

3.25 miles for the circuit, a little more if you wish to explore the village. Largely on minor roads with some track and field paths. No stiles, but two field gates can be awkward, in one case due to a combination lock put in place to try to deter rustlers. Set in undulating countryside. Includes Llanfilo church and village, the settlement of Tredomen and passes the sites of two hillforts.

Park near the church, which is well worth a visit either before or after your walk (grid ref: 119 333).

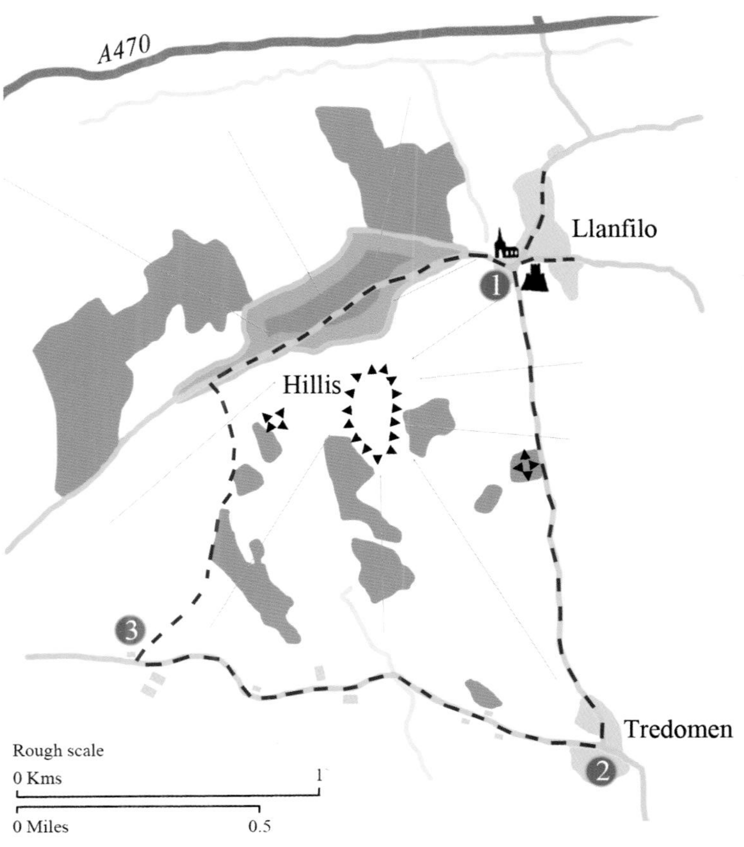

LLANFILO CHURCH

The sub-circular churchyard and dedication to St Beilo, the daughter of Brychan, indicate that there was once a Celtic church here. The settlement itself is not mentioned in any documents till the late 1300s, though its citizens appear as witnesses in charters before this date, including Robert de Llanfilo, who was constable of Brecon during the 1100s. Mentions in documents in the late 1300s and throughout the 1400s suggest that it was by then a fairly populous settlement, and subsequent archaeological work confirms that Llanfilo was larger then than it is now.

The nave and chancel are unusual in that they are of roughly similar length, and much of their medieval core was probably retained when the church was extensively restored in 1913. The tower was completely rebuilt in 1881, though it is believed to be a copy of its predecessor. Two large carved stones, probably dating to the Norman period, were reused in the work of 1913, one above a now blocked priest's door on the north side of the church and the other as a wall-plate in the porch to support the roof timbers.

The church contains two rare stone altar slabs, a probable pre-Norman 'boulder' font with two bevels cut around the outside at the top as decoration, a carved rood screen and loft dating from c.1500, an earlier vaulted roof, Breconshire's oldest surviving bell, now resting in the chancel and believed to have been cast in Worcester between 1380 and 1400, and Jacobean altar rails and box pews dating to 1684.

The rood loft rather dominates the screen, because it has been considerably altered in relatively recent years. Originally divided into 15 panels, each of which held a carved figure, by the early 1900s the figures had been removed and the central part fitted with two large triangular pilasters aligning with the frame of the doorway below, with a plain space between them. Following W.D. Caröe's restoration of the church in the early 1900s, four additional triangular pilasters were added to divide the front of the loft into the five present bays. Each of these now holds a figure under a carved hood, these being (from left to right) St Peter, St James the Great, the Virgin and Child, St Luke and St Paul. The figures were carved by Nathaniel Hitch between 1926 and 1930. The trails on the beams above and below the loft front are original, featuring above a trail of pomegranates and a series of circles encircling trefoils and below a vine trail and a pomegranate trail. The depiction of the pomegranate indicates a post 1501 date for the original work, the fruit being a symbol of Aragon, and so of Katherine of Aragon, who arrived in England in that year to marry Prince Arthur, the elder brother of the future Henry VIII.

Outside the churchyard lies St Filo's Well, a reputed holy well that was the village water supply but is now unloved as a concrete and brick cistern.

❶ With your back to the lychgate at the entrance to the churchyard, turn right and walk uphill, immediately passing a small moated site on the left-hand side of the road, rather hidden behind vegetation. Its location close to the church suggests it might have been the site of an ecclesiastical building or of an early manor house. Continue uphill along the road, ignoring the turning to the right, and keep following the road uphill and then downhill, past another moated site which is obscured by trees (the first stand of trees you come to on your right, just after which is the entrance track for Lower Hillis Farm) and then past an old school house on your left and into Tredomen.

TREDOMEN
The 'Tre' part of the name indicates a farm, hamlet or estate, and 'domen' normally infers the presence of a mound, often a castle motte. No such mound is extant today, though it is possible that one was obliterated by the later buildings. However, the name Tredomen only appeared in that form from 1595, so it could be a misconstruing of an earlier name. It was at this time that Tredomen was the home of Sir Edward Awbrey, high sheriff of Brecknockshire in 1583, 1589 and 1599.

Middle House (the second house reached on the left as you enter the village) is probably the oldest building in the settlement, the house dating from the early 1600s, though some of the farm buildings may have an earlier core. What was Upper House (the first house on the left as you enter the village), which is now used as a barn, has elements of 17th- and 18th-century date, whilst Tredomen Court is a mixture of 16th- and 17th-century work. (To see Tredomen Court you'll need to turn left in the village and walk along past the large stone barn till you reach its driveway.) The tithe survey of the mid 1800s shows Tredomen Court as the focal point of the settlement, suggesting that this was the centre of the local manorial estate. Various building platforms in neighbouring fields and thin strips suggesting tenement plots, coupled with information gleaned from old maps, suggests that the manor was once the core of a modest thriving settlement which has since shrunk to its current size.

2 Turn right on the road signposted Brecon, just before Tredomen Court. You will be keeping on this road for a little over a mile. Walk through Trefeithan, then cross a stream, and shortly thereafter, beyond a pond, you will come to a set of barns on your left (named The Buildings, Trefeithan Court). Opposite the entrance to these, and just before a house on your right (called Pen Pentre), go through the field gate on your right.

3 Follow a track across this field to a gate on its far side and then continue to follow the track across the next field to a stream on its far side marked by a line of trees. Cross the stream and follow the track round to the left. Go through one gate and then another, keeping on the track as it wends its way along the foot of an oak-clad slope to its right. At the end of this wood, you leave the track, the path climbing across the hillside to aim for the left-hand corner of another wood further up the slope. At this corner the path turns slightly left to head for a gateway in the field boundary opposite at a junction of hedges.
Go through (or climb over) this gate. The path then

HILLIS HILLFORT

With the ramparts largely wooded, it is difficult to discern this hillfort. Oval in shape, it measures some 330m north to south and 130m east to west, the ramparts, made of stone rubble, following the contours of the hill. There are two entrances, one in the north-east and one in the south, the former being the more complex, and both having inturned ramparts. The centre of the hillfort is crossed by a bank, which may or may not be an original feature. If it is original, it may be that the northern part of the enclosure, the one with the more complex entrance, which appears to have been approached by a causeway, was home to people, whilst the southern section served by the simpler entrance may have been used for corralling stock.

Some 200m to the west lies a smaller hillfort (named as a 'settlement' on the OS map) of similar proportionate shape and also divided by a bank running east/west, though with less well defined embankments. Whether the two sites were occupied in tandem is unknown.

follows the hedgerow on your left up to a gate which leads out onto a piece of common. (The gate may be closed with a combination lock to protect against rustling.) Turn right on the road that crosses the common, and follow it back into Llanfilo. You may want to walk to the right-hand side of the common, near its crest, to get the best view of Hillis hillfort.

You may wish to explore Llanfilo by heading up the lane opposite the church's lychgate and then returning and strolling down the road from the church.

LLANFILO

One of the earliest buildings that still stands is Penmaes Farm, reached along the lane roughly opposite the church's lych gate. Just before you reach Penmaes, a stone gateway leads into a field on the right beyond which may have stood an early manor house, perhaps the forerunner of Penmaes farm, or ecclesiastical building. The medieval village street stretched downhill from the church at least to and probably beyond Penishapentre Farm. On the west side of the street there are many vacant plots which probably once sustained houses and either side of Penishapentre are the remains of building platforms and trackways. To the north of St Antony's on the east side of the street an earthwork platform probably marks the site of another house.

Walk 20
Llanelieu

7.25 miles on lanes, tracks, grassy paths on open access land and paths through fields and woods, some of which can be wet and boggy (even in dry weather in patches), so wear appropriate footwear. Set in undulating country and with the occasional short steepish section. Has great views throughout much of the walk and takes in the atmospheric church of Llanelieu, and slightly distant views of Neolithic tombs. There is the Three Horseshoes pub in Felindre, which you may wish to visit at the end of the walk. (Please note that at the time of writing the pub is open in the evening between Wednesday and Sunday and at lunchtime at the weekends; check for latest details on 01497 847304.)

Park near the village hall in Felindre or in its car park (grid ref: 187 368).

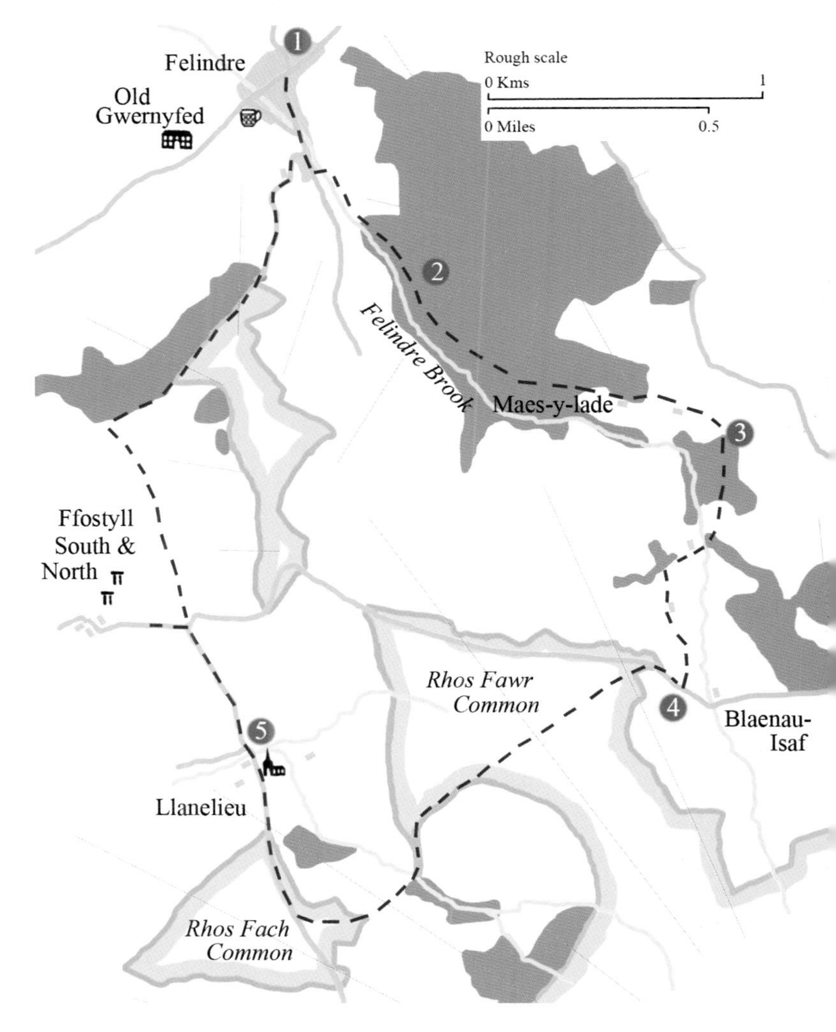

1 With your back to the entrance to the village hall's car park turn right on the road and then immediately left. When you reach the T-junction ahead, turn left and walk up to the end of the group of houses soon reached on the left. Here a sign on the right-hand side of the road points to a bridleway on the left-hand side, and this you take, following a wide track.

❷ After several hundred yards, where the track you're on levels off, a dirt track branches off to the left and heads more steeply uphill, and this you take. After a while, follow this across the track (which has doubled back on itself up the hillside) and then take the right-hand fork where it splits a little further on. This will lead you to a gate onto a track above a small field.

Follow the path to another gateway into a small field. Initially keep following the field boundary on your right, but where a path heads away from the boundary and slants uphill across a corner of the field, follow that and it will lead onto a track that circles above the buildings of Maes-y-lade. The path leads into another small field which you cross to go through a field gate into the next field, then keeping ahead to aim for a barn further along

the hillside. Cross a lane and then take the track to the left of the barn, passing over the stile at its end to enter a field. Walk along the field boundary on your left, passing two stiles to reach the far side, where you cross a stile into some woodland.

3 Across the stile the path turns left to cross a marshy 'ford' then heads downhill through the fairly open woodland: the route is well waymarked by posts, some of them bearing a yellow cap, and crosses several small streams. In due course you cross the slightly wider Felindre Brook. Keep on ahead and on the far side of this patch of ground cross a stile to the left of a field gate, then cross the brook again, just below a house. The path then heads uphill, initially following the boundary of the house's garden, through a field. At the top far right-hand corner of the field go through the field gate on your right, then cross the stile on your immediate left. Then follow the line of the old track through fields and the remnants of old hedgerows to pass above a stone barn (see photo on opposite page). Keep following the lines of old field boundaries on your left and downhill, to leave the fields near Blaenau-Isaf by a gate onto a road.

4 Turn right on the road and follow it onto Rhos Fawr Common. Here turn half left away from the road and walk up onto the crest of the common where you should find a grassy track that heads roughly towards Pen-y-fan, the highest point on the horizon ahead of you, with that of the nearer Mynydd Troed slightly to the left. If these are shrouded in cloud, your line should roughly parallel the face of the Black Mountains on your left. After about a third of a mile you reach an internal corner of the common. Here, keep ahead, shadowing the boundary with a field on your left. This will lead to a tongue of the common. Follow this, and drop down to cross a stream, then walk up the track on the far side. At the top of the rise, turn right on the gravel track and follow it to a road.

Turn right on the road and this will lead through Rhos Fach Common and then downhill to Llanelieu, where you bear right to visit the church.

LLANELIEU CHURCH

Built in the 13th century and restored in the early 20th, the church is now in the care of the Friends of Friendless Churches. The round churchyard suggests that the religious site has Celtic origins, and two pillar stones carved with Celtic-style crosses that now stand against the west wall of the porch add credence to this idea. The lichen on these now largely hides, on one, an incised ring-cross with four small rings in the angles and, on the other, a cross ringed with three circles. They have been dated to between the 7th and 9th centuries.

The church's gem is its double screen. This stands as matching triple arcades, 6 feet apart. Timbers connecting the screens would have supported a floor for a rood loft, whilst the eastern arcade still supports a tympanum composed of boards some half an inch thick. This still bears its red background colour on which are stencilled white roses, the westernmost screen having red flowers painted onto a lighter background. The position of the rood (usually a cross and a depiction of the Crucifixion) can still be seen in the shape of a cross near the top. Cut into the tympanum are seven assorted 'squints' which would have allowed those in the loft to see the priest officiating in the chancel. The western triple arcade would have supported a parapet forming part of the screen facing the congregation. The rood loft would have been reached by a wooden staircase at its northern end, and there may have been a second staircase at the southern end, but any evidence for this has been obscured by the addition of the pulpit. Originally there would have been altars placed under the screen on either side of the nave passage, wainscotting helping to enclose the spaces, whilst, in 1869, it was recorded that the loft was topped by a 'coved and boarded' roof or ceilure.

On the walls are some wall paintings which were covered in limewash for a time, but are now exposed to view again. They include, on the west wall, a much damaged depiction in black of Adam and Eve and the Tree of Life, with a serpent's head, and stencilled flower patterns. The royal coat of arms and panels of text were later additions, painted in the late 1600s.

5 On leaving the church, turn right and walk down through the churchyard to a gate that leads to some steps back out onto the road near Llanelieu Court.

LLANELIEU COURT

This lies at the T-junction near where you leave the churchyard. It is thought to date to the 15th century with later additions, and includes two late medieval gothic arches that have been claimed to have been part of a monastic cell belonging to Llanthony Priory. There is little evidence that there were other buildings in the vicinity, except for one cottage that lay close to the churchyard, yet there was a pound for holding stray stock between the church and the court that was demolished at the beginning of the 20th century. Stocks to the immediate south of the churchyard, which were marked on early editions of the Ordnance Survey map, have also gone, whilst records indicate that a yew near the churchyard was used as a whipping post, the felon's hands inserted into holes bored in the wood and held in place by a bar.

Turn right on the road and follow it till you reach a T-junction. (To get the best view of the burial chambers of Ffostyll North and South, you may wish to turn left on the road and walk along for some 75 yards, looking half-right across the field to your right into the field beyond its hedgerow; you may be able to spot the two 'barrows', one with a small tree on its top. Then return to the junction and turn left.) The circular walk crosses this junction to

FFOSTYLL NORTH AND SOUTH

These are a pair of Neolithic long barrows that lie some 70m apart from each other, the one to the north orientated east/west, while that to the south runs north/south. The arrows in the photo show the locations of the two barrows. These barrows are amongst the largest and most prominent of those clustered around the northern end of the Black Mountains (though difficult to see from local roads and paths!), and this might suggest that they were the final resting place of individuals of importance to the local inhabitants. Excavations carried out in the early 1920s by C.E. Vulliamy, each only lasting a few days, did not necessarily support this view. Though both barrows had been damaged as a result of 'mining' for stone, in the southern barrow an entire cist burial with its roof slab was unearthed. At the bottom of this cist was found a layer of burnt bones, ascertained to be those of goats, oxen and pigs. Above this layer was a considerable amount of human bone 'in the utmost confusion; only in a few instances were they in anatomical relation to each other, and by far the greatest number were split and broken', according to the excavation report. Analysis of the bones concluded that they were those of at least nine individuals of a variety of ages, including a male aged about 40, an old woman, a young child aged about 6 and a 7-month-old foetus. It was estimated from the assemblage that the average stature of an adult would have then been 5ft 4ins (1.62m), but in the absence of carbon dating in the early 1920s, no suggested date was given for when these individuals would have lived. In 1922 Vulliamy excavated the chamber at the northern end of the cairn and discovered more cremated remains, including those of an adult and a young child, together with fragments of crude black pottery. The absence of pieces of bone that would have made an entire human being made him wonder if the barrows were where the bones of those who had died were finally interred, perhaps having spent some years buried in other locations.

The northern barrow was found to comprise three chambers, though with no evidence for passages leading to any of them. The chambers again included the remains of humans as well as those of horses, dogs, oxen and pigs, and this time some of the human remains did preserve their anatomical relationship with each other. The individuals were thought to include a female with rheumatoid arthritis, a large male and two children aged 11 and 6.

pick up the track on the far side and follow this along (if you didn't venture a short way down the road, you may be able to spot the two 'barrows' of Ffostyll North and South in the field beyond the hedgerow on the far side of the field on your left). Having passed some field gateways, the track will gain a rougher surface and drop downhill, to then turn right and head along the hillside. After a while you will pass through a gate onto another common. Keep to the left-hand track here and follow it along the foot of the common, and in due course it will gain a tarmacked surface and lead you back down to Felindre. Immediately after the lane leaves the common through another gate, look over the gate to your left to see the house called Old Gwernyfed (see p.220). (The photograph shows this view.) When you reach a T-junction in Felindre, turn left and then take the first right to return to the road junction near the village hall.

Walk 21
Capel-y-ffin

9.75 miles, but can be split into a short valley walk or a long upland walk. It includes the various Christian sites in the valley, together with The Vision, a farm that was part of the inspiration for Bruce Chatwin's novel On the Black Hill, *plus a long upland walk above the Grwyne Fawr Reservoir. There is a lovely valley walk back to Capel-y-ffin, passing waterfalls. There are plenty of streams and a few stiles to cross in the valley part of the walk, and reaching the plateau top above Capel-y-ffin involves a steep climb.*

There are spaces for some 10 cars to park off the road in the vicinity of the church at Capel-y-ffin and the road junction just to the south of the church (grid ref: 255 314).

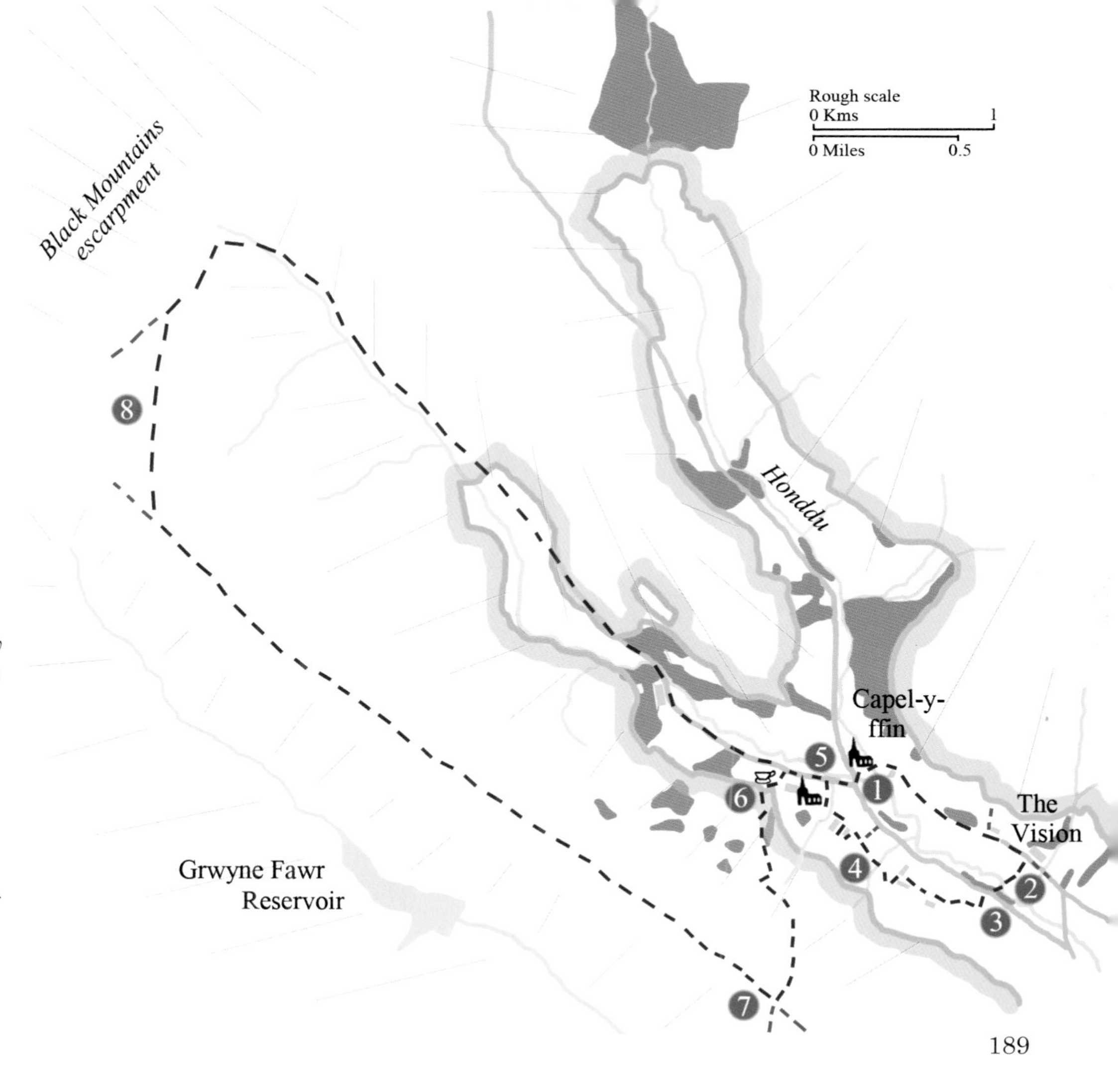

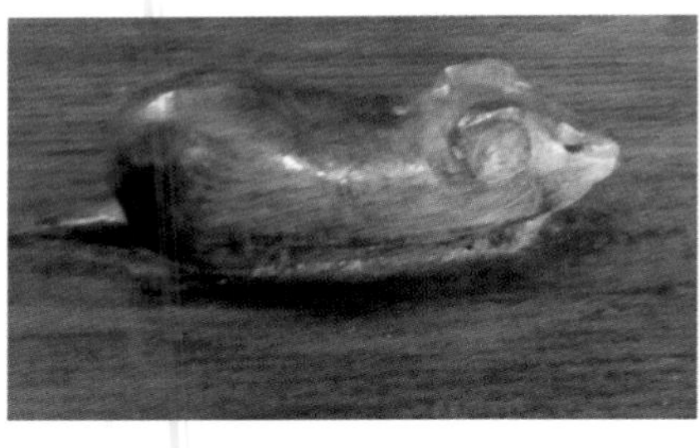

CAPEL-Y-FFIN CHURCH

The dedication is to St Mary the Virgin, which relates to a tale of how, sometime in the 1100s, a woman saw a vision of the Virgin Mary in the field where a church was then built. The ancient yews around the churchyard suggest that the site has a much older religious history, however – in his diary Francis Kilvert, Victorian curate of Clyro, describes the church as 'squatting like a stout grey owl among its seven black yews'. One of these to the south-west has an estimated age of 1,500 years, and the grove could have sheltered the site of a Celtic saint's cell.

The current building is not medieval but dates to a reconstruction in 1762 and is one of the smallest churches in Wales, measuring just 26 x 13 feet internally. It originally served as a chapel of ease within the parish of Llanigon to the north, but is now the centre of its own parish. There is a wooden gallery, an ancient font, and wooden font cover with the carving of a mouse. The porch was added in 1817. Outside are gravestones carved by Eric Gill (see also p.196) and his pupil, Laurie Cribb. The name Capel-y-ffin means 'chapel of the boundary' since the settlement lies close to the boundary between the old dioceses of St David's and Llandaff.

To do just the short valley walk simply follow points 1 to 4, turning right when you reach the road at the end of point 4). If you wish to concentrate on the hills and prune off some of the historical part in the valley, walk up the no through road at the junction near where you parked and follow the walk from point 5.

You can choose to visit the church before or after your walk, but before could be best as your boots might be clean then (or you could take them off and leave them in the porch to be on the safe side).

❶ Take the signed footpath through a field gate onto the track just to the right of the church as you approach it and on the same side of the road. This will soon lead you across a stream and to a chapel and thence into what was once a farmyard. The path crosses this, heading to the left of the house and then continues along the hillside. The path is well waymarked (and initially signed as leading to join the Offa's Dyke path on the ridge above you). The path will soon kink left and then right to follow a short length of field boundary on your right and then enter a larger field. Continue along the hillside across the field, rising slightly uphill (there's likely to be a

BAPTIST CHAPEL
A stone tablet on the outside wall of the chapel states: 'Messrs William and David Prosser brought the Ministry of the Gospel to their house in the Year 1737. And secured this place for that sacred use for the time being. Both died near the end of the year 1780.' It would seem that the Prosser brothers initially let their house be used for Baptist services before they had it rebuilt as a proper chapel in the 1760s. The chapel was run in conjunction with one in the Olchon valley on the other side of the Black Mountains ridge to the east, and by the 1790s the congregation amounted to some 40 souls. The first ministers were all long-serving: Joshua Andrews between the years 1745 and sometime in the 1780s, followed by George Watkins inthe early 1830s and then Morgan Lewis, who only ever ministered here, though he served as a preacher in an area that extended from Machynlleth to Hereford, being known as one who spoke 'in a lively and passionate way'. Just two services a year have been held in more recent times.

rough outline of the path in the grass) to reach a stone stile on the far side of the field. Cross this (and the rails on its other side) and then shadow the field boundary on your left across the next field to another stone stile in the far left-hand corner. Cross this and again follow the field boundary on your left, which will lead you to another stone stile which you cross. Then head down the bank on the far side by some stone steps.

Cross the stream and keep following the track ahead. When it reaches an old barn on your left the path joins the tarmac lane ahead that slants slightly downhill. This will soon lead you to a collection of footpath signposts near a second gate across the lane pointing in three directions: one in the direction you've come from, one pointing up some steps to the path that joins the Offa's Dyke path, and one pointing ahead to Llanthony, which is the one you take (so staying on the tarmac). Within a few yards you'll come to a field gate across a stone track on your left, the private entrance to The Vision farm. You will get better views of the farm looking back to it from a bit later in the walk (and also in winter rather than in summer).

❷ Carry on along the tarmac, but in a few yards take the footpath off to the right over a stile, signposted for the valley road. Cross the stile and head down the field to another stile. Cross this, and then cross the corner of the next field to a stone stile in the fence on the far side. Over this, cross the footbridge, then walk for some 80 yards

THE VISION

The farm became famous through Bruce Chatwin's novel *On the Black Hill*, which tells the story of twin brothers Lewis and Benjamin Jones, who together farmed 'The Vision', the name apparently taken from the farm at Capel-y-ffin. The Black Hill of the novel's title is the name of the highest point on the ridge of the Black Mountains above the farm. The conjunction of names could be a happy accident, for Chatwin was to explain that the Black Hill was also the name of a hill near Clun in Shropshire near which he was staying when he wrote what became the opening chapters of the book. The twins in the novel were actually based on brothers who lived at Newhouse Farm, just to the east of Hay Bluff on the English side of the border, whom Chatwin had met when he was staying with Penelope Betjeman, wife of John Betjeman, who lived near them. In the book, the Black Mountains exert a somewhat heavy and brooding presence, and 'The Vision' farm is in a different location to that here.

along the bottom of the bank on the left to then turn left when you reach a gap in the trees, where you walk up to a field gate and stile that leads out onto a road.

3 Cross the road and go through the field gate almost opposite, then follow the field boundary on your right uphill. You can get a better view of The Vision if you look back across the valley from this field. Near the far right-hand corner of the field, cross the stile on your right and then follow the field boundary on your left. This will lead to a small footpath gate out onto tracks near some dilapidated barns. Your route passes these barns to their right, then joins a wide track on which you turn left to follow it towards the house and recently converted barn further along the hillside. At the end of the converted barn on your left, walk up the bank to a footpath gate.

Through the gate, walk along the track as far as you need to be able to climb the bank on your right, for the footpath you want continues to roughly follow the contour of the hillside. Once in the field above the bank, cross it, following the field boundary on your right. This will lead to a field gate into the next field, where you again keep to the field boundary on your right. At the far end of the field, you drop down to a stream which you cross, and then cross a stile. Follow the path into the next field and once in it, turn left to walk up the edge of the field to a stile in the top fence. Cross this, and then follow the field boundary on your right.

4 Towards the end of this field you have a choice. The route ahead has a potentially difficult stile in the middle of a stream (at least after rain!), unless it's been replaced, but it does take you close to the ruins of the monastery and then to a pleasant path downhill by the stream. If this sounds daunting you can take the signed footpath through a gate in the fence on your right reached about 100 yards short of a ruined stone barn. Follow the track down to the road on which you turn left, and left again at the junction near where you parked, to rejoin the route at the point where a footpath leads off through an arched gateway on your left, reached after a few hundred yards (and then go to point 5 to continue the circular walk).

If you are happy to tackle the possibly daunting stile, carry on ahead to the ruined barn at the far end of the field. There is a stile in the corner of the field, but it is obscured by vegetation and fencing and carries (or should carry) a warning about the dangerous wall of the barn above the stile. Therefore, turn left at this point and walk alongside the barn to use the field gate at its far end to leave the field. Through the gate, turn right and follow the track into a field on the far side of a new barn (don't go through the next gate across the line of the track). You now want to continue roughly following the contour of the hillside across this field. After a few yards you should find yourself once more following a field boundary on your right. At the far end of this field the path will drop down to a stream with a stile in the middle of it (unless it has been repaired recently). Cross both stream and stile and walk up the path on the far side. You can take a few steps further up the bank to come close to the walls of the monastery, but the path follows the stream downhill, crossing it at one point by an old stone bridge and then passing out through a stone arch onto a road.

5 This is where the routes reunite, so you either turn left on the road or continue walking along it, depending upon which route you took. Keep an eye out for the remains of the monastery on your left, followed by a white-painted building.

MONASTERY AND WOODEN CALVARY

As a young man, Joseph Leicester Lyne was drawn to the Church of England, but having become a curate, he soon fell out with the church's hierarchy. In 1862 he expressed the following view: 'Souls are perishing by thousands close to our doors. The Church of England, as she is at present, is wholly unable to grapple with the task. ... Communities of men – call them colleges, monasteries, or whatever you please – appear to be the most suitable for the object in view. These men should be unmarried and altogether unshackled by earthly cares and domestic ties. Such establishments must be governed by rule. The rule of St Benedict has received universal sanction, and the veneration of thirteen centuries. It is suitable in almost every way for all ages and times, and is consistent with the most faithful loyalty to the English Church.' Styling himself Father Ignatius, he looked for a site where he could put this view into practice. Having failed to buy Llanthony Abbey further down the valley, in 1869 he purchased 32 acres at Capel-y-ffin on which to build his monastery, styling it Llanthony Tertia (Llanthony Secunda had been founded outside Gloucester when the original Llanthony was threatened by Welsh attacks). With the help of fellow monks and local masons he succeeded in building his monastery, which continued until his death in 1908, Lyne being buried in his church.

Lyne's convictions seemed to be confirmed by a series of visions seen in the late summer of 1880. On August 30th, two monks, on separate occasions, saw the Host appear on the altar in the church, and later that day four boys playing in a nearby field saw a female figure glide across the ground, identifying her as the Virgin Mary. Over the following two weeks, the figure was seen a further four times, on the last occasion by Father Ignatius himself. August 30th became a day of pilgrimage to the monastery, with people coming from far and wide, often walking from the railway stations at Hay to the north and Llanvihangel Crucorney to the south. The wooden Calvary which the walk passes was installed on a piece of ground acquired by Hilda and Irene Ewens, daughters of Father Ignatius's sister Harriet, in remembrance of the apparitions. The buildings were not finished at the time of Father Ignatius's death and with his demise the group of adherents soon dispersed. The church proved to have been poorly constructed and fell into disrepair.

Looking for a place of seclusion away from urban life, from August 1924 to October 1928 the controversial artist Eric Gill and his family lived in the domestic buildings of the former monastery, where Gill established a community of artists. Secluded it was, the only visitors being the doctor, who travelled by horse, and the occasional postman. There was no electricity, water came from a stream, and dining in the winter was by candlelight and necessitated wearing trenchcoats. One of the artists was David Jones, who painted the local scenery and was for a time engaged to Gill's daughter, Petra. Amongst other work whilst here, Gill designed the Perpetua and Gill Sans typefaces and worked on a number of sculptures. He was to look back at this time as one of his most creative periods, as did David Jones. But the conditions were dispiriting, and in 1928 the community left for a farm near High Wycombe in Buckinghamshire.

Just past the end of the field in front of the monastery and the associated white-painted building, take the track off to the left and you'll soon come to a wooden Calvary on the right. Keep right at the fork soon reached beyond this at a sign for the Grange Trekking Centre to pass by some chalets used in connection with the riding centre. At the far end of the track, which gains a tarmac surface near a house that might offer refreshments, don't go through the field

gate ahead of you, but turn sharp left onto the concreted track and follow it up to a gate out onto the open hillside.

6 Here you initially have a choice of routes: straight up the hillside following the edge of the conifer wood on the left, or the more used zig-zagging path up the hill-side, aiming, in due course, for the near top corner of the conifer woodland, where the two routes rejoin. The path now heads towards the steep hillside and is pretty clear on the ground. If you look ahead you can see its course making a zig-zag up the steeper part of the slope (shown in the photograph above). Follow this path and after a bit of a puff, the path will start to level out, passing a cairn

on your immediate right. Keep following the path, which has been repaired in places with stone rainwater channels and a gravel surface, and it will lead you to a junction of paths near another stone cairn on the ridge. You may want to turn left at this junction to visit the cairn, but the circular route turns right.

7 You now have a long and largely level walk along this ridge, passing above the small Grwyne Fawr Reservoir and its dam in the valley on your left.

GRWYNE FAWR RESERVOIR

With the expansion of the steel and coal industries in what was then western Monmouthshire, there was a need for an increased water supply. The problem was finding a site of sufficient altitude to collect the water and pipe it to the point of use. The site in the Grwyne Fawr valley was chosen because, at 1,725ft above sea level, it was high enough to allow water to be gravity fed to Abertillery and the surrounding areas. Building work started in 1912, but it was found that the road leading up the valley could not take the weight of the traction engines used to haul the necessary goods to the site. Negotiations with landowners to build a railway failed and then the advent of the First World War put the plans on hold. Work recommenced in 1919, the route of a railway to connect to the main line at Llanvihangel Crucorney having been agreed.

The 173ft-high dam wall was formed of large boulders weighing up to 5 tons each encased in concrete and then faced with dressed stone, and a 16-inch diameter steel pipeline was laid in a tunnel drilled through Coity Mountain to a reservoir in Cwmtillery, some 17 miles almost due south. The dam was completed in February 1928, after which the railway was dismantled, the trackbed being resurfaced to form a road. The reservoir, which could hold 400 million gallons (1,800 megalitres) of water, has recently been decommissioned, as lack of management of the surrounding catchment area allowed peat sediment to build up in the reservoir, resulting in discolouration of the water, and it was deemed uneconomical to remedy the problem.

After some 3 miles the path will slightly descend from one of the 'peaks' you cross in following the path, the path at this point being noticeably sunk into the ground due to the erosion of the ground. Here you will see that the path divides. You want to take the right-hand option, which is a largely green sward and will swing you in a gentle arc towards the northern escarpment of the Black Mountains. (As you go, look out for the path on the far side of the valley over to your right – you should see signs of a small path just above the steeper drop into the bottom of the valley: this is the line of your route back that you take in due course.)

8 Keep on the path and it will eventually drop down and join a path that runs along the top of the escarpment. Turn right on this and follow it along, and as you

start to rise on it, keep an eye out for a path that heads off to the right. This is fairly faintly marked at first, but don't worry about taking the wrong path, for as you head into the valley, most paths tend to lead you to the one that soon becomes very obvious on the ground, being a small path leading down the valley and perched above the stream on its left-hand side. If the weather has been wet recently, you should see some small but vibrant waterfalls along its length and in side streams flowing down from the far hillside. The path will gradually widen to a track, then lead between a cottage and some farm buildings where it will also gain a tarmacked surface. You now just follow this road back to where you parked.

Walk 22
Hay-on-Wye

6.5 miles on a mixture of paths, lanes and tracks in generally good order. A handful of stiles. Set in undulating country with one longish steady ascent. Takes in sites around Hay and Cusop as well as the site of Mouse Castle to the west.

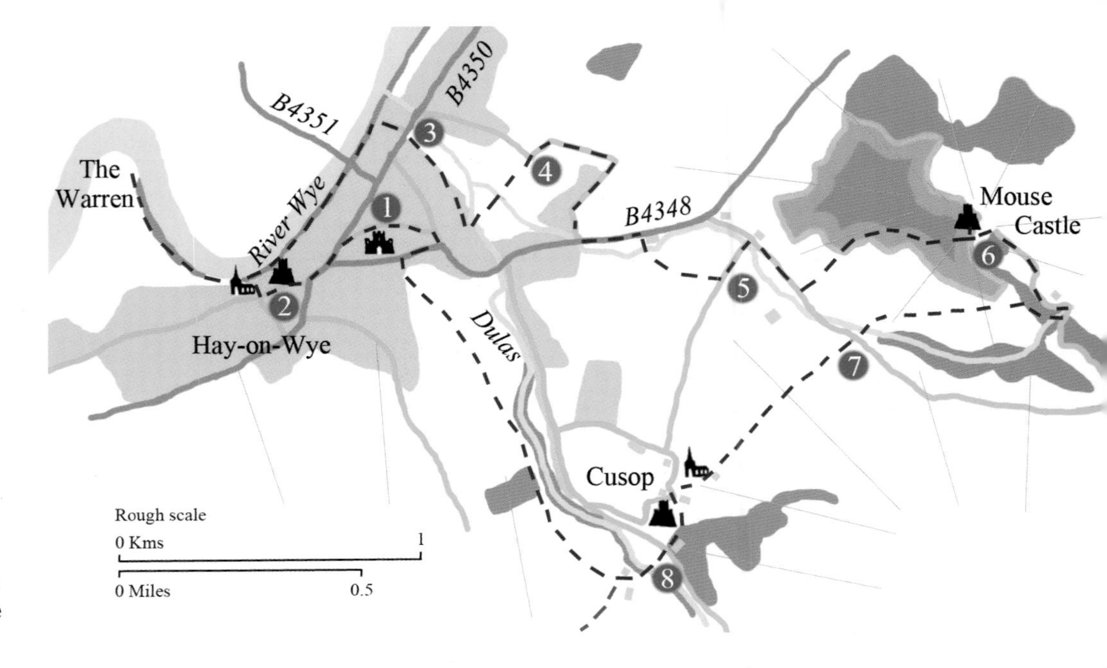

1 To start the walk, with your back to the new castle entrance in the square in Hay, turn left and walk along Castle Street. When you reach the T-junction, turn left (still on Castle Street) and cross the road, noticing the blue plaque on the wall by Jones Home Hardware store about the site of one of the old gates of the walled town. Just past the Blue Boar Inn, the road you're on becomes Church Street, passing Hay Cinema Bookshop on your left. Take the road off to the right (called Swan Bank) just this side of the Swan at Hay Hotel. Almost immediately you pass a mound on your right that is the site of the first castle, and soon reach an entrance into the churchyard.

HAY CASTLE

The first castle was probably constructed on the small motte near the church (passed later on in the walk) by one of the followers of Bernard de Neufmarché, who led a devastating attack on the Welsh territory of Brycheiniog in the late 1090s. This was followed by a stronger castle on the present site, probably commenced by Earl Miles of Hereford, for in 1155 his son Roger granted a house within the castle precinct to Brecon Priory. On Roger's death without heirs, the castle passed to William de Braose and became a favourite residence of his wife, Maud or Matilda St Valery. In the later struggles between the de Braose family and King John, the castle changed hands three times, on the last occasion both castle and town being burned by King John. Rebuilt by Reginald de Braose, the castle was attacked in 1231 by Llywelyn Fawr. The town was again burned but the castle may have survived, for two years later it became the base for Henry III in his campaigns first against Walter Clifford and then Llywelyn. In 1263 Henry granted the castle to the Mortimers, but the following year its constable surrendered it to Simon de Montfort, who was then seeking to bring the Mortimers to heel and make them accept the new system of government under the Provisions of Oxford and their successor terms. The Mortimers retook the castle the following year, and shortly after that Simon de Montfort met his death at Evesham. The castle continued to be used over the next 135 years, unlike several of its neighbours, and was garrisoned under the command of Sir John Oldcastle against the forces of Owain Glyndwr in the early 1400s. By 1461, however, the antiquarian John Leland reported that it was in in decay, though he noted that the town walls remained strong and included three gates along with a postern.

The castle remains comprise a roughly oval ringwork measuring some 70m by 80m at its widest and built on a small natural knoll that has been scarped to make its sides steeper. The earliest structure is the four-storeyed tower that still stands next to the gateway above the market place; this has been partially rebuilt and buttressed since its construction. A wooden palisade probably originally crowned the rest of the knoll. Either the original tower contained a gateway (as at Ludlow Castle, where the gateway was walled up and is now the castle keep), or it stood alongside the gateway and provided protection to it. At some point the palisade was replaced with a stone wall, of which little survives and which seems to have had just one tower along its length. The mansion that abuts the early tower was built around 1660 and was badly damaged by fires in 1939 and 1977.

HAY CHURCH

When the church was first built, the site of Hay Castle was the nearby motte, which probably explains why the church was built here rather than near the current centre of town. The church was for many years without a resident vicar, starting from the times of the English Civil War when no-one was appointed for several years, after which it was usually held jointly with other parishes to east and west, or the appointed vicar lived elsewhere and appointed a curate in his place. In 1825 that curate was the wealthy Humphrey Allan. He organised the rebuilding of the church by the architect Edward Haycock the elder in 1833, the tower, dated to the 15th century, being the only part of the earlier building that remained largely untouched, though the castellations were added later. Allan was followed by a resident vicar, Archdeacon William Bevan, who took up residence in Hay Castle and remained as vicar for 56 years. In his time the chancel was extended. Extensive refurbishment was carried out in the early 2000s, including reroofing much of the building and installing a kitchenette and toilets. The interior still retains its gallery which is supported by cast-iron columns. The badly worn recumbent figure near the north-west corner of the church is believed to be that of a monk – possibly an early priest of the parish.

2 Having visited the church, return to where you entered the churchyard and once through the gate, immediately turn left down a path. This soon leads under an old railway line to a path high above the River Wye, on which you turn left to head for The Warren.

HAY RAILWAY

The Hay Railway started life as a horse-drawn tramway of 3ft 6in gauge for the transportation of coal from a wharf on the Brecon and Monmouthshire canal at Brecon to Hay, and subsequently to Eardisley and Kington in Herefordshire. L-shaped runners were used for the rails, the wheels of the trams carrying the coal fitting outside the upright of the L so that the trams were easily guided by the rails. The section from Brecon to Hay was completed in May 1816 and that to Eardisley by December 1818.

The line between Hay and Eardisley was sold to the Hereford, Hay and Brecon Railway in 1860, with the engineer Thomas Savin completing the railway in 1864. Ownership of sections of the railway between Hay and Brecon was initially in the hands of several different companies. The line was bought by the Midland Railway, who used it as a link in a through route from Birmingham to Swansea, to compete with the Great Western Railway. They ran the line essentially for the transport of goods, with local passenger traffic as an incidental aspect of the line's work, and trains for passengers between Hereford and Swansea were discontinued in 1931. The line was never a huge commercial success and as road traffic burgeoned it became economically unviable. It was completely closed to passengers on 30 December 1962, and to freight in 1964. You follow the railway's route between The Warren and the road bridge across the Wye.

THE WARREN

The area is so-called because it is thought to have been used to breed rabbits in medieval times. A proposal in the early 1970s to turn it into a caravan park prompted a campaign to purchase the meadow and retain it for public recreation, something it had provided for many years. The Hay Warren Trust was formed and continues to look after the site, part of which is now a Site of Special Scientific Interest. From around 1815 the meadow was crossed by the Hay Tramway, along which horse-drawn trams trundled, carrying Welsh coal from a wharf in Brecon on the Monmouthshire and Brecon Canal to Hay, Eardisley and Kington. The shingle beaches were popular bathing spots in Victorian times, then for soldiers recovering in the First World War, and they remain popular with swimmers and paddlers today.

Once you have passed through the entrance gate to The Warren, take the path that slopes off downhill to the right and continue along it till you reach Hay's pebble beach, near some rapids.

From The Warren, return along the path towards Hay, but rather than turning back up the path to the church, keep ahead, noticing the various carved sculptures of animals and birds along the way, some by the path, others by the old railway line which runs parallel to and above the path. The path will lead you under the road bridge that crosses the Wye and to a small car park which is often used by canoeists. Leave the car park via its access lane and walk up to the B4350.

3 Cross this, heading slightly to the right, to then take the set of stone steps up the bank on the far side of the road. Here you join the Wye Valley path for a while. Walk ahead, looking out for the remains of the old town walls to your immediate right, somewhat obscured by vegetation. The path will eventually lead into a residential area. Having passed alongside some houses, it follows the Wye Valley path, which makes a hairpin turn left down a tarmacked lane. This leads to more houses and some communal open space on the right. Keep ahead and use the footbridge to cross the Dulas Brook, which forms the English/Welsh boundary hereabouts.

Once across, head up the bank to the corner of the house on your left and cross the field on a path which bears slightly right; this will take you to a small metal footpath gate. Go through this, then head down to the next stream, crossing by a bridge made from a large slab of rock. Then go a few more steps downstream before heading up the far side of the dingle and taking the small metal footpath gate into another field. Through the gate you turn right to cross to the corner of this comparatively narrow field where there is another small metal footpath gate. Go through this to emerge onto a road, on which you turn right.

4 Follow the road as it twists and turns (you leave the route of the Wye Valley path at its first bend) past Nantyglasdwr Farm, to reach the B4348. Turn left along

this (there is a pavement), crossing the road when you reach a bungalow that is partly hidden by a fence on the far side of the road, to go over the stile just this side of it.

The path follows the boundary of the bungalow down to a stream which you cross using stepping stones, and once up the bank on the far side, the path turns slightly left, crossing the field and aiming for the right-hand side of the collection of farm buildings a few fields ahead. Having crossed the stile in the hedgerow you reach, the path then follows the line of the sunken track across this next field to leave it by a stile alongside a field gate. Over the stile, turn left on the road.

5 Walk along the road, bearing right when it forks to meet a more major road, on which you turn right. After about 250 yards, just past the old walled entrance to the farm on your right, go through the old metal kissing gate on your left to enter a field. Walk up this field, taking a line that initially stays roughly parallel to the fence on your left. Having passed some of the woodland to your left, you will reach a stile to enter the wood itself.

Here, follow a well-worn path which turns slightly right and continues uphill to meet a wider forestry track. Turn right on this. After a while your path leaves this track and bears left, initially heading up some steps, to continue climbing the hillside. Keep left when the path forks, then ignore a path that runs downhill to a footpath gate and keep going, to soon reach another footpath gate on your immediate right that leads out of the woodland. You will need to go through this gate to continue the circular walk, but if you wish to see Mouse Castle, turn left on the path here and follow it up to the top of the hill, where the well-preserved motte can be seen, then return to this gate.

MOUSE CASTLE

The motte of this castle stands on a headland with steeply sloping ground falling away on all sides except towards the north-east, making for a fine defensive spot and also a good observation point (at least it would be if it wasn't surrounded by trees!) The motte stands some 4 to 5m high and is some 15 to 20m in diameter at its top; interestingly, it would have been better placed towards the edge of the western bank to maximise use of the natural defences. Outside the moat around the motte there is an outer rampart that varies in height around the circuit of what would have been a bailey, but stands about 3m high and 10 to 12m wide to the north and east of the motte. The entrance to the castle was to the south-east of the motte, represented by a hollow way. There is some speculation that the castle might have been built on the site of an Iron Age hillfort.

The castle is believed to have been constructed in the late 1000s on the orders of Roger de Lacy, and its plan is indicative of such a date, for the site would have served very well as the most north-easterly point of Norman penetration into this part of Wales prior to the Normans' successful campaign in Brycheiniog in 1090.

6 Go through the gate and walk along the path, which will soon lead you out onto a rough lane, on which you turn right. Follow the lane till you come to where it makes almost a U-shaped bend as it crosses a stream (sometimes dry). About 30 yards beyond the bend, take the footpath off to the right, this following a fence on your left. The path first doubles back on the lane you've been following, then crosses a footbridge and heads through the woodland to lead you to a gate out into a field. Continue along the edge of the field for about 30 yards, keeping an eye out for a waymarking post hard against the fence. Here you turn left and then head half-left down the slope, to reach a gateway on a bend in the hedgerow below you. Go through the gateway.

Once in the next field, your target is the metal field gate on its far side, set just to the right of a large oak tree that stands beyond the field in some rough ground. To the right of this field gate you will find a stile which you cross, to then initially follow the fence line on your left and then aim directly at the farm buildings in the valley ahead of you. About 200 yards short of the far side of the field you will once more come close to the field boundary on your left. When this fence bends round to the left, follow it downhill and you will come to a footbridge. Cross this bridge, then head up the bank on the far side to cross a stile out onto a road.

7 Cross the road and the stile on the far side to enter another field. Cross the corner of the field to the hedge about 100 yards in front of you, then turn right and follow it to reach a stile in the corner of the field that you come to. Cross this to enter a much larger field, which the path crosses to the mid-point on the far boundary. It is difficult to give a landmark to aim for, though the line of the path may be evident across the field, but as you cross the field you should be able to make out a small metal footpath gate to the right of a house and its outbuildings: this gate is your target. Go through the gate to enter the church-yard of Cusop church.

CUSOP CHURCH
Under the large yew tree by the south-east corner of the church lies the grave of William Seward, a follower of the Methodist preachers Wesley and Whitfield who in 1740 was injured by a mob when preaching in Hay and died a week after the incident. The church itself is Norman, but was much restored in 1857.

RICHARD BOOTH
In 1962 Richard Booth opened a bookshop in Hay, then a quiet and slightly run down town. With an extrovert character and an ability to persuade, he soon acquired the household libraries of landed families who were downsizing, as well as importing thousands of books cleared out from American libraries and institutions. Soon he had several bookshops in the town, and other people came and set up their own bookshops, bringing the total number to about 30, some of them specialising in particular themes or subjects. To help put this burgeoning Town of Books on the map, on April Fools' Day in 1977 Richard Booth dressed in fake ermine robes and a homemade crown and walked the streets declaring that he was now King of Hay and that the town was an independent state. The stunt garnered huge publicity, which he followed up with other regal nonsense. But behind it all there was a deep conviction of the importance of supporting localism, before such a word was in common parlance, and a dread of the dead hand of bureaucracy.

He bought the castle in the 1960s when it was just about still habitable, but a fire badly damaged it in 1977. By his own confession he inherited one fortune, made two and lost four, and by 2007 he no longer owned any bookshops, though there is still a Booth's Bookshop in Hay. He died in 2019.

Leave the churchyard by the path that leads to its lych-gate, passing the gravestone of Richard Booth, self-styled 'King on Hay' en route. At the gate, turn half left and take the path (just to the right of a white gate and cattle grid) which heads into some woodland. Notice the earthworks of Cusop Castle on the right at the start of this path. Follow the path as it bends right and drops down past a recently renovated mill building.

CUSOP CASTLE

The remains consist of an irregular oval-shaped 'courtyard' with the remains of a ditch, and a possible entry near the middle of the north-east side. Foundations of a curtain wall have been found on the bank, and there is evidence of buildings on the south side. It is said that portions of the gateway were still standing in the early 1800s. It probably represents the remains of a fortified mansion or pele tower with its origins between the 12th and 14th centuries.

CUSOP MILL

A water corn mill is recorded as operating on a leat diverted from the Dulas Brook in the 1330s. Also in the 14th century, a fulling mill, the water powering hammers for beating cloth after weaving to consolidate the fabric, is recorded in Hay and was probably also sited on the Dulas Brook. At least two paper mills were built on the brook, one near Llangwathan, further up the brook from where you cross it on this walk, and one near Cusop. These mills were probably short-lived and had probably ceased production before the end of the 19th century. Cusop Mill is on the left as you head down the hill to cross the lane and the brook. This three-storey mill was built in the early 1800s of rubble stone with a slate roof and attic lit by a lunette in a central pediment. It is believed to have ceased milling in the early 1900s, but a turbine was put in to generate electricity in the 1920s. A mill is shown here on Taylor's map of 1754, and a corn mill on the OS map of 1889. The mill leat is about 200 yards long and crossed the road by a culvert to a large stone-lined terminal pond which is now a lawn.

8 Cross the road you meet in the valley bottom to walk up the drive of Lower House, once more crossing Dulas Brook. When the drive approaches some houses, the footpath swings right and goes up some steps to a footpath gate, which you go through. The path then zig-zags up a short bank to another gate which you go through to enter a field. Here you join Offa's Dyke Path, which you'll follow back into Hay. So, take the right-hand signed section of Offa's Dyke Path (i.e. that into Hay rather than up onto the Black Mountains!) and cross the field to a footpath gate on its far side. Cross the next field, leaving it by a path between trees and cross the following fields, shadowing the Dulas Brook dingle to your right, and at one point crossing another brook by a footbridge. In due course you'll reach a narrower field where the path splits: here you want to follow the path which goes alongside the metal field fence on your left down to a gate into the next field, in which you follow the old hedgerow on your right towards the edge of Hay. At the end of the field, go through the footpath gate out onto a gravelled track and follow it along till it meets the B4348. Cross this, then simply follow the stone wall on your left in an arc, turning left down Castle Lane to return to the square in front of the castle.

Walk 23 Three Cocks & Little Lodge

6 miles on lanes, and paths through fields which can be muddy and wet. A few stiles. Set in gently undulating countryside. Includes two churches (one a ruin), a Neolithic tomb site, a castle site and an old mansion.

You can start this walk either from the lay-by near the church on the A438 situated between Three Cocks/

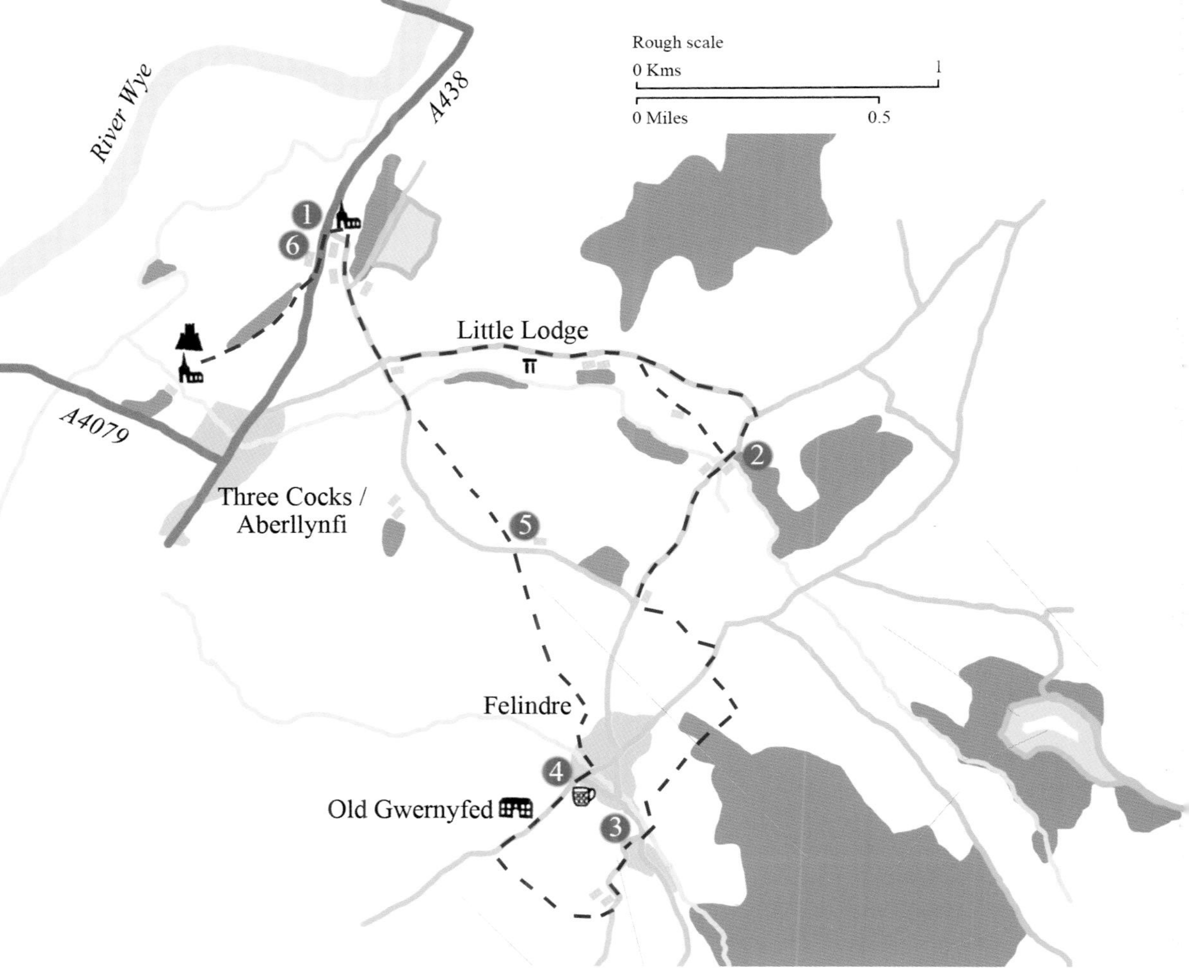

SS CYNIDR AND PETER, GLASBURY

The Norman church, probably built on the site of an earlier church dedicated to St Cynidr, lay somewhere near the present junction of the Afon Llynfi with the Wye, though the Wye has changed its course hereabouts on several occasions. A flood shortly after the restoration of the monarchy in 1660 undermined the church steeple, and washed open the graves and swept away the bones, leaving the community, under the leadership of the then vicar, to rescue what they could of its furnishings and some of the building stone and start afresh.

A new site was given by Sir Henry Williams of Gwernyfed, one of the major local landowners, and work on the construction of a new church began in 1663 and was completed in 1665 and dedicated on St Peter's Day that year. Next to nothing remains of that church apart from the lower courses of the chancel walls and the altar rails, for by the 1820s the building not only needed a major overhaul but was also considered too small for the size of the parish. A new church, designed by Lewis Vulliamy, a London architect who had relations living in Glasbury (see under LITTLE LODGE LONG BARROW, overleaf), was rather austere, as little expense could be spared. Started in 1836, the church was finished in 1838. This building had further work carried out in 1881, including replacing the flagstones with encaustic tiles.

J.W. Hobbs, reminiscing about his years as the booking clerk at Three Cocks railway station between 1902 and 1905, wrote that there were good congregations at the church, comprising 'chiefly the gentry, retired people, visitors at the Hotel, and some of the large farmers. Most of the working classes were chapel, except those employed at Gwernyfed or Tregoed [large nearby estates]. The strongest chapel was the Baptist at Glasbury, which was always full on Sunday nights, and often packed. Baptisms used to take place about once a year in the River Wye, which runs alongside the chapel. The chapel was the chief source of social entertainment. ... The two Glasbury chapels and Felindre combined and held two entertainments in each chapel every winter. These always had to be arranged for the week of the full moon, so as to have moonlight on the way home.'

Aberllynfi and Glasbury (grid ref: 177 385), or, if you wish to start or end from a pub, at the Three Horseshoes in nearby Felindre. (Please note that at the time of writing the pub is only open in the evening between Wednesday and Sunday and at lunchtime at the weekends; check for latest details on 01497 847304.) We have described the walk as starting from the church on the A438 (point 1 on the map and directions), but if you want to start from the pub then commence at point 4.

1 Enter the churchyard to see the church (the entrance door is on the far side from the A438). Having visited the church, turn right out of the door and then left to head to a corner of the churchyard, leaving it by a gate, and then turn left on a minor road. Keep along this, keeping right at the first road junction and then turning left at the crossroads.

Pass the electricity substation on your right, followed by a long field. Near the crest of the hill you will reach a field gate on your right followed by a hedge that acts as a boundary between fields running away from the road downhill. Immediately past this hedge, stop and look through the gap in the hedgerow to see the remains of Little Lodge Long Cairn.

LITTLE LODGE LONG BARROW

The site of this Neolithic long barrow was excavated in 1929 by C.E. Vulliamy, an author and biographer whose parents lived in Glasbury. He found unburnt human remains together with the bones of red deer, sheep and cattle. Evaluation of the human remains by a team from the British Museum ascertained that they belonged to four adult males and one male youth.

The original roughly oval mound, now much mutilated and with several of the stones that formed the chambers visible, measures some 58m long north to south and between 12 and 22m wide, and now stands to a maximum of 1m high. The excavation revealed traces of chambers at the narrow southern end and at the centre of the mound. One of the southern chambers retains its form and measures roughly 2m by 1.4m, though it is narrower at one end than the other. It still retains five stones forming the side of the chamber, all standing less than 1m in height. Adjacent are some stones that formed part of the side of an adjoining chamber. To the west of the chamber are three further stones appearing just above ground level; their function has not been determined.

The largest and most clearly visible stone, some 3m long, 0.5m wide and 1m high, forms part of the main chamber. Other stones nearby relate to chambers in this vicinity, and some stones at the northern end of the mound would have formed part of the kerbing that ran around the whole monument.

Continue on along the road and pass a farm on the right. At this point you have a choice: you can either keep to the road till you reach a T junction where you turn right, or, at the first field gate past the farm, go through this and enter a field. The footpath crosses this field aiming for a point roughly in line with the left-hand end of the group of buildings comprising a farmhouse and allied outbuildings seen across the field. Here, not quite in the corner of the field, you will find a small gate that leads out onto a gravelled track. Cross this, heading to another small gate in the hedgerow ahead, located just above an outbuilding. Go through the gate onto the lane that serves the farm. Cross this and go through another small gate into the field on the other side of the lane. The path now heads to the far right-hand corner of this field, though you won't

see the stile which you cross to leave the field till you are all but right above it. Turn right on the road on the far side of the stile.

❷ The two routes have now rejoined, the road passing through a group of buildings that include what was Tregoyd Mill by a stream, and then rises uphill. In due course a road will join the one you're on from the right. Just past this junction, and just past a cottage on your left at this point, turn left along a bridleway. This will lead you between fields out to another road.

Turn right on this and look out for a stile on your left, reached after 50 yards. Cross this, and then cross the length of the field to a stile just to the left of the far right-hand corner. Over this, the path turns right and twists through a patch of bracken to a stile into another field. Once in the field, ignore the footpath sign up the hillside, for your path crosses the field, heading only slightly uphill to its far side where you will find another stile into a piece of woodland. Follow the path through the woodland to a stile on its far side. Over this, the path slants down to the field boundary below you and follows it along the hillside to enter an area with some trees. Here it soon bends to the left above a steep bank above a stream. Follow the path along the top of this bank and when you reach an area shaped by a small disused quarry on your left, the path drops down to the right to leave this patch of open woodland by a stile onto a track. Turn right on the track, and right again when you reach the road.

OLD GWERNYFED

The original house that stood here was replaced *c.*1450 and this latter forms the core of the existing building. Around 1600-1605 the house was modernised to the prevailing standards of the time, with the addition of three projecting wings, one at each end and one in the centre, to form a ground plan of the letter E for Elizabeth. 1605 saw the wedding of Sir Henry Williams, the son of the house's new owner (who was a wealthy lawyer), to Eleanor Whitney. A bardic poem celebrating the event shows that the house now had a hall, parlour, kitchen, wine cellar, brew-house, poultry houses and kennels for hunting dogs. A new spiral staircase had been built, believed to have been constructed around the mast of a wrecked ship of the Spanish Armada washed up on the Welsh coast. Outside, extensive gardens were laid out.

A fireplace that carries a date of 1680 indicates later alterations, but sometime after 1720 the Williams family moved their main residence to Llangoed Hall further up the Wye Valley, and Old Gwernyfed became a tenanted farmhouse. The south wing was gutted by fire in 1780 and a large chimneystack was added to the north-west façade in the early 1800s. At this time the estate passed into the hands of the Wood family by marriage, and decades later they built a new home they named Gwernyfed Park, which was eventually to become the site of Gwernyfed High School. In turn, the house passed to the Hore-Ruthvens by marriage in the early 1900s. In subsequent decades the estate was much reduced by sales, and Elyned Hore-Ruthven (née Wood) took up residence in Old Gwernyfed. When she died in 1965, the house was first rented out, then sold. It changed hands again in 2013, and since then a major restoration programme has been undertaken.

❸ Take the second turning to the left off this road (i.e. not the cul-de-sac, but the road reached soon afterwards), and follow it to a farm. Keep to the road through and past the farm, the road bending left and then right to pass above the farmhouse. When the road then bends left, your route lies through the field gate on the right. Cross the field you enter along the line of a track to reach a stile into the next field. Your route now keeps following field boundaries on your right, leading slightly downhill at first, passing through field gates in the corner of fields, till you reach a field gate on your right that leads out onto a road. Turn right on the road and you will soon reach Old Gwernyfed on your left. Keep on along the road and you'll come to the Three Horseshoes pub.

❹ With your back to the pub entrance, turn right and walk along the road (or just keep walking along the road if you started at the church) and you'll soon come to a footpath sign off to the left just this side of the white-painted Bridge House. Follow the lane (which is the start of the path) down to a footbridge across a wide stream. In the field on the far side Ordnance Survey maps show the footpath heading off across the field, but modern custom and practice shows that a headland path has been made round the edge of the field, so turn right once in the field and follow this along the field boundary, till you come to an old metal kissing gate alongside an old metal field gate on your right, through which you go into another field. Again follow the path alongside the field boundary on your right to the far side of the field where you cross a stile into the next field. This time the path crosses the field, heading for the far right-hand corner, where you will find another metal kissing gate that leads out onto a road.

5 Cross the road to a footpath gate and enter a large field. Initially aim for the second telegraph pole from the right that stands in the field, from which you head to a junction of field boundaries just below it to go through a small metal gate into the next field. Follow the field boundary on your right to the far end of the field where you go through another small metal gate (set not quite in the corner of the field) to enter the field beyond. Cross this, aiming for the left-hand corner of the electricity substation you can see ahead of you. On the far side of the field you will find a field gate through which you go to join a road. Turn right on the road and follow it up to a crossroads. Go straight over this and then bear left at the next junction which will lead you down to the church on the A438.

6 The full walk continues to see the remains of Three Cocks'/Abellynfi's motte and bailey castle. When you reach the main road, cross it and turn left to walk along the road's pavement, passing first a pair of cottages on your right and then a single house called Ashville. Immediately past the latter, go through the small gate on the right into a field. Shadow the field boundary on your right across the field to its far corner, where you pass into the next field, immediately above a strip of woodland that runs along the slope of an escarpment. Follow this field boundary along till you reach a field gate on your right, which you go through to then turn left and walk across a narrow patch of ground (probably around some brambles) to reach a small gate which you go through to enter the area of the bailey of the castle, with its motte to the right. If you cross the bailey you will come to the stonework outline of the original church here, now partly buried in a group of trees.

Return to the main road by the same route and go to point 1 if you started the walk at the Three Horseshoes.

ABERLLYNFI CASTLE, CHAPEL AND SETTLEMENT

The castle is known to have existed by 1233, for in that year it was taken by Royalist forces fighting for Henry III, who was in conflict with Walter Clifford. Clifford then held Cantref Selyf, an area that included Bronllys and lands along the western side of the Wye between Three Cocks and beyond Crickadarn near Erwood. Soon retaken, the castle remained in the hands of the Kinnersleys, its erstwhile lords, for several generations.

The castle is of the motte and bailey type, the motte lying at the northern end above an escarpment that drops down to the Wye's floodplain. Some loose stone remains on the motte, suggesting that a stone tower might once have been built upon it. South of the motte are the remains of a large bailey, which the footpath crosses. The remains of St Eigon's chapel lie some 50m south-east of the castle. (The photo shows the view across the bailey to the motte. The remains of the chapel are to the left of the photo.) Some 20m by 8m, they appear to define a simple, two-celled building which may have served as a chapel to the castle, even though outside the castle walls, but in any case also served the local community, though there appears to have been no churchyard. Records show that Sir Henry and Lady Eleanor Williams of Old Gwernyfed (see p.220) had an elaborate tomb in this chapel, whilst the register for Glasbury church records that marriages and baptisms were carried out here until at least 1695. By the end of the 1700s, however, it was noted that the chapel contained some mutilated monuments of the Williams family, including one lacking a head, showing that the building was falling into disrepair and had suffered vandalism by that date.

If there was a medieval settlement at Aberllynfi, it is likely to have been in the area near the chapel and the castle, though there is no clear sign now of any such habitation. If there was a settlement here, its centre clearly shifted over time to focus on the main road between Hay and Brecon, as trade developed on what is now the A438. The first mention of the Three Cocks Inn was in 1754, and it is quite possible that this date marks the start of the present village of Three Cocks.

Walk 24
Llyswen

3.25 miles mainly on tracks and paths, including those across grassy open access land. Some stiles. There is a steady ascent and a more undulating descent. Includes passing by the probable site of the original Llys Wen.

The walk starts from the church in Llyswen, near which there are a couple of parking places (grid ref: 134 380), though you may wish to start from either of the pubs and park there, if using the pub before or after the walk.

> LLYSWEN
> The name Llyswen translates as 'White Palace', and it is believed that it may have started life as a local centre of power in the 6th century AD, though the name could also refer to the palace of Rhodri Mawr, a 9th-century prince of renown. Where this might have been built is uncertain, though tradition assigns it to a field near Dderw to the south-east of the village. The settlement is reputed to have had a Norman castle, but if so, nothing of it remains. The site most favoured for this castle is an alleged motte, scheduled as an ancient monument, that lies some 400m to the south-west of the village. However, the origin of these earthworks is uncertain, and it may even be a relatively modern feature.

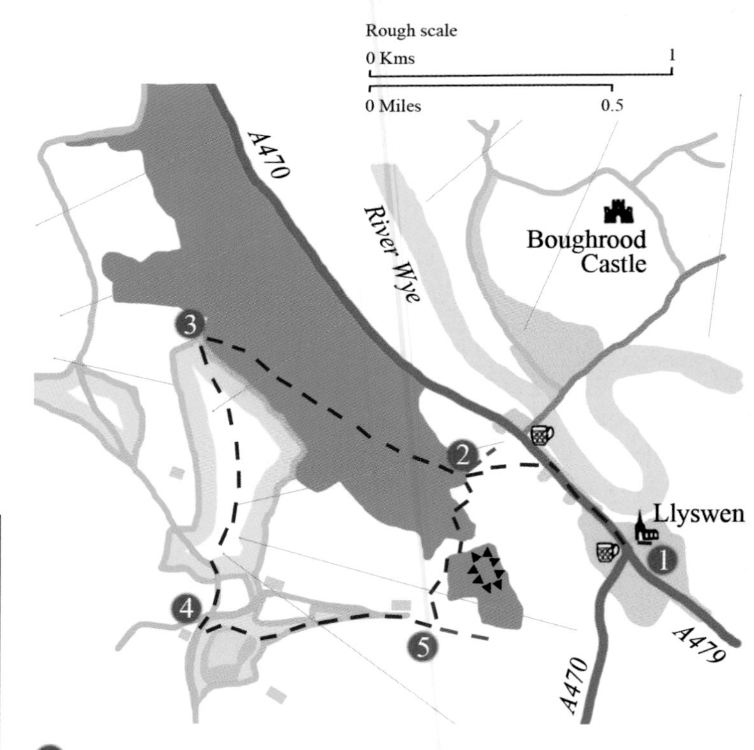

❶ With your back to the gates into the churchyard, walk up to the A470 and turn right along the pavement. Just past the gateway to the Old Rectory on the left-hand side of the road, you'll come to a housing development on the right called Glan yr Afon/Riverside. Here, cross the A470 and go up some steps and through a small metal gate by a footpath sign into a field. Cross the bottom corner of this

field to a stile on the far side (about 25 yards to the left of a metal field gate) and once over the stile, head to the far uphill corner of the next field.

2 Cross the stile here and you'll find yourself at a crossroads of paths. Ignore the stile to your left and the path that heads back downhill to your right and carry on ahead to follow a path that slants uphill across the hillside. This will become a grassy path that leads onto a flat area crossed by forestry tracks. Head diagonally across this area to continue along what is now a track. Within 20 yards you'll reach a fork – keep right, still heading uphill and slanting across the hillside. When there is another fork in the track (there's a waymarking sign between the

LLYSWEN CHURCH

It is claimed that an early Christian Clas site (one comprising religious and domestic buildings) at Llyswen was granted to the See of Llandaff *c.*560 AD. If so, the sub-circular shape of the present churchyard suggests that this might have been the site referred to, as circular churchyards often indicate an early Christian site, many such sites which now have an irregular shape having lost some of their original ground. The only difficulty with this theory is that the space would have been too small for the building of the usual range of buildings associated with a Clas church. The church is dedicated to St Gwendoline, a 9th-century saint believed to have been buried at Talgarth. It was rebuilt in its entirety in the early 1860s, though the font might be a survivor from the earlier structure.

two paths) keep to the left and you will soon reach a gate out onto a common.

3 Through the gate, head up the slope to the remains of a large fallen tree. Just before the tree, take the grassy track off to the left. (If the way is blocked by the fallen tree, walk round it in a clockwise direction and join the grassy track on the far side of the blockage.) Keep on this broad track across the common (on a clear day you'll eventually see Pen-y-fan ahead of you) until you reach a road. Turn left on the road and walk along it (or initially the common alongside it) until you reach a converted chapel and a red telephone kiosk (now used as a community noticeboard).

4 With your back to the telephone kiosk and the converted chapel to your right, walk round the edge of Brechfa Pool, keeping it to your right, till you meet a gravel track. The pool has unfortunately become infested with New Zealand Pygmy Weed, which can smother local wildlife and is difficult to remove, so it's important not to get it on your boots or clothing (or your dog!), so that you

THE SITE OF LLYS WEN / WHITE PALACE?

This structure's position on a steep slope makes it unlikely that it was ever a 'hillfort' as such. It is more likely to have been the original site of the Llys or 'palace' from which Llyswen takes its name, although such 6th to 9th century sites are notoriously difficult to find because of the scarcity of literature about their origins and precise location. The site is roughly rectangular, which again would be unusual for a hillfort, with its strongest banks or ramparts on the northern uphill, and so more vulnerable, side. Later openings have been made in these ramparts, with a pond created in the south-west corner, making analysis of the site even more difficult.

don't inadvertently aid its spread. Turn right on the track and follow it for about a hundred yards, then just before a metal field gate on the left, turn left on a wide grassy track that follows the right-hand edge of the common, and this will lead you onto a minor road near the end of the common. Follow this to its end, reached in a matter of yards, pass the entrance to a house on your left, and continue on the path that continues ahead and downhill.

5 After a few hundred yards you will come to a stile in the fence on your left. Cross this and cross the field about 45 degrees right of straight ahead to a footpath gate on its far side. Go through this and up the path beyond it into the next field. Turn slightly left to cross this to a stile on the far side, passing between some small fenced-off areas where trees have been planted, to reach a stile into the next field. Over this, turn right and head downhill, aiming to the left of the corner of the wood on your right, and heading almost straight for Boughrood Castle, a 'stately' home in the valley bottom (if visible – it's occasionally lost in mist or cloud). The photograph on the opposite page shows the descent towards the site of Llys Wen, with Boughrood Castle roughly central. From the corner of the wood, follow its edge down to the corner of the field where you cross a stile into another wood. This can be the best place to observe the earthworks in the woodland on your right that might once have formed part of the original Llys Wen, or White Palace.

BOUGHROOD CASTLE

The original Boughrood Castle was built in the 12th century. The remains include a motte, badly damaged by the construction of Castle Farm but retaining traces of masonry on its top, though these may have been further disrupted by relatively recent landscaping, and the ghost of a bailey. The current 'castle' was built in 1817 by Francis Fowke, who had made his money while working for the East India Company. Unlike the 'Honourable' which sometimes accompanies the name of the company, Fowke appears to have made his money by largely dishonourable means – bribes, rake offs from army contracts and dealing in opium. His lack of morals extended into his love life; he fathered 16 illegitimate children, all but one of them by Mary Lowe, a London actress who became his mistress when she was aged 20. Francis died in 1819 and the castle passed to his eldest son, another Francis, whilst the inheritance was due to be shared equally between all his children, a request that was not fulfilled. Francis, meanwhile, remodelled the castle, removing the battlements that his father had built. The family inheritance was still a matter of dispute when the executor of the elder Francis's will died, leaving accumulated debts and instructions that the castle was not to be sold till the youngest of the children had reached the age of 21. In 1833, the castle and most of its lands were sold to Walter Wilkins (de Winton) of nearby Maesllwch Castle (in Herefordshire), and it has since changed hands several times.

Over the stile, walk diagonally downhill through the woods to a stile in the fence that separates the woodland from the field below. (The stile is about halfway along the bottom fence-line. Depending upon fallen trees, it's possible to descend directly at about 45 degrees, or you can follow the narrow footpath which initially leads along the contours of the hill, keeping your eye open for the stile, which you should be able to spot through the trees on your right, and then pick a route down to it.) Once over the stile, walk down to the bottom left-hand corner of the field, cross another stile, and then another immediately found on your right. From here, retrace your steps from the start of the walk, crossing the field and going over a stile a little to the right of a field gate, then cross the next field to a gate in the far left-hand corner to return to the A470.

Walk 25
Erwood & Crickadarn

3 miles. On minor roads, tracks and cross field paths. Some stiles. Set in undulating countryside, there is one slightly awkward ascent due to a steep bank, and a boggy patch to cross to reach the site of Crickadarn Castle. Also includes two churches and the site of a mill.

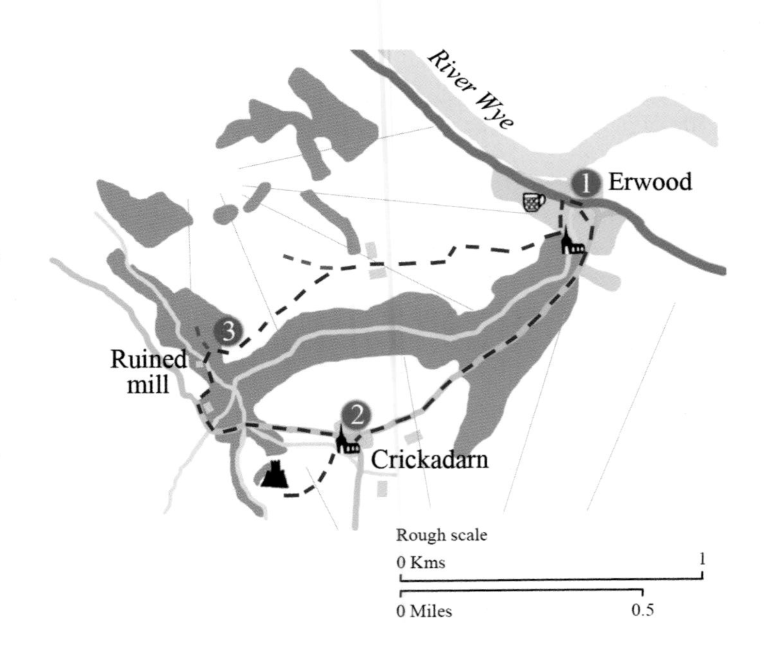

There are some parking spaces near the public toilets in the dip in the A470 in the centre of Erwood. If there is no space here, follow the A road south (away from Builth Wells) for about 100 yards and take the road off to the right. There may be some spaces in front of the houses above you on the left as you start to head up this road.

The walk is described as starting from the parking area near the toilets in Erwood (grid ref: 096 431).

ERWOOD

No mention of Erwood has been found in medieval documents, the first dated reference appearing in 1608 when 'Errwd' is mentioned, believed to be a reference to Erwood Hall or its successor. The present Erwood Hall dates from 1800, perhaps encasing some earlier elements. It might well be that the medieval settlement of Crickadarn, clustered near its castle and visited later on in this walk, 'migrated' downhill as times became more settled, perhaps as the Civil War ended, so that its residents could benefit from improvements to the main road between Builth Wells and Brecon close to the Wye, and the trading opportunities that this provided. The presence of a market hall in such a small settlement certainly supports this suggestion, even though the current one was built at the end of the 19th century.

ERWOOD CHAPEL OR HEPHZIBAH ENGLISH BAPTIST CHAPEL

This was built c.1827 but its internal orientation was rotated through 90 degrees just a few decades later. It is a listed grade II building due to its painted gallery. Hephzibah is a Hebrew word meaning 'My delight is in her', and several Baptist chapels take this name from its use in a prophesy in *Isaiah* Chapter 62, which says 'But you shall be called Hephzibah', meaning that a day will come when God's people will know the unbroken presence and love of God.

❶ With your back to the toilets, turn right and then immediately right again to walk up a narrow tarmacked lane. At the T-junction at its top, turn right, soon reaching the chapel.

From the gate to the chapel you turn right to walk up the road, but you can cross and follow the track through the grass on the opposite side of the road as it cuts off a corner of the road. Thereafter, continue following the road uphill and into Crickadarn. Go ahead at the T junction to enter the churchyard and visit the church.

CRICKADARN CHURCH

St Mary's church was probably built in the 13th century, traces of work of this date remaining in the north wall of both nave and chancel. The rest of the nave and chancel appears to have been largely rebuilt in the 15th and 16th centuries, the latter century also seeing the addition of the tower and porch. In 1810 it was noted that the seating was irregular, that the front of an oak rood loft survived and that the architecture was 'vile'. By 1865 new seats had been provided, only the beam of a rood loft remained, and the outer walls of the nave and chancel were whitewashed. Since then the church has been much restored, first in 1867, then in 1895 and again in about 1914. Inside the church are the remains of a Royal Coat of Arms painted on the north wall, probably those of one of the first three King Georges.

On leaving the church, turn half-right and walk over to the corner of the churchyard. Here you will find a kind of stile created out of a couple of gravestones. Through this, a short length of path leads to a stile which you cross and then head over a short stretch of boggy ground into a field. Follow the field boundary on your right and then the stream which is a continuation of the line, crossing it by the 'causeway' soon reached. At this point you are looking at the mound that is the site of Crickadarn castle. The footpath should continue on from here, but has been fenced across, with nothing done by Powys Council in the three years we have been writing to them about it, nor about the state of the path in general. You therefore now need to return the way you've come to rejoin the road in front of the church.

CRICKADARN CASTLE

Little is known about this castle, and little evidence of its existence remains. It may have been built by the Clifford family, for Walter Clifford is mentioned as holding land at Clettwr, the name of the nearby brook, in 1252. However, land in the vicinity had been granted some 80 years earlier to Dore Abbey, a large Cistercian abbey in south-west Herefordshire of which part is now a parish church, suggesting that a castle had been built here by that date. The top of the site has been scarped and ditched to form a roughly circular top some 60m in diameter. Much rubble stone litters the site, and this could be part of the remains of a ringwork that once surmounted the scarped mound, but little trace of mortar has been found. The entrance was probably on its eastern side, where a natural causeway heads in the direction of the church. It is likely that the field in which the castle now stands was quite marshy, creating a naturally defensive feature.

2 Turn left on the road and follow it along, descending to cross a stream then rising uphill to pass Verlands, a house on the right. Immediately past the end of the grounds of this property, as the road starts to bend left, take the signposted path (hopefully it still will be) off to the right that leads steeply down a gully into a wood. Follow this and it will lead you to a footbridge across a stream by the ruins of a mill.

Over the bridge, head straight up the bank and round the roots of a fallen tree, where the line of the path becomes more visible. The path climbs uphill to the left and you'll soon reach a post marking a split in the path. You want the right-hand path, which leads you uphill, the way being fairly clear on the ground though at some times of the year it can be slightly obscured by bracken. The path keeps going in broadly the same direction from this point, up and across the hillside, levelling out briefly at one point, and staying close to the edge of the steep drop

down into the valley below. The path will become clearer towards its end and lead you up to a stile which you cross to enter a field.

3 The path now roughly parallels the field boundary on your right to cross the field to a gate into the next field. Again stay parallel with the field boundary on your right and cross this field to reach a gate into the field beyond. Keep on much the same line across this field, heading for its far top corner and leaving it across a stile a few yards to the right of a field gate. Here, and on the track through the farm, in good weather you'll have fine views to the right of Hay Bluff and the Twmpa or Lord Hereford's Knob in the Black Mountains.

Over the stile you'll join a gravel track on which you turn right and walk into the farmyard of Maescletwr. Keep ahead, passing to the right of the farmhouse on what becomes a tarmacked lane, and follow this downhill. Where the lane bends to the left just above Erwood, you'll see a bench on your right. Take the path behind the bench and drop down into the centre of the village on what becomes a lane between houses. When you reach the main road the Wheelwrights Arms is to your left (along with the current Market Hall built in 1898), the toilet block to your right.

Walk 26
Builth Wells

4.75 miles on lanes, tracks and field paths. Few stiles, though some gates can be awkwardly tied. Takes in aspects of the town including the castle site, and enigmatic earthworks on Garth Hill, which are reached after a gentle ascent.

The walk starts from the Wyeside Arts Centre near the bridge across the Wye.

1 With your back to the arts centre and the mural to your right, cross the road and turn right up Broad Street (the high street). Go past Kings Head Lane, reached on the left after 70 yards, and past the next single shop, then turn left into a little seating area which has a statue of a Celtic goddess and a map of the town. Continue uphill from this area to join Kings Head Lane as it continues uphill to reach a T-junction.

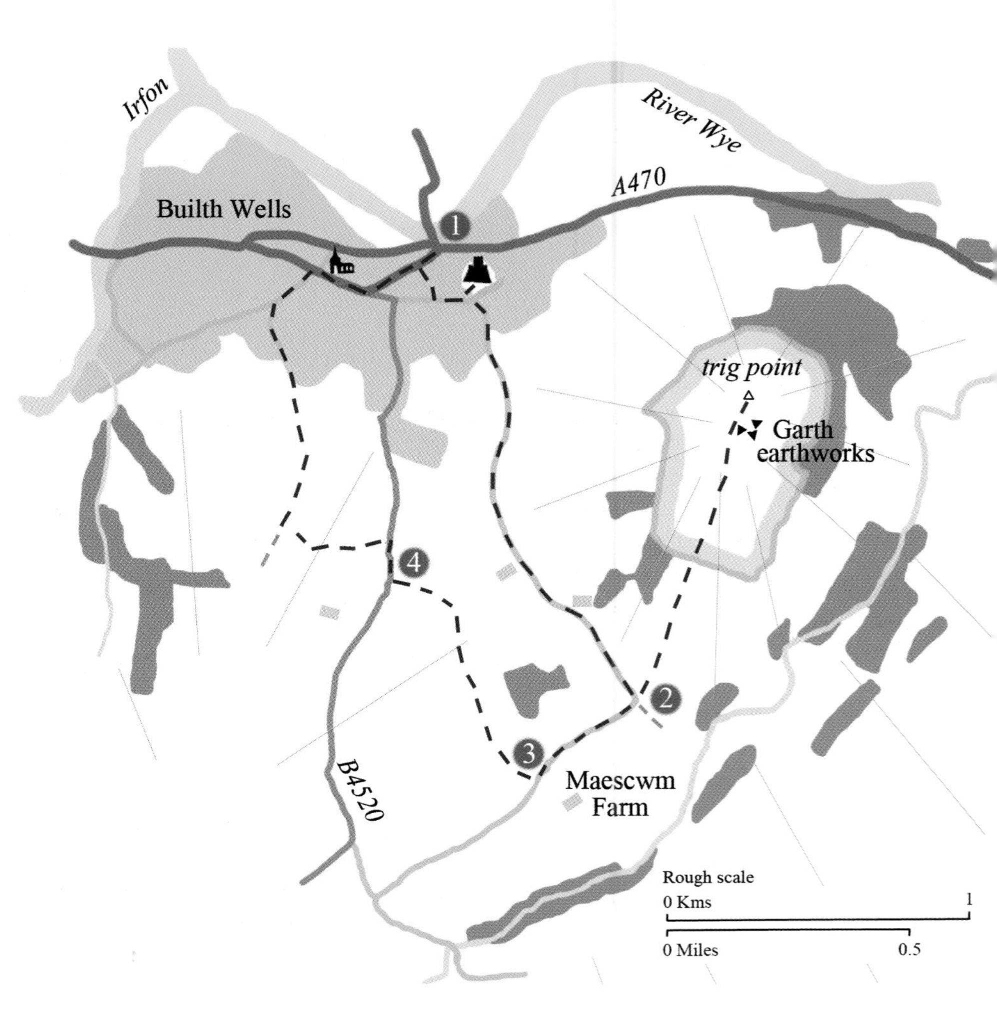

BUILTH WELLS

The first settlement is believed to have been to the north of the current town and to have formed part of the territory known as Rhwng Gwy a Hafren – the land between the Wye and the Severn. It was with the arrival of the Normans in the 11th and 12th centuries that the current town began to take shape, focused on an important ford across the Wye. Indeed, the first part of the town's old name, Llanfair yn Muallt, refers to the foundation of a Norman church dedicated to St Mary, (Llanfair means 'St Mary'), though the original oval shape of the churchyard suggests that a Celtic foundation predated this church. The second part of the name, Muallt or Buallt, refers to the wooded pasture of the surrounding countryside used for rearing oxen or cattle. The Norman town was laid out along two streets connecting the castle at the south to the church at the north and would originally have been protected by a thorny hedge. Its original settlers were probably mainly Welsh, with a smattering of English people and Flemings. Builth became the centre of a Marcher lordship and therefore had its own laws outside of those of England or Wales. Often on the front line in the wars between Welsh princes and Norman English lords, the town and castle suffered damage, notably in 1260. In 1282, the death of Llywelyn ap Gruffydd nearby (see under MURAL on next page) saw the start of a period of greater stability and peace for the local population, though under largely alien overlordship.

In 1691 a fire destroyed 41 houses in the town, which explains why little of the medieval period remains. In 1770 the current bridge was erected. In the later 1800s the springs near the junction of the Irfon and Wye – one saline, a second chalybeate and a third sulphurous – were developed, with pump rooms erected along with saline and sulphur baths, together with facilities for showering or immersing oneself in vapour from the springs. This led to a period when the town became a summer spa, served by the new railways. The town's position at a junction of main roads and railway lines, with stations at both Builth Wells and Builth Road some 2 miles away, also meant it became a centre for handling stock, both cattle and sheep, and subsequently the site of a major agricultural showground and home of the Royal Welsh Show, still held each summer. The station at Builth was closed in 1962, but that at Builth Road remains.

WYESIDE ARTS CENTRE

The town gained the epithet 'Wells' in the 1860s, but it was a poor relation to spas elsewhere, with no assembly rooms, concert hall or market hall. During the 1870s a group of residents formed a committee with the aim of constructing a building that would house all three facilities, and it was erected on the site of a row of old cottages. The Assembly Rooms were located upstairs, and later became home to a cinema. In the 1920s the building passed into private hands, but in the 1960s the person who had inherited the building appreciated that it needed repair and updating and the charitable Wyeside Arts Centre Ltd was formed and acquired the premises. The centre has been refurbished this century and continues to offer a range of live performances and films. Note the terracotta medallions of Shakespeare, Haydn and Mozart on the south façade.

MURAL

This shows the last days of Llywelyn ap Gruffydd, prince of Gwynedd, leading up to his death at Cilmeri, two miles away, in December 1282. Llywelyn, having defeated an English force close to the Menai Straits, had come to Builth to discuss affairs with local Welsh leaders. One story says that he may have been lured this way by the Mortimers, who were related to Llywelyn by marriage, suggesting that they wished to discuss terms. Either way, the English, led by the Mortimers and John Giffard, learned of his presence with only a few supporters, and set out to kill or capture him. Folklore tells that a local blacksmith reversed the direction of the horseshoes on Llywelyn's horse to try to confuse the English, only, in some versions of the story, to then betray that fact. Another story has it that Llywelyn sought safety in Builth Castle, but that he was refused entry, its garrison fearing the strength of English arms in the vicinity. Others say that Llywelyn found the castle to be in English hands. After a while the English caught up with Llywelyn's party and during the subsequent fight he was killed by Adam de Francton.

Turn left here and immediately after four red and yellow brick Victorian houses (the last two being pairs of semis) turn left again down a very short tarmacked 'lane' at the end of which a stile leads you on to the site of Builth Wells Castle.

BUILTH WELLS CASTLE

The first castle on this site was built in timber by the de Braose family in the 11th century. During the conflicts between King John and this family, in 1208 the castle was placed in the care of the sheriff of Gloucester by the king. The Welsh helped the de Braoses retake the castle in 1215, but with the crowning of the new king, Henry III, in 1216 and the reconciliation of the de Braoses with the English Crown, the Welsh seized the castle the following year and restored it to the de Braose family, only to besiege it again in 1223, when it was relieved by royal troops. In 1229 it was taken once more by the Welsh, and this time they destroyed it. It was rebuilt by the English Crown in the early 1240s, this time in stone, and again besieged on several occasions between 1256 and 1260, when the Welsh destroyed it for a second time. In 1276 Edward I included it in the ring of castles he constructed to surround the old territory of the princes of Gwynedd, including those at Aberystwyth, Harlech, Caernarvon and Conway. On a much smaller scale than the other castles, Builth Castle comprised a great tower on the motte, surrounded by a wall with six towers. The motte, reached from a bailey to its south-east, was surrounded by walls and contained a twin-towered gateway on the eastern side. Part of the original bailey to the south-west was separated by the construction of a wide ditch outside the new walls. A drawbridge from the gateway spanned the moat that surrounded the castle, some of it still water-filled to the south-east. Presumably springs on the hillside filled the moat. Although it was smaller than the other 'Edwardian' castles, £1,666 was spent on the castle's construction, a considerable sum for the time. Records show that many of the workmen – masons, carpenters and carters – came from the local area, their surnames reflecting settlements to the south of Builth and to the south-east in Herefordshire. The new castle was besieged in 1294, but held out thanks to a relieving force. In subsequent years it became a muster point for forces going to serve in France. It was held by Lord Richard Grey of Codnor throughout the Owain Glyndwr rising. After the fire of 1691, the castle appears to have been dismantled to provide materials to help rebuild the settlement. The motte remains the prominent feature of the site, together with two baileys, the larger to the south-east, separated by a ditch. The entrance to the motte lay at the northern end of the larger bailey.

When you've seen enough of the castle earthworks, return to this stile and back down the 'lane', turning left at its end to carry on along the road on which you were previously walking. Take the next road off to the right, Newry Road, which is soon reached. Keep on this road for about a mile until it makes a sharp turn to the right, with a no through road continuing ahead.

GARTH HILL EARTHWORKS

This has been described as a small hillfort that roughly follows the contours around the hill, but the only clear structure visible is a length of bank and ditch to the immediate right of the path as you approach the summit. Ordnance Survey maps suggest that the earthworks are those of a small enclosure to the immediate right of the path; might this have been the location of a small Iron Age farmstead? That would seem unlikely, as farmsteads of this period were usually located lower down such slopes. The site has never been archaeologically investigated and remains a mystery.

② At this point, cross the stile on the left and follow the path along the field boundaries and old hedgerows on your left up onto the top of Garth Hill. As you near the top you might be able to pick out a bank to the immediate right of the path, these being the remains of earthworks (see the photo in the text box on the left). The path ends at the trig point, where, in clear weather, you can gain good views over Builth and the surrounding countryside.

You need to return down the hillside to the road by the same way that you came up. When you reach the road carry on straight ahead, following the road till you reach the entrance lane for Maescwm Farm on your left. Immediately opposite this is a gate into a field on your right.

3 Go through this gate and walk across this field to a gate on its far side (you might need to divert round a spring in the middle of the field). Once through this gate, the path follows the field boundary on your right to the next corner of the field where you go through a foot-path gate into another field which contains a scattering of mature oaks. To cross this field, your path starts by heading to the left of the oak immediately through the gate and on to the left of the next nearest oak. From here it continues roughly contouring the slope towards the far side of the field. As you approach this, you should be able to see the stile in the fence below you that you need to cross, though it may be partially hidden by nettles in summer.

Once across this stile the path follows the line of the old hedge on your left downhill passing through a gateway at the bottom into the next field. Here the path turns a little to the right to cross the next field, aiming for a gateway on the far side that is about 40 yards to the right of an oak in the far hedgerow. Through the gateway follow the old hedge on your left to reach a gate on the far side of the field that you go through to reach the B4520.

4 Turn right on the road and take the first field gate on the left, which is reached after 150 yards. Through this gate follow the field boundary on your left up to a gate into the next field, where you follow the line of the old track ahead of you, passing to the left of some straggler remnants of a previous hedge, across a corner of this field.

When you reach the hedge ahead, turn half-right and follow it along to a gate that will lead you out onto a wide grassy track.

Turn right on the track and this will lead you down into Builth, the track becoming stony in its later stages. When you reach a road, keep ahead on it, joining the entrance road to a school and then turning right at a T-junction quickly reached. This will lead you down to another T-junction where again you turn right.

Builth Wells' parish church is over on the left, but we have never found it open. Carry on along the road, following it as it bends left and it will lead you back into Broad Street and so down to the Wyeside Arts Centre.

ST MARY'S CHURCH

The original church may have been a Celtic foundation, replaced in due course by a Norman church. When this might have been built is unclear, but it was certainly by 1283, for in that year a dispute arose between the church and the chapel in the castle as to the number of services to be held in each. The oldest part of the present church is the tower, which dates from about 1300, the remainder dating to a major rebuilding carried out between 1873 and 1875 which replaced structures built in 1793, these themselves having replaced the earlier medieval nave and chancel. The nave and chancel of 1793 stood on the eastern side of the tower and were left standing while the Victorian additions were made to its west and then taken down, allowing the church to be continuously used during the building work.

Index